Elementary
English
Grammar

THE UNIVERSITY
OF BIRMINGHAM

COLLINS
COBUILD

HarperCollins*Publishers*

second edition 2003

© HarperCollins Publishers 1995, 2003

HarperCollins Publishers
Westerhill Road, Bishopbriggs, Glasgow G64 2QT, Great Britain

www.cobuild.collins.co.uk

Collins®, COBUILD® and Bank of English® are registered
trademarks of HarperCollins Publishers Limited

ISBN 0-00-714309-5

The Cobuild Series

Publishing Director	Lorna Sinclair Knight
Founding Editor-in-Chief	John Sinclair
Editorial Director (1st edition)	Gwyneth Fox
Editorial Director (2nd edition)	Michela Clari
Managing Editor	Maree Airlie
Lexicographers	Kerry Maxwell, Alison Macaulay
Editor	Maggie Seaton
Cartoonists	Ela Bullon, Ham Kahn, Duncan McCoshan

Acknowledgements

We would like to acknowledge the assistance of the many hundreds of individuals and
companies who have kindly given permission for copyright material to be used in the
Bank of English. The written sources include many national and regional newspapers in
Britain and overseas; magazine and periodical publishers; and book publishers in Britain,
the United States and Australia. Extensive spoken data has been provided by radio
and television broadcasting companies; research workers at many universities and other
institutions; and numerous individual contributors. We are grateful to them all.

Note

Entered words that we have reason to believe constitute trademarks have been
designated as such. However, neither the presence nor absence of such designation
should be regarded as affecting the legal status of any trademark.

A catalogue record for this book is available from the British Library

Typeset by Digital Imaging, Glasgow and Rosetta Publishing, Peebles

Printed and bound in Great Britain by The Bath Press, Bath

Contents

Contents

Introduction

Writing an elementary grammar of English is a difficult undertaking. It is important to identify the basic patterns of the language and to organize and exemplify these in a way which is accessible to the elementary learner. It is important to provide teachers and learners with a clear authoritative statement. But it is also important to make statements and offer examples which give a true reflection of the language.

Of course a grammar is not a course in itself. It should be seen as an invaluable supplement to the day-to-day work in the classroom and as a useful resource for self-study. To help with this we have organized the material into four 'cycles'. In each cycle we illustrate first the grammar of the verb group, secondly the noun group, and finally adverbials. In determining the content of each cycle we have tried to reflect the priorities revealed in most teaching materials at this level.

The verb section **Cycle 1**, for example, deals with the basic tense uses, question forms, and patterns with *There* as subject. In **Cycle 4**, on the other hand, there is work on complex sentences with clauses of time, purpose, reason, condition, and so on. After each Cycle there is a Review section which revises the work of that cycle in detail and goes on to incorporate work from previous cycles. It is hoped that this cyclical organization will help teachers to fit work on grammar conveniently into their existing teaching programme. For self-study purposes there is a full answer key to all the exercises in the book.

At the end of the text we have included specific sections on spelling, numbers, and pronunciation. All of these are of central importance to the elementary learner. In the Appendices supplement we have looked in more detail at different aspects of verbs, nouns, adjectives and prepositions, as well as listing the most common prefixes and suffixes to help with word-building. We have also included a full glossary of grammar terms, which gives simple, clear explanations of the most important grammatical terminology. The *Collins COBUILD Elementary English Grammar* gives elementary learners all the information they need to become confident in English.

UNIT 1 *Am/is/are*

1 **The verbs *am*, *are* and *is* are followed by:**

A noun group: Mr. Brown **is** a teacher. It **isn't** my book. **Are** you a student?

An adjective: She's **tall.** I'm **tired. Are** you **happy**? They're **hungry.**

An expression of place or time: Mary's **at home.** It's **six o'clock.** It's **on the table.**

An expression of age: I'm **sixteen.** She's **fourteen years old.**

2 **The forms of the verb are as follows:**

Positives		
Statements		**Questions**
Full form	**Short form**	
I **am** late.	I'm late.	**Am I** late?
You **are** next.	You're next.	**Are you** next?
My mother **is** here.	My mother's here.	**Is your mother** here?
She **is** at home.	She's at home.	**Is she** at home?
My brother **is** out.	My brother's out.	**Is your brother** out?
He **is** fifteen.	He's fifteen.	**Is your brother** fifteen?
It **is** on the table.	It's on the table.	**Is it** on the table?
We **are** right.	We're right.	**Are we** right?
They **are** my parents.	They're my parents.	**Are they** your parents?

Negatives			
Statements			**Questions**
Full form	**Short form (1)**	**Short form (2)**	
I **am not** late.	I'm **not** late.		**Aren't I** late?
You **are not** next.	You're **not** next.	You **aren't** next.	**Aren't you** next?
She **is not** in.	She's **not** in.	She **isn't** in.	**Isn't she** in?
He **is not** at home	He's **not** at home.	He **isn't** at home.	**Isn't he** at home?
It **is not** here.	It's **not** here.	It **isn't** here.	**Isn't it** here?
We **are not** happy.	We're **not** happy.	We **aren't** happy.	**Aren't we** happy?
They **are not** ready.	They're **not** ready.	They **aren't** ready.	**Aren't they** ready?

UNIT 1 Practice

A Write answers to these questions. Use full sentences for your answers. Use short forms.

1 How old are you?

2 Are you a teacher?

3 Where are you now?

4 Is it morning, afternoon or evening?

5 What's the weather like - is it warm or cold?

6 What day is it?

B Put a tick (✔)beside these sentences if they are true. Put a cross (✗) if they are not true:

1 The exercise book is on the table.

2 The ball is on the chair.

3 The big book is on the table.

4 The shoes aren't under the table.

5 The pen and pencil aren't on the chair.

6 The shoes are under the chair.

7 The ball and the book are on the chair.

8 The pen and pencil aren't on the table.

C Correct these sentences:

1 The big book is on the table.   _The big book isn't on the table. It's on the chair._

2 The shoes are on the chair.

3 The exercise book is on the chair.

4 The ruler and the pen are on the chair.

5 The pencil's next to the ruler.

6 The ball and the book are on the floor.

D Correct these sentences about yourself:

1 My name is Kim.   _My name isn't Kim, it's_

2 I'm three years old.

3 I'm from Scotland.

4 I'm a pop singer.

5 I'm English.

Now write the same things about a friend of yours:

6 _His/Her name isn't Kim, it's_

7

8

9

10

5

UNIT 2 | Present continuous

1 The form of the present continuous is:

am/is/are + '*-ing*'

For the negative you add *not* after *am/is/are*:
I **am not working** at the moment.

You can use the short forms *aren't* and *isn't*:
We **aren't going** by bus.

I'm **not playing** today.

It **isn't raining** now.

2 You use the present continuous:

a to talk about an activity or something happening now:

They**'re talking**; they**'re not eating**.

It**'s raining**, but it**'s not snowing**.

The kids **are playing** tennis; they**'re not working**.

b to talk about a temporary situation:

I**'m living** with my friends at the moment.
We**'re staying** at a wonderful hotel.
I**'m not feeling** well today.
My sister**'s working** as a waitress for a month.

c to talk about a future plan:

Mike **is coming** home on Thursday.
They**'re having** a party next week.

d to talk about change, development and progress:

Life **is getting** easier thanks to technology.
Do you think your English **is improving**?
Inflation **is rising** and unemployment **is getting worse**.

e with *always* to criticize or complain about what someone does:

You**'re always interrupting** me!
My father **is always losing** his car keys.

We're going to the theatre tomorrow.

MAY

You're always leaving your clothes on the floor!

A Are these sentences 'Present activities' ___(PA)___ or are they 'Future plans' ___(FP)___?

1 Be quiet. I'm trying to relax. _____
2 We're having a party soon. Can you come? _____
3 Who is making that noise? It's terrible! _____
4 They're going to a restaurant tonight. _____
5 Are you working now? _____
6 What are you doing tomorrow? Do you want to come to a match? _____
7 They're learning English now. _____
8 I'm wearing my new jeans. _____
9 Is the sun shining? _____

B What are you doing now? Write true statements using *I am ...-ing* or *I'm not ...-ing*:

1 wear jeans _____
2 study English _____
3 sit at home _____
4 watch TV _____
5 smoke a cigarette _____
6 talk with friends _____
7 relax _____
8 listen to music _____

C Look at the picture and complete the sentences using these verbs:

eat push shine buy walk read listen to wear

1 The boy _____ sweets.

2 The businessman _____ across the road.

3 It's a fine day. The sun _____.

4 A jogger _____ music on a personal stereo.

5 The man at the bus stop _____ a newspaper.

6 The woman in the park _____ a pram.

7 No-one in the picture _____ a hat.

8 Some customers _____ fruit.

D Match the questions and answers:

1 Where are you going on holiday this year?   To Malta probably.
2 What are you doing this evening?   We're going camping.
3 Why are you learning English?   I'm watching a video.
4 Are you doing anything this week-end?   Because it's useful.

Now give your real answers to these questions.

UNIT 3 Present simple

1 You use the present simple:

a **to talk about things that are always true:**
It **gets** cold in winter here. Water **boils** at 100 degrees.
February **is** the shortest month.

b **with words like** *never/sometimes/often/always* **or**
time expressions like *every day/at the weekend* **to**
talk about regular and repeated actions, and habits:
We **often go** to the cinema on Fridays.
My parents **never eat** meat. I **get up** late at the weekend.

I **read** the newspaper every day.

c **to talk about general facts about our lives:**

We **live** in a small house in Bristol.

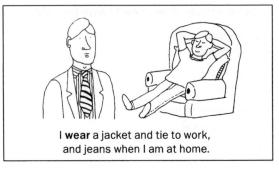

I **wear** a jacket and tie to work,
and jeans when I am at home.

2 The form of the verb changes with *he/she/it*:

I **work** from 9 to 5.
You **work** very hard.
She **works** in the supermarket on Saturday.
He **works** for my father in our office.
We **work** for the new company in the centre of town.
They **work** in uniform.
She **enjoys** English classes. He's a student, he **reads** a lot.

My father sometimes **smokes** a pipe.
It **smells** awful!

3 With verbs that end in *-o/-s/ch/sh* the present simple form is *-es*:

He **goes** out every weekend. She **watches** a lot of TV.
The film **finishes** at 9.30 tonight.
He **does** everything for his children.

4 With verbs that end in *consonant + y*, the *he/she/it* present simple form is *-ies*:

study – He **studies** languages at university.
fly – The plane **flies** twice a week.

BUT: *I play – he plays I buy – she buys*

Note: have – has:

They **have** everything you want in that shop.
She **has** a house in St James' Square.

He **stops** and **has** a cup of coffee at eleven o'clock.

UNIT 3 Practice

A Complete these sentences with:

go   goes   do   does   have   has   like   likes   live   lives

1 I _____ a lot of friends in London.

2 My son _____ in Los Angeles, so I _____ there every year to see him.

3 Most people _____ going on holiday.

4 The new BMW sports car _____ a top speed of 220 km per hour.

5 The sun _____ down in the west.

6 The Smiths are very kind. They _____ a lot of work for people in hospital.

7 He's so clever! He always _____ well in exams.

8 More than 11 million people _____ in Tokyo.

9 My neighbour _____ rock music, unfortunately.

B Complete the sentences using the correct form of the verb in (brackets):

1 Tony is a great reader. He _____ lots of books. (read)

2 Pat's favourite music is reggae. He _____ to it all the time. (listen)

3 My father is a businessman in an international company. He _____ all over the world. (travel)

4 The Strongs are farmers. They _____ in the country. (live)

5 I have a friend called Fabrice. He _____ from France. (come)

6 The hotels here are very expensive. The rooms _____ a lot! (cost)

7 My mother is good at languages. She _____ French, German, Russian and Arabic. (speak)

8 Andrea is a tourist guide. She _____ everything about the history of the city. (know)

C Give your answers to these questions:

1 I always get up before seven o'clock, but Steve normally gets up late.
And you?

2 Steve goes to bed late. I normally go to bed before midnight.
And you?

3 I play sports every day. Steve never plays sport.
And you?

4 Steve visits his friends in the evening. I usually visit my friends at the weekend.
And you?

5 I like classical music and blues. Steve likes rock and roll.
And you?

6 Steve wears jeans every day.
I wear smart clothes.
And you?

Do/does and *have/has* in questions and negatives

Cycle 1

1 You use *do* and *don't* to make questions and negatives in the present simple tense:

A: **Do you know** Peter?
B: Yes. We are old friends.

A: What's that?
B: **I don't know.**

A: **Do you like** this music?
B: Yes. It's great.

A: **Do they enjoy** the theatre?
B: No. **They don't go out** very often.

A: **Do they live** here?
B: No. They live next door.

2 You use *does* and *doesn't (does not)* for questions and negatives with *he, she* or *it*:

A: Is Helen at home?
B: Helen? **She doesn't live** here.

A: **Does David go** to university?
B: No. He's still at school.

A: 'Oh dear. I'm sorry.'
B: 'Don't worry. **It doesn't matter.**'

He **doesn't speak** English.

3 Often the negative of *have* is *don't have* or *doesn't have,* but you can also say *haven't* or *hasn't:*

I haven't any money.   She's got some, but **he hasn't** any.

4 Often the question forms are *Do you have ...?* and *Does he have ...?* But you can also say *Have I ...? Have you ...? Have they ...? Has he/she/it ...?*

A: **Have you** any children?
B: Yes. Two girls and a boy.

A: **Has he** any brothers?
B: No. But he has two sisters.

5 In Britain, you often use the form *have got* instead of *have:*

I haven't got any money.

She's **got** some, but **he hasn't got** any.

A: **Have you got** any children?
B: Yes. Two girls and a boy.

A: **Has he got** any brothers?
B: No. But he's got two sisters.

Have you got any children?

What's the matter?

I've got a headache.

UNIT 4 Practice

A Write down whether you do these things or not:

1 Study English _I study English._
2 Play cricket _I don't play cricket._
3 Speak French _____
4 Study Japanese _____

5 Go to England every year _____
6 Like jazz _____
7 Live in a flat _____
8 Live in a house _____

B Now think of a good friend. Write down whether he or she does those things:

1 _She doesn't study English._
2 _She plays cricket._
3 _____
4 _____

5 _____
6 _____
7 _____
8 _____

C Write down questions you could ask someone about these things:

1 Watching television every day _Do you watch television every day?_
2 Buying a newspaper every day _____
3 Going abroad on holiday every year _____
4 Working in an office _____
5 Living alone _____
6 Liking rock music _____
7 Playing the piano _____
8 Living in a big city _____

Write true answers to the questions:

9 _I don't watch TV every day._
10 _____
11 _____
12 _____

13 _____
14 _____
15 _____
16 _____

D Rewrite these questions and negatives without do/does:

1 I don't have any friends in England. _I haven't any friends in England._
2 Do they have a big house? _____
3 He doesn't have much money. _____
4 They don't have any pets. _____
5 Does she have any nice new clothes? _____

Now do them again with have got:

6 _I haven't got any friends in England._
7 _____
8 _____

9 _____
10 _____

11

UNIT 5 Present perfect (1)

1 The form of the present perfect is:

have/has + past participle

2 You use the present perfect tense for something which happened in the past but has an effect in the present:

A: 'Are you going to the film tonight?'
B: 'No. I**'ve** already **seen** it.'

A: 'Why isn't John at work?' (present)
B: 'Don't you know? He **'s had** a bad accident.'

3 Often it refers to the very recent past:

Karen **has** just **passed** her exams.   I**'ve** just **seen** your mother at the shops.

4 You use the present perfect for something which started in the past and is still going on:

I know London very well. I**'ve lived** there for five years.
He's her closest friend. He **has known** her **since** they were children.

or to ask questions about the past up to the present:

A: **Have** you **heard** of Boris Becker?
B: Yes. He plays tennis.

A: **Have** you **been** to America?
B: No. But I**'ve been** to Canada.

A: How many times **has** she **been** to England?
B: I think she**'s** only **been** once.

> Have you ever seen a Yeti?
>
> No. Have you?

or for something which still hasn't happened but is expected to happen:

A: May I borrow your book?   A: Do you know Henry?
B: I'm sorry. I **haven't finished** it yet.   B: No. We **haven't met** yet.

⚠ WARNING:
You do not use the present perfect in a clause with a past time expression:

They've just finished work. They finished **ten minutes ago**.
I've read that book. I read it **last week**.

5 Exercise: Find the words *already, just, since, yet, ever* on this page. Which uses of the present perfect do they go with?

UNIT 5 Practice

A Match the questions and answers:

1 Do you know Michael?
2 Where's Andreas?
3 Are you going out tonight?
4 Is James at home?
5 Is Maria at the University?
6 Do you want a sandwich?
7 Are Linda and Sam coming tonight?
8 Can I borrow your grammar book?

a No. I haven't done my homework.
b No thanks. I've just had lunch.
c Yes. We've met many times.
d No. He has gone on holiday.
e No. We haven't invited them.
f He's gone to the shops.
g I'm sorry, but I've lost it.
h No. She hasn't finished school yet.

B Have you heard of these people, been to these places, seen these films or read these books?

1 Brazil _I haven't been to Brazil._
2 Don Quixote _____
3 Honolulu _____
4 Andre Agassi _____

5 Emilio Zapata _I've heard of Emilio Zapata._
6 Oliver Twist _____
7 Madrid _____
8 Charlie Chaplin _____

Now think of some to ask your friends: Have you seen/ read/ heard of/ been to?

C Write under the picture what has happened to these people:

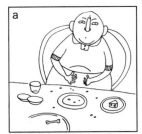
a

He's eaten too much.

b

c

d

e

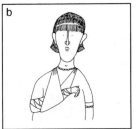
f

g

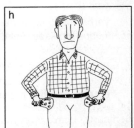
h

Here are some ideas to help you: ... broken her arm; ... had an accident; ... lost all his money; ... fallen down; ... lost their way; ... eaten too much; ... won a prize; ... caught a fish.

UNIT 6 Present perfect (2)

1 **You can use the present perfect after words like *when, after, until, as soon as,* to talk about something in the future:**

Tell me **when** you **have finished**.   I'll write to you **as soon as** I **have heard** from Jenny.

[For a note about the present simple in sentences like this see Unit 11]

2 **If you say someone *has gone* to a place you mean they are still there:**

A: Where are the children?   B: They'**ve gone** to school.
Ken and Angela **have gone** to London for a holiday.

If you say someone *has been* to a place you mean they went there once but they are not there now

The children **have been** to school. They're back at home now.
I'**ve been** to Paris but I'**ve** never **been** to Rome.
[See Unit 5-Practice, Exercise B]

3 **Look at questions and negatives with *have* in Unit 4, sections 3 and 4:**

Now look at questions and negatives with the present perfect:

A: **Have** you **found** your book yet?   B: No. I've looked everywhere, but I still **haven't found** it.
A: **Have** you **seen** Bill lately?   B: No. I **haven't seen** him for a couple of months.

4 **Some verbs are usually used in continuous forms because they talk about actions that go on for some time. The following verbs are examples:**

drive live make stand study travel watch wait walk work

You often use the present perfect continuous
form with these verbs to emphasise how long
something has been going on up to the present:

We've **been travelling** for three hours.

He's **been working** very hard.

She's **been watching** TV all day.

*[For verbs not normally used in the
continuous form see Unit 66]*

I've been waiting here for ages. BUS STOP

5 **You can use the present perfect continuous tense to show that something is still going on:**

Compare: I **have read** your book. I enjoyed it very much.

and: I'**ve been reading** your book. I'm enjoying it very much.

6 **You can use the present perfect continuous to show that something is or was temporary:**

I **have been working** as a ski instructor, but now I'm looking for a new job.

UNIT 6 Practice

A In these time expressions the present simple refers to a time in the future.
Change present simple to present perfect:

1 When I finish Oliver Twist I will read Don Quixote.

   When I have finished Oliver Twist I will read Don Quixote.

2 You can do the shopping after you make the beds.

3 Don't go out before you do your homework.

4 I'm going to stay in class until I finish my essay.

B Write out these dialogues putting the verbs in the present perfect question form or
negative form:

1 A: (Your sister/ pass her exams)?

   B: I don't know. (She/not get/the results)

   Has your sister passed her exams?
   I don't know. She hasn't got the results.

2 A: (Your brother/go/to America)?

   B: No, (he/not go/yet)

   _____?
   No, _____ .

3 A: (Peter/start/ school)?

   B: No, (he/ not start/ yet)

   _____?
   No, _____ .

4 A: (You/read/the newspaper)?

   B: No, (I/ not read it/yet)

   _____?
   No, _____ .

C Write under these pictures what these people have been doing:

He's been waiting for a bus.

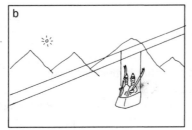

UNIT 7 Was/were

1 You use *was* (negative *was not* or *wasn't*) as the past of *am* and *is* with:

A noun group: He **was a good student**, now he's a teacher.
My favourite book when I **was a child was Robinson Crusoe**.

An adjective: My grandfather **was** very **tall**.
I **wasn't happy**.

An expression of time or place: It **was three o'clock**.
He **was at school** in 1999.

An expression of age: He **was twenty** in June.
She **was nineteen** when she married.

2 You use *were* (negative *were not* or *weren't*) as the past of *are* in the same way as *was*:

> Dear Sue,
>
> We're in Florida now.
> We were in Miami
> yesterday. The weather
> was fantastic.
> We were on the beach all
> afternoon.
>
> Love,
>
> _____
> _____
> _____
> _____ ,
> _____
> _____

3 You can use *was*, *were*, *wasn't* and *weren't* for questions:

Were you here yesterday?
Who **was** that man?
You walked fifty kilometres – **weren't** you tired?
When did we arrive? **Wasn't** it on Friday?

4 Exercise: Complete this chart by filling in the blank boxes:

	Present	Past (positive)	Past (negative)	Past (question)
I	am busy	was busy	wasn't busy	Was I busy?
He				Was he there?
She		was angry		
It	is cold			
We				Were we late?
You	are sad			
They			weren't at home	

UNIT 7 Practice

A Match the questions with these answers:

I was in town.   I was in bed, but I wasn't asleep.   No, I was fine, but my brother was ill.

It was really hot.   No, I was with a friend.

1 A: Where were you yesterday at 3 p.m.?   B: _____

2 A: Were you alone?   B: _____

3 A: What was the weather like yesterday?   B: _____

4 A: Were you ill last week?   B: _____

5 A: Were you in bed asleep at midnight?   B: _____

B Now write your real answers to the same questions.

C The pictures show a room before and after a robbery.

Complete the sentences with *was* or *were* with the following objects:

1 The vase _____ on the table on the right.

2 The video recorder _____ under the television.

3 The paintings _____ on the wall behind the desk.

4 The books _____ on the shelf near the door.

5 The camera _____ on the desk.

Before:

After:

D Are these statements true or false? Correct the false statements:

1 Winston Churchill is the Prime Minister of Britain. _____

2 Charlie Chaplin was a famous musician. _____

3 Cities are smaller now than in 1900. _____

4 The world record for the 100 metres sprint is 10 seconds. _____

5 Istanbul was the capital of Turkey before Ankara. _____

6 Latin is the most useful international language. _____

E Complete the sentences using *was, wasn't, were* or *weren't*:

1 'Where _____ you yesterday?' 'I _____ ill so I stayed at home.'

2 I left school when I _____ 17 and started university when I _____ 18.

3 The film we saw last week _____ terrible.

4 'What _____ the weather like yesterday?' 'Oh, it _____ terrible.'

5 'We've just finished the exercise.' '_____ it difficult?'

6 I called my parents half an hour ago but they _____ in.

UNIT 8 | Past simple

1 You use the past simple to talk about things that happened in the past:

I **stayed** in that hotel last week.
He **worked** all night and finally **finished** the project when the secretaries **arrived** in the morning.

2 You also use the past simple to talk about the general past, and about regular actions in the past :

We **lived** in Rome for a year when I **was** a child.
Our friends often **visited** us there.

3 For most verbs, the past simple form ends in *-ed*.

Some verbs have an irregular past form:

Can you match these 20 irregular past simple forms and their infinitives?

begin _____   give _____

break _____   go _____

buy _____   have _____

come _____   make _____

do _____   pay _____

drink _____   say _____

drive _____   see _____

eat _____   take _____

find _____   tell _____

get _____   write _____

did   found   went   told   drove   bought
    saw   came   had   paid   got
    ate   broke   took   began   drank   said   made
                     wrote   gave

4 For all regular and irregular verbs (except *be:* see Unit 7), the form is the same for all persons: *I/you/he/she/it/we/you/they said.*

5 You use *did ... + infinitive* to form questions in the past:

Did you **get** home all right?
Did he **go** out last night?
Did you **tell** them about the party?
Who **did** you **see**?
Where **did** you **buy** that hat?
When **did** she **arrive**?

6 You use *did not* (or *didn't*) + *infinitive* to form negatives in the past:

I **didn't understand**, so I asked a question.
He **didn't give** me his address.

They **didn't buy** anything.

Practice

A Use the verbs from section 3 opposite to complete these sentences:

1 I _____ Mike in the street yesterday.

2 When I was in Spain, I _____ this sombrero as a souvenir.

3 After the concert we _____ home by taxi.

4 He opened the packet and _____ a chocolate biscuit.

5 Have you got that letter Bob _____ us last week?

6 My uncle _____ me a couple of interesting books for my birthday.

7 Ivor _____ his leg and was taken to hospital in an ambulance.

8 I _____ it all myself!

B Underline the past simple verbs in the following:

The police are looking for a man who stole £25 and a jacket from a crowded fashion shop in Brighton last week. The man, who was between 20 and 25, with short brown hair, took the jacket from a staff changing-room. 'I'm not worried about the money, really,' said the victim, Sally Walker, 25, who works in the shop. 'But the jacket cost me £150. I got it when I was on holiday in Turkey.' The police do not think the man is dangerous, but warned the public to be careful.

C Complete the questions for the answers on the right:

1 When _did she buy_ the jacket?   When she was on holiday

2 Where _did she go_ on holiday?   Turkey

3 What _did he steal_ steal?   A jacket and £25

4 Where _did he steal them_ from?   From the staff changing room

5 How much _did the jacket_ cost?   £150

D Frances is a manager of a busy company. Look at her diary for yesterday, then write about what she did or didn't do:

e.g. She had a meeting with the bank manager.
She didn't have time to write a letter to Gerry.

E What about you? Which of these activities did you do yesterday?

watch TV   have a shower   cook a meal
read a paper   make a phone call   write a letter
play a sport   speak English   listen to music
go out   visit a museum

e.g. I didn't watch TV yesterday.
I wrote a letter to a friend yesterday.

8.30	Buy paper and magazine for mother ✓
9.00	Have meeting with bank manager ✓
10.00	Call Export International ✓
10.15	Write to Gerry ✗
10.30	Talk with Jan and John about new products ✓
11.30	fax ISB in Munich about training course ✗
12.00	write letter to Directors of XYZ to confirm meeting ✓
1.00	meet David for lunch ✗
2.00	take taxi home ✓
2.30	pack suitcase ✓
4.00	take train to London ✓

Past continuous
(Review Unit 2 on Present continuous)

1 **The form of the past continuous is:**

was/were + *'-ing'*

2 **You use the past continuous for an action which was interrupted by another action:**

I **was reading** the newspaper when the doorbell rang.
They **were flying** from London to New York when the accident happened.

WARNING: **If two things happen one after the other you use two verbs in the past simple tense:**

As soon as he **saw** me he **waved**.

I **woke up** when my alarm clock **rang**.

3 **You use the past continuous for an action which was still in progress at a particular time:**

At 2.15 we **were** still **waiting** for the bus.   It was just before midnight. We **were talking** quietly.

4 **You often use the past continuous to set the scene for a story or for a series of events:**

It was 1975. We **were living** in a small house in Liverpool.
On the day I had my accident, I **was preparing** for my examinations.

5 **You use the past continuous to show that something was changing, developing or progressing:**

The children **were growing up** quickly.

We **were learning** quickly.

Practice

A Complete the following sentences. You should put one verb in the past simple and the other in the past continuous:

1 I (meet) _____met_____ Peter while I (shop) _____was shopping_____ this morning.

2 We (walk) _____ home this evening when it suddenly (begin) _____ to rain.

3 I (hurt) _____ my back when I (work) _____ in the garden.

4 I (stay) _____ in Oxford, so I (go) _____ to see Tim.

5 Ken (do) _____ his homework last night and he (forget) _____ to telephone home.

6 We (live) _____ in Greece when our first daughter (be) _____ born.

7 She (work) _____ in the library when she (see) _____ Maria.

8 We (go) _____ to the opera when we (stay) _____ in Milan.

B Complete the following sentences using the past simple or the past continuous:

1 When he (hurt) _____ his back he (go) _____went_____ to see the doctor.

2 When she (hear) _____ the news she (begin) _____ to cry.

3 We (listen) _____ to the radio when Fred (come) _____ home.

4 I (hear) _____ a strange noise and the dog (begin) _____ to bark.

5 Everyone (talk) _____ and suddenly the lights (go) _____ out.

6 I (have) _____ a nice hot shower when the doorbell (ring) _____ .

7 I (have) _____ a nice hot shower when I (get) _____ home.

8 The children (play) _____ happily when mother (arrive) _____ home.

UNIT 10 Past perfect
(review Units 5 and 6 on Present perfect)

1 **The form of the past perfect is:**

had + past participle

2 **When you are talking about past time, you use the past perfect for something which happened earlier and has an effect on the time you are talking about.**

I didn't go to the film with my wife because I **had** already **seen** it.
John wasn't at work because he **had had** a bad accident.

3 **Often the past perfect refers to something which had happened very recently:**

It was July. Karen **had** just **passed** her exams.   I told Rosa I **had** just **seen** her mother at the shops.
I was feeling very tired because I **had** just **finished** work.

4 **You use the past perfect for something which started earlier and was still going on at the time you are talking about:**

I knew London very well.
I **had lived** there for five years.

He was her closest friend. He **had known** her since they were children.

or to talk about the time up to the time you are talking about:

A: In 1987 **had** you **been** to America before? B: No, but I **had been** to Canada.
I didn't know anything about rock'n roll. I **had** never **heard** of Elton John.

or for something which hadn't happened at the time you are talking about:

She wanted to borrow my book but I **hadn't finished** it.
I didn't know Henry. I **had** never **met** him before.

5 **You use the past perfect continuous tense to talk about something which had been going on for some time:**

We **had been travelling** for three hours.
She **had been watching** TV all day.

or for something that was still going on or something that was temporary:

I **had been reading** her book.
I was enjoying it very much.

I **had been working** as a ski instructor,
but I was looking for a new job.

UNIT 10 Practice

A Match the questions and answers:

b 1 Did you know Michael?
a 2 Where was Luis?
h 3 Did you go to the cinema last night?
c 4 Did you see James and Leila?
d 5 Were you feeling hungry?
e 6 Were you locked out?
f 7 Did you have any money left?
g 8 Did you know Paris well?

a He had gone to the shops.
b Yes. We had met many times before.
c No. They had gone away for the day.
d Yes. I hadn't eaten since breakfast.
e Yes. I had forgotten my key.
f No. I had spent everything.
g Yes. I had been there twice before.
h No. I hadn't finished my homework.

B Make sentences from these parts:

e 1 I couldn't understand very much
g 2 We didn't know where to go
a 3 I didn't enjoy the film very much
H 4 Everything was very wet
i 5 They knew they would be late
b 6 They were very brown
j 7 We were tired out
c 8 John couldn't open the door
d 9 I had to go to the bank
f 10 I couldn't see very well

a because I had seen it before.
b because they had been working in the sun.
c because he had lost his key.
d because I had spent all my money.
e because I hadn't been learning English very long.
f because I had forgotten my spectacles.
g because we had lost our map.
h because it had been raining all day.
i because they had missed the last train.
j because we had been working all day.

C Complete these sentences with one verb in the past simple and one in the past perfect:

1 I (go) ___*went*___ home as soon as I (finish) ___*had finished.*___ work.

2 Everybody (go) ___*had gone*___ out for the day. There (be) ___*was*___ nobody at home.

3 Bill (live) ___*had lived*___ in Leeds ever since he (be) ___*was*___ a boy.

4 After I (eat) ___*had eaten*___ I (order) ___*ordered*___ a cup of coffee.

5 He (feel) ___*felt*___ awful. He (catch) ___*had caught*___ a bad cold.

6 He (take) ___*took*___ the book back after he (read) ___*had read*___ it.

Present tenses used for the future

1 When you are talking about something in the future, which is arranged for a definite time, you use the present simple. There is usually a time expression in these sentences:

The next train **arrives** at 11.30.   The meeting **starts** straight after lunch.
We **have** a holiday tomorrow.   We **leave** at two o'clock tomorrow afternoon.

2 In statements about fixed dates in the future you normally use the present simple:

Tomorrow **is** Tuesday.

It's my birthday next month.

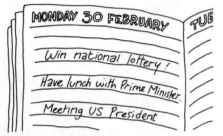

Monday **is** the thirtieth of February.

Friday **is** my birthday.

3 When you talk about people's plans or arrangements for the future, you often use the present continuous tense:

I'm **seeing** Jill next week.

They're **getting** married before Christmas.

We're **having** a party next week.   I'm **doing** my homework this evening.

4 When you are not sure about arrangements, you talk about the future using the present tense of verbs like *hope, expect, intend, want* with a *to-infinitive* clause:

We **hope to see** you soon. He **wants to catch** the last bus home.
Henry **expects to be** at the station to meet us tomorrow.

5 After the verb *hope* you often use the present simple to refer to the future:

I **hope** you enjoy your holiday. June **hopes** she passes her exam all right.

6 Present tenses are often used to refer to the future in clauses with *if* and with time words like *when* and *before*:

You won't get lost if you **have** a good map.   Have a drink **before** you **go**.

* There is a deliberate mistake on this page. Can you find it?

A Look at the letter below. Underline all the verbs in the present tenses. Put a bracket round those which refer to the future:

Dear Monica,

Many thanks for your letter. I am pleased you are enjoying your holiday. When (do you come) home? It will be great to see you again.

We are going to Greece this year - next Friday in fact. I am trying to get everything ready in time, but it is very difficult with three small children. Our plane leaves at six o'clock on Friday morning, so we are taking a taxi to the airport at four o'clock in the morning - I hope the children behave themselves and get ready quickly without too much trouble. Peter has three weeks holiday this year so when we get back from Greece we are staying with his mother in Brighton for a week. She has a big flat in a block right next to the sea. The children love it.

Lydia is starting school this September. I hope she likes it. Jimmy hates going to school. He shouts and screams every morning. Perhaps he will be better when Lydia starts. Thank you for your news. I am very pleased to hear that Isobel has done so well at University. What is she doing next year? Has she decided yet? What about the twins? When do they leave school?

Give my love to Norman. I am sorry about his accident. I hope he gets better soon.

Much love,

Teresa.

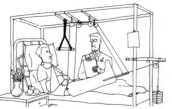

I hope he gets better soon.

We are taking a taxi to the airport at four o'clock.

B Answer these questions using the present simple or the present continuous:

1 What day of the week is your birthday on? *My next birthday is on a Friday.*

2 What time does this lesson finish? _____

3 What are you doing tomorrow morning? _____

4 How many English lessons do you have next week? _____

5 What day is it the day after tomorrow? _____

6 What is the date next Thursday? _____

7 What are you having for supper tonight? _____

8 What are you doing after your lesson? _____

9 When is the next national holiday? _____

10 How old are you on your next birthday? _____

UNIT 12 | *Will and going to*

1 When you **know** that something will happen in the future, you use the present simple or the present continuous:

The next train **arrives** at 11.30.   We're **having** a party next week.

2 When you are **predicting** what will happen, you use *will* or *going to*: *predicting*

The weather tomorrow **will be** warm and sunny.   I think it's **going to rain.**

3 When facts or events in the present situation mean that something is likely to happen in the future, you normally use *going to*:

4 When something is clearly going to happen very soon, you use *going to* for a warning:

'Watch out, we're **going to crash!**'

'Be careful, you're **going to drop** those glasses.'

5 When you are making a promise or an offer, you use *will*: *promise*

I'll **ring** you later tonight.   I'll **come round** and help you later.

6 When you are telling someone about a decision you have made, you normally use the present continuous or *going to*:

I'm **staying** at home tonight.   I'm **going to do** some work.

When you are talking about a decision someone else has made, you normally use *going to*:
She's **going to write** you a letter.   They're **going to call** in and see us.

7 When you are telling someone about a decision you have just made, you normally use *will*:

Ken lives near here.   I think I'll **go** and see him.
A: Did you know it's Winnie's birthday?   B: Really? Thanks. I'll **send** her a card.

A Match these sentences:

1 It's very cold.
2 The children are really tired.
3 I feel awful.
4 She's bought a new dress.
5 Oh dear, I've missed my train.
6 There's a big queue.

a I think I'm going to be sick.
b I'm going to be late.
c We're going to have some snow.
d It's going to be very crowded.
e They're going to fall asleep.
f She's going to look very smart.

B Complete these dialogues using *will* or *going to*:

1 A: Dad, (you/lend?) (1) _will you lend_ me the car next week? Annette and Andy (have) (2)
_____ a party and they've invited me.

B: I'm sorry, your mother and I (see) (3) _____ that new film at the Odeon. We probably (not
get back) (4) _____ until ten o'clock.

2 A: What (you/do?) (5) _____ this summer?

B: We haven't decided yet. Perhaps we (share) (6) _____ a house with my parents in the Lake
District. They (borrow) (7) _____ a cottage from some friends for a few weeks.

A: (there/be?) (8) _____ enough room for you and the children?

B: Oh no. The children (not come) (9) _____ They (take) (10) _____ a trip to
Singapore. They (stay with) (11) _____ Andrew's brother for a month.

A: That (be) (12) _____ exciting. I'm sure they (have) (13) _____
_____ a wonderful time.

C Complete the following using *will* or *going to*:

'Wait a minute. (I/open)

_____ the door
for you.'

'(I/write) _____
every day.'

'Help (I/fall)

_____ !'

'Oh dear (We/get)

_____ wet.'

'You have a rest this evening.
(I/cook) _____
the supper.'

'I think (I/get into trouble)
_____ .'

UNIT 13 *There*

1 You use *there*:

When you want to say that something exists: ✓

Once upon a time **there** was a little girl called Red Riding Hood.
In the forest **there** was a wicked wolf.

When you want to talk about an activity or event: ✓
There was a party last week.   **There**'s a football match tomorrow.

When you want to talk about a number or amount: ✓

There was a lot of trouble
at work this morning.

In the kitchen **there** was a large table
and four chairs.

2 When the noun which comes after *there* is singular, you use *is* or *was*:

There is a book on the table.   **There was** an extra English class yesterday.

You use singular with two nouns joined by *and* if the first noun is singular:
There was a man and two women.   **There was** a table and some chairs in the room.

When the noun which comes after it is plural you use *are* or *were*:
There are three beds in the room.   **There were** two big beds and a little bed.

3 If you want to make a question you put *there* after *is; was; were*:

Is there anyone at home?   **Were there** many people at the meeting?
Are there some oranges left?   **Isn't there** a good film on TV tonight?

or before *be* or *been*:

Will **there be** enough time?   Could **there be** anyone there?
Has **there been** anyone here?   Will **there be** any children there?

4 Common expressions with *there*:

There are a few ...	**There** are a lot of ...	**There** isn't/wasn't any ...	**There** aren't/weren't any ...
There's/are no ...	Is/are **there** any ...?	Was/were **there** any ...?	**There's** nothing to do.
There's plenty to eat.	**There's** nowhere to go.		

UNIT 13 Practice

A Answer these questions using *there*:

1 How many people are there in your class? *There* _____
2 How many people are there in the room? _____
3 Are there any pictures on the walls? _____
4 Is there anything on your desk? _____
5 How many people are there in your family? _____
6 How many small beds and how many big beds were there in the room? _____

B Rewrite these sentences to begin with *there*:

1 We have an English class every day. *There's an English class every day.*
2 A meeting will be held at three o'clock. _____
3 An accident happened this morning. _____
4 A lot of people came to the concert. _____
5 Three books lay on the desk. _____
6 Lots of children will be at the party. _____

7 We have nothing to eat or drink. _____

8 Three people waited in the shop. _____

C Complete the dialogue using expressions with *there*:

there was nobody at home   there's a good film   Is there anything good
I don't think there'll be anything   There wasn't anything

A: _____
  on TV tonight?

A: Do you think _____
  on at the cinema?

A: Shall we go round and see Joe and
  Pamela?

B: No, _____
  very interesting.

B: I don't know. _____
  _____ last week.

B: Let's telephone first. Last time we went
  _____ .

29

What ...?

Cycle 1

1 You use a question form after *What* ...?

What does he want?   **What** have you done?   **What** will they say?

2 You use *What* ...?

to make or ask about plans:

What are you doing tomorrow?   **What** are you going to do?   **What** shall we do?

to find out what happened:

What happened?   **What** did you do?   **What** did you say?

to ask someone to repeat or explain something:

What do you mean?   **What** did she mean?   **What** does it mean?   **What** does 'repeat' mean?
I'm sorry, **what** did you say?

to find out about a problem of some kind:

What's the matter?   **What**'s wrong?   **What**'s up?   **What** happened?

to find out what something is like:

What sort of dog is it?

'**What** does he look like?'

What kind of ... is it?   **What** sort of ... is it?   **What**'s it like?   **What** colour is it/are they?
What does he look like?

to make a suggestion:

So Monday's no good.   **What** about Tuesday?   **What** about some lunch?

to introduce a new idea or a new topic:

I'm ready for lunch.   **What** about you?   So Tom's OK.   **What** about Marie?

to ask about time:

What time is it?   **What** time do you finish work?

3 We often use *What do you think* ...? for questions. There is no question form after *What do you think* ...?

What do you think they will say?   **What** do you think it means?

UNIT 14 Practice

A Rewrite these questions leaving out the words ... *do you think* ... :

1 What do you think they are going to do?   *What are they going to do?*

2 What work do you think he does?   _____?

3 What do you think it means?   _____?

4 What time do you think they will arrive?   _____?

5 What colour do you think she wants?   _____?

B Match the questions and answers:

1 What did it look like?   a It's very big. It has four bedrooms.

2 What's your new house like?   b He was very wicked.

3 What's your new job like?   c It's great! But it's hard work.

4 What was the wolf like?   d It looked very nice.

5 What's it like learning English? e I don't know really. I've just started.

C Complete the dialogues below by adding one of the following nouns:

colour   kind   sort   language   size   work   time   day

1 A: What ___sort___ of person is he?   5 A: What _____ is your car?
  B: He's very quiet, but he's really nice.   B: It's sort of light blue.

2 A: What _____ does the next train leave? 6 A: What _____ do they speak in Austria?
  B: I'm not sure. I'll have to check the timetable. B: Mainly German I think.

3 A: What _____ shoes do you take?   7 A: What _____ of food do you like?
  B: I don't know. Those look about right.   B: I love Chinese and Indian food.

4 A: What _____ is it today?   8 A: What _____ does your mother do?
  B: It's Monday.   B: She's a doctor.

D Use these phrases to make six short dialogues to go with the pictures:

A: What's wrong?/What's the matter?

B: a It's my leg. I think it's broken.   d I think I've run out of petrol.
   b I haven't any money. I've spent it.   e I've lost my key. I can't get in.
   c I didn't sleep very well last night.   f I feel awful. I've eaten too much.

UNIT 15 *Wh-* questions

1 You use a question form after a *wh-* word. Look at these common expressions:

Where ...?
Where is she now? **Where** are you going? **Where** shall I put this? **Where** do you live?

When ...?
When can you start? **When** did she arrive? **When** does she leave?

Why ...?
Why do you want to know? **Why** don't you buy a new one? **Why** did you do that?

Who ...?
Hello, **who** is it? **Who** was that? **Who's** been eating my porridge? **Who** did you see?

How ...?
How do you know? **How** do I get to your grandmother's house? **How** much is it?
How many people are there? **How** long is it? **How** old is Peter now?

2 In conversations, we often use short questions:

A: We're going on holiday.
B: **Where** to?
A: Florida.

A: I have to go out tonight
B: **What** time?
A: About half-past seven.

A: It's a long way to walk.
B: **How** far?
A: Nearly ten miles.

A: These shoes are cheap.
B: **How** much?
A: Only twenty-five pounds.

A: I'm very angry.
B: **Why?**
A: I've lost my passport.

A: I saw a friend of yours.
B: **Who?**
A: Antonia.

3 Other ways of asking questions:

When Where What Who How Why	do you think ...?	I wonder	when ... where ... what ... who ... how ... why ...

These forms are very common when the speaker is not sure if the other person knows the answer.
Study these examples. Notice the word order.

How old is Jack's brother?
I wonder **how** old Jack's brother is.
How old do you think Jack's brother is?

Where do Bill and Jenny live?
I wonder **where** Bill and Jenny live.
Where do you think Bill and Jenny live?

Why did she do that?
I wonder **why** she did that.
Why do you think she did that?

'I wonder **who** it is.'

A Make up dialogues from these boxes:

A: Let's go and see Peter and Mary some time.	B: What?	A: Italy I think
A: They live in that big house on the corner.	B: Who?	A: Well, we could go this weekend.
A: We could probably get there quite quickly.	B: When?	A: You know – those friends of Michael's.
A: I'm afraid I've lost it.	B: Where?	A: Well, we could take a taxi.
A: I think they're away on holiday.	B: How?	A: My library book. I don't know where it is.
		A: I don't know. I think I've left it at school.

B Rewrite these sentences with *Wh_____ do you think...?* or *I wonder ...?*

1 What's she like?   1 _I wonder what she's like._

2 What did she mean?   2 _____

3 Who does this belong to? 3 _____

4 Why are they so late?   4 _____

5 What does he want?   5 _____

6 How old is he?   6 _____

7 Where have they gone?   7 _____

8 What will they say?   8 _____

C Here are some answers. Can you find possible questions on page 32?

1 Last month.   5 Next week.   9 On that table.

2 In Scotland.   6 By bus.   10 Turn left here.

3 £1.30.   7 In the office. 11 To the shop.

4 To Glasgow.   8 For a holiday.

'What do you think it means?'

D Rewrite as ordinary *wh-* questions:

1 How long do you think it will take?   1 _How long will it take?_

2 I wonder how much it will cost.   2 _____

3 What do you think it means?   3 _____

4 I wonder where they come from.   4 _____

5 I wonder when they will arrive.   5 _____

6 I wonder where he's gone.   6 _____

UNIT 16 Count nouns

1 Most nouns are COUNT NOUNS in English. This means that they have a singular and a plural form. You add *-s* to form most plurals:

singular	plural
I haven't read a **book** for ages.	**Books** are cheap here.
Where's the **bus stop**?	We need more **bus stops**.
I need a **holiday**.	We get three **holidays** a year.

2 You add *-es* to nouns ending in *-ss, -s, -ch, -sh* or *-x* to make the plural:

I'm in **class** A.	I have two **classes** today.
Which **bus** do you take?	There are no **buses** on Sundays.
It's a Swiss **watch**.	He can repair **watches**.
That's my **dish**.	He washed the **dishes**.
Put the **box** down.	Where are the shoe **boxes**?

You add *-es* to most nouns ending in *-o*:

Is that a **potato**?	I had some **potatoes** for lunch.
I want a **tomato**.	I don't like **tomatoes**.

(But just add *-s* to *photo, radio* and *piano*)

He washed the **dishes**.

3 Nouns ending in *consonant + y* change to *consonant + ies*:

Which **country** are you from?	We visited ten **countries**.
This is a photo of me as a **baby**.	I can hear **babies** crying.

(But for *vowel + y*, just add *-s*: day – days/boy – boys)

4 Some common count nouns are irregular. Can you match the singular and plural forms of these nouns?

women sheep feet men fish mice children teeth people

child _____	fish _____	sheep _____
foot _____	man _____	tooth _____
mouse _____	person _____	woman _____

5 You use plural nouns without determiners such as *this, that, the, a* to talk about things or people in general:

My brother doesn't like **spiders**.   **Computer games** are expensive.

Children start school at the age of 6.   **Cars** cause pollution.

UNIT 16 Practice

A Give the plural of these nouns:

baby   _____   box   _____   child   _____

shoe   _____   shop   _____   day   _____

church   _____   foot   _____   radio   _____

sandwich   _____   city   _____   story   _____

B Label the pictures using the plural of these nouns:

photo   fish   mouse   watch   tooth   bus   box   baby   sheep

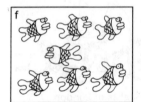 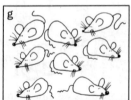 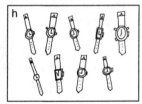 

a   b   c   d   e

two buses   _____   _____   _____   _____

  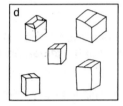 

f   g   h   i

_____   _____   _____   _____

C Match the sentence parts:

1 Buses are
2 The bus is
3 Women
4 That woman is
5 Watches were
6 My watch is
7 Most students work
8 A student in my class comes
9 Books are
10 There is a book

very hard all year.
a Rolex.
made of paper.
invented a long time ago.
about geography on my desk.
going to the station now.
from near Buenos Aires.
work as well as men.
cheaper than taxis.
my neighbour.

D Complete these questions using these words:

months   days   day   hours   hour   minutes   week   weeks   year   year

1 'How many _____ are there in a _____?'   'Seven'

2 'And how many _____ are there in a _____?'   '52'

3 'How many _____ are there in a _____?'   '24'

4 'How many _____ are there in an _____?'   '60'

5 'How many _____ are there in a _____?'   '12'

UNIT 17 — Singular, plural and collective nouns

1 Many common nouns are SINGULAR NOUNS. This means that they are only used in the singular form:

a Sometimes they are singular because there is only one of them in the world. You normally use them with *the*:

the air the sun the moon the sky the dark the world the future the past

The sky is very cloudy. It's difficult to see **the sun**.

b Many nouns formed from verbs are used as singular nouns to talk about common daily activities. You normally use them with *a*:

a bath a fight a rest a wash a shower

'Do you want **a drink**?' 'Yes, great. But I need a quick **wash** first.'

2 Some nouns are called PLURAL NOUNS because they have no singular form or because they have a special meaning in the plural. You normally use these with *the* or possessives like *my, his*:

your clothes her feelings the pictures my travels
the sights his likes and dislikes the police

The police are coming. They'll be here in a minute.
I've met a lot of interesting people on **my travels**.

In three days we saw all **the sights** of London.

3 Some tools and clothes with two similar parts are plural nouns:

glasses trousers pants tights jeans pyjamas shorts scissors binoculars scales tweezers

Where are my **jeans**? What colour are your **pyjamas**?

You can also say *a pair of* + singular verb:
A large **pair of sissors was** on the table.

4 Nouns for special groups of people or things are COLLECTIVE NOUNS, and can have a singular or plural verb because you can think of the group as one idea, or as many individuals:

army audience company enemy family gang government group public staff team

My **family is** in Brazil. His **family are** all strange. Do you know them?

UNIT 17 Practice

A Complete these sentences using these singular nouns:

the sun   the sky   the moon   the past   the future
the dark   the air   the world

2 It's a beautiful day. There isn't a cloud in _____ .

3 I sleep with the light on because I'm afraid of _____ .

4 What do you think cars will look like in _____ ?

5 The first astronauts to walk on _____ were American.

6 It's not good for your eyes to look directly at _____ .

7 Heathrow is the busiest airport in _____ .

8 There's a bad smell in _____ . Have you been cooking?

1 Travel was much slower in _____ .
Now everyone has fast cars.

B Match the sentence parts:

1 I'm very thirsty. I'd love   a wash.
2 The doctor felt exhausted. He needed   a drink.
3 Mrs Small is taking her dogs for   a fight.
4 Listen to the shouts. Someone is having   a sleep.
5 We played tennis, then had   a walk.
6 My hands are dirty. I need   a shower.

C ANAGRAMS. Look at the pictures in 3 opposite and put the letters of the objects in the right order:

a pair of S R O S S I C S   a pair of W E Z E T E R S
a pair of C L I R A B O N U S   a pair of M A J A P Y S
a pair of S L A S G E S   a pair of S H I G T T

D Now complete these sentences using your answers to C:

1 Can I borrow _____ to cut this paper, please?

2 Jack went to the opticians to get _____

3 She wore _____ under her jeans to keep warm in winter.

4 He used _____ to get a small piece of wood out of his finger.

5 To keep warm in bed at night, many people wear _____ .

6 _____ will help you see things that are a long way away.

E Complete the sentences using: *staff/team/audience*:

1 Which is the best football _____ in your country?

2 The _____ of this school is excellent.

3 I'm afraid no-one can help you at the moment, the _____ are all in a meeting.

4 Are your _____ all professionals?

5 The _____ isn't very big tonight: there are only 10 people in the cinema.

6 The _____ were singing and dancing everywhere in the concert hall.

UNIT 18 Uncount nouns

Most nouns in English have a singular and plural form (e.g. one bed, two beds), but many common things cannot be counted directly. These are called UNCOUNT NOUNS.

1 Uncount nouns:

a **do not have a plural form:**
We bought a lot of **food** at the supermarket.
There's going to be some **rain** at the weekend.
Milk is good for you.
If you need to change **money**, go to the bank.

b **take a singular verb:**
Electricity is dangerous.
Rice is the basic ingredient of Eastern cooking.
Water is more important than food in the desert.

c **cannot be used with** *a/an* **or a number:**
My uncle started **work** when he was fourteen..
Last winter we had **ice** on the lake.

d **can be used with** *the/this/that/my* **etc**
(but not with plural words such as *these/those***) to
talk about something specific:**
What's **the food** like in that restaurant?
I like **music**, but I didn't like **the music** we heard today.
I gave you **that money** for clothes, not chocolates!

We bought a lot of food at the supermarket.

2 With uncount nouns you use the words *some, much* and *any* to talk about a quantity of something:

Mrs Pick went out to buy **some bread**.
There's not **much petrol** in the car, so we'd better go to a garage.
We haven't had **any rain** here since April.

3 Some nouns can be uncount nouns and count nouns. As uncount nouns they have a general meaning, and you use them as count nouns to talk about a particular example:

A shop near me sells 20 different **cheeses**. I hate **cheese**.

There's a **hair** in my soup! Val has long dark **hair**.

It's made of **glass**. I had a **glass** of Coca-Cola.

There's a **hair** in my soup.

UNIT 18 Practice

A Put these uncount nouns in the right categories:

· snow	· dinner	· petrol	· toast	(ice
· food	· milk	·· maths	· lunch	· coffee
· wood	· aerobics	· butter	· physics	· breakfast
· metal	· glass	· bread	· gold	tea

1 substances: _snow_____

2 liquids: _____

3 meals: _____

4 types of food: _____

5 sports/subjects: _____

B Now use some of the uncount nouns from A to complete these sentences:

1 The car ran out of _____ a kilometre from our home.

2 We got up early, had _____ , then drove to the airport.

3 _____ is a very valuable metal.

4 A lot of people keep fit by doing _____ , which is exercising to music.

5 They say that the English drink a lot of _____ .

6 When we woke up, everything was white: the ground was covered with _____ .

C Complete the sentences using the following words:

glass/glasses	paper/a paper	business/a business
two sugars/sugar	cheese/a cheese	a grey hair/hair

1 Sam went out to buy _____ to read.

2 _____ is made from trees.

3 They say that mice like _____ .

4 Camembert is _____ from France.

5 You don't always need a lot of money to
start _____ .

6 Do you prefer long or short _____ ?

7 I was very worried when I found I had _____ .

8 _____ is bad for your teeth.

9 'How do you like your tea?' 'White with
_____ , please.'

10 After the accident the road was covered
with broken _____ .

11 We had a coffee and two
_____ of mineral water.

12 '_____ is always good in the holidays,' said the toy-shop
owner.

UNIT 19 A/an/some

1 You use *a* with singular nouns. Put *a* in front of the singular nouns in this list:

_____ week	_____ book	_____ person	_____ tables
_____ sports	_____ people	_____ tomato	_____ cup
_____ dog	_____ house	_____ parents	_____ children

2 You use *a* with count nouns, not uncount nouns. Put *a* in front of the singular count nouns in this list:

_____ box	_____ work	_____ job	_____ news
_____ banana	_____ honey	_____ traffic	_____ holiday
_____ teacher	_____ hat	_____ water	_____ furniture

3 You use *an* with words that begin with *a, e, i, o, u*. Put *an* where necessary:

_____ elephant	_____ apple	_____ cat	_____ aunt
_____ beach	_____ test	_____ opinion	_____ idiot

4 You also use *an* in front of words that begin with *h* if the *h* is silent:

an hour   a hospital   an honour   a hope   an honest man

5 You use *a* in front of words that begin with *eu* or *u* if the first sound is pronounced /ju:/. Compare:

a European country   a university   an ugly face

6 You use *a/an* when you are talking about a person or thing for the first time:

There is **a man** at the door. (=I don't know which man)
I need to buy **a new shirt**. (=not one specific shirt)

7 You use *a/an* to talk about jobs:

My father is **an engineer** now, but he was **a soldier** before.
I worked as **a secretary** last summer. This year I want to be **a shop assistant**.

8 You use *a/an* instead of *one* with some numbers:

a hundred pounds   half a kilo   a million people
a litre of wine   an hour   a thousand times

9 You use *some* with plural nouns and uncount nouns to talk about more than one object, if the number isn't important:

I want **some apples, some wine, some potatoes** and two **oranges**.

Some friends gave me some information about good hotels.

A Match the two parts of these sentences:

1 I've been waiting for you for	a hundred people.
2 This car can do 140 miles	half an hour.
3 Those apples cost 50p	a few times.
4 We're having a party for about	a lot to do.
5 Sue has been to Germany	a month.
6 We're very busy in the office. There's	a kilo.
7 We normally go to the cinema once	an hour.

B Look at the pictures. Who can you see? Complete the sentences using these words:

a student   a nurse   a tourist   a musician   students   nurses   tourists   singers

1 He looks like _____ .   5 He's _____ .
2 I think she is _____ .   6 They are _____ .
3 They look like _____ .   7 She is _____ .
4 I think they are _____ .   8 They are _____ .

C Look at the pictures, then make complete sentences using *a/an* or *some* and the words given, e.g.

There – telephone – living room.   *There's a telephone in the living room.*

1 There – small table – kitchen.   5 There – tv – living room.
2 There – lot of pictures – living room.   6 There – plants – both rooms.
3 There – flowers – living room.   7 There – guitar – living room.
4 There – lamp – corner of the living room. 8 There – people – living room.

UNIT 20 *The*

1 Review *a/an* in Unit 19.

2 You use *the* with a singular noun when the person you are speaking to knows which person or thing you are talking about:

I had a book and a magazine with me. I read **the book** first. (=the book I had with me)

He bought a new shirt and a tie. **The tie** was very expensive. (=the tie he bought)

I spoke to **the headmaster** at school this morning. (=the headmaster of my school)

'Is there life on **the moon**?' (=there is only one moon)

'Dad said I could borrow **the car** tomorrow.'
(=my father's car)

I left the fruit in **the kitchen**. (=the kitchen in our house)

The president is coming next week. (=the president of our country)

She went into her room and locked **the door**. (=the door of her room)

Who is **the woman** next to Mary?

She was talking to **the man** who lives next door.

You use *the* with a plural noun when the person you are speaking to knows which group of people or things you are talking about:

Where are **the children**? (=our children)

He bought two shirts and a tie. **The shirts** were quite cheap. (=the shirts he bought)

Have you washed **the cups and saucers**? (=the cups and saucers we have been using)

3 You use *the* when you are talking about a system or service:

I spoke to her on **the telephone** yesterday. I heard it on **the radio**.

4 You can use *the* with a singular noun when you want to make a general statement about something:

The tiger is a very dangerous animal. My favourite flower is **the rose**.

⚠ WARNING: You do not use *the* when you use a plural noun to make a general statement, or when you make a general statement about an uncount noun:

Tigers are dangerous animals. **Roses** are my favourite flowers.

Rice is very expensive in England. **Platinum** is more valuable than gold.

UNIT 20 Practice

A Complete these sentences. Put *a/an* in one blank and *the* in the other:

1 I was speaking to _____*a*_____ friend on _____*the*_____ telephone.
2 _____ headmaster is moving to _____ new school.
3 My sister is taking _____ children to _____ party.
4 He ate three sandwiches and _____ large cake. _____ cake was filled with cream.
5 I heard _____ great programme on _____ radio this morning.
6 The first man on _____ moon was _____ American.
7 There's some hot water in _____ kettle. Can you make _____ cup of tea?

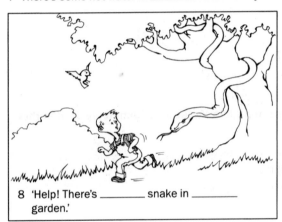

8 'Help! There's _____ snake in _____ garden.'

9 'Look, there's _____ big kite in _____ sky.'

B Fill the blanks using *a, an* or *the*:

Police have been looking for (1) _____ eight-year old boy who tried to hold up (2) _____ sweet shop with (3) _____ gun, *writes David Ward.*

The boy threw (4) _____ carrier bag at (5) _____ shopkeeper and ordered her to fill it up. 'I don't know whether he wanted me to fill (6) _____ bag with sweets or money,' said (7) _____ shopkeeper. 'I am not sure if (8) _____ gun was real or not,

but I don't think it was (9) _____ toy gun.' The boy went into the shop and bought (10) _____ bar of chocolate for 25p. 'He gave me (11) _____ 50p piece and as I gave him his change (12) _____ man came in. (13) _____ boy waited until (14) _____ man went. Then he threw (15) _____ plastic carrier bag at me, pointed (16) _____ gun at me and said: 'Put everything in.'

UNIT 21 Other uses of *the*

1 With places you use *the*:

a with names using *Union/Kingdom/States/Republic*:
The United States The United Kingdom The Republic of China

b with mountain ranges and groups of islands:
The Alps The Rockies The Canaries

c with rivers, seas, oceans:
The Thames The North Sea The Atlantic Ocean

d with hotels, cinemas, theatres, museums:
The Hilton Hotel The Odeon The British Museum

2 You use *the* with points of the compass:

It's much colder in **the north** of England than in **the south**.
A: Where do you come from? B: I'm from **the north-east**, near Newcastle.

3 You use *the* with adjectives to talk about groups of people. Adjectives commonly used in this way are:

the rich the poor the young the old the blind the disabled the dead
Life nowadays is very difficult for **the poor** and **the disabled**.
There was a garden for **the blind**. All the flowers had a very strong scent.

4 You use *the* with superlatives (see Unit 64).

She is **the oldest daughter**. It was **the best film** I had ever seen.

5 You use *the* to talk about a family:

The Kennedys are probably the most famous family in the USA. We live next door to **the Browns**.

6 You use *the* with:

a musical instruments:

He's learning **the guitar** and **the piano**.

b positions:

in the corner   at the top

in the middle

on the left   on the right

at the bottom

⚠ WARNING: You do not use *the* when you are talking about one particular instrument.
We bought Helen **a new violin** for her birthday. A: What's that? B: It's **a trombone**.

UNIT 21 Practice

A Match these questions and answers:

the Ritz   the Andes   the Nile   the Clintons   the guitar   the Odeon   the south west

1 Which instrument does Paul McCartney play? _____

2 What's the nearest cinema to your house? _____

3 Which part of the country do you live in? _____

4 What's the longest river in your country? _____

5 Who are your neighbours? _____

6 Which is the biggest hotel in your town? _____

7 Which are the biggest mountains in your country? _____

B Now give true answers to the questions.

C Complete these sentences by adding *the*. You must put one *the* in the first sentence, two in the second, three in the third and so on:

1 Excuse me, can you tell me time please?

2 What's name of nearest cinema?

3 We went to cinema last night. Unfortunately we were late so we missed start of film.

4 Name of river that flows through middle of London is Thames.

5 Weather in north of England will get worse on Thursday and Friday. At weekend temperature will be 3 degrees and there will be snow during night.

6 We live near sea in south of England. Every day in afternoon we walk dogs in woods for a couple of hours. Scenery is so beautiful.

7 I read in encyclopaedia you gave me that Mount Everest in Himalayas is highest mountain in world. Longest river in world is Nile in Africa.

8 I was thinking of girls we met in street when we were going to a party in house next to restaurant where Michael works. One came from Republic of Ireland. We invited them to party but they couldn't go because they were flying to United States next day.

UNIT 22 Possessives

1 Can you match these possessive adjectives to the right pronouns?

their   your   her   his   our   my   your   its

I _____   It _____   You _____   We _____

He _____   You _____   She _____   They _____

2 You use the possessives:

a when you say that something belongs to someone:

'That's **my** car.'

They showed us **their** holiday photographs.

b when you talk about relationships:

Sarah is **my sister**. Have you met **their father**?   What's **your friend** called? He hasn't seen **his parents** today.

c when you talk about a part of the body:

Arlene broke **her arm** last week, did you know?   **My head** hurts.

d when we talk about clothes:

Take **your** hands out of **your pockets**!   Have you seen **my jeans**? I can't find them.

3 You can also use *noun + 's*:

a with a name:

I was in **Mark's** new house last night.   Sidney is **Jane's** brother.

b with a singular noun (normally referring to people):

It's my **uncle's** birthday next Monday.
Sam asked if he could borrow his **friend's** car.

c with an irregular plural noun:

Children's clothes are expensive.

d to talk about people's houses, and common shops:

I slept at **David's** last night.   He went to the **chemist's**.

4 With a regular plural noun, you just add an apostrophe ':

Sinatra was my **parents'** favourite singer.

Colston College is the best **boys'** school in the region.

UNIT 22 Practice

A Complete these sentences with possessives:

1 I don't live with _____ parents now.

2 Rosa wanted to give _____ father a CD for _____ birthday.

3 Jessica went upstairs and started to wash _____ hair.

4 I know the Spencers but I've never met _____ son.

5 We're having a party in _____ house on Friday. Can you come?

6 Good morning, ladies and gentlemen. Can I have _____ attention, please?

7 France is famous for _____ wine and _____ cheese.

8 I don't know much about the Amazon and _____ history.

B What's wrong?

There is a problem in each of the pictures here.
Complete the sentences:

1 He's forgotten _____ . (trousers)

2 The cup is missing _____ . (handle)

3 They've lost _____ . (keys)

4 Patricia can't remember _____ . (number)

5 'Excuse me, is this _____ ?' (animal)

6 'Excuse me, can you give us _____
    back?' (ball)

C Rewrite these questions:

e.g. What's the name of your mother? – *What's your mother's name?*

1 What's the name of your best friend?

2 What's the favourite colour of your mother?

3 What's the address of your neighbour?

4 Do you know the first name of your teacher?

5 What is the main export of your country?

6 What food is the speciality of your region?

D Now write your real answers to the questions starting as follows:

1 My _____ .

2 My _____ .

3 My _____ .

4 His/Her _____ .

5 My _____ .

6 My _____ .

UNIT 23 | Demonstrative adjectives

1 With singular nouns you use *this* to talk about something near you, and *that* to talk about something further away:

This water tastes strange. **That building** is 200 years old.

'Have you got **this shirt** in **that colour**?'

'**This coffee** isn't mine!'

2 With plural nouns, you use *these* to talk about objects near you, and *those* to talk about things further away:

I don't like **these shoes** much. **These chocolates** are very nice!

'Can I have some of **those apples**, please?'

'Aren't **those people** strange!'

3 You use *this* with *morning, afternoon, evening* (but not *night*), *week, month, year* and *century* to talk about the present time, and *that* to talk about the past:

Are you busy **this evening**? We could go out.
I'm afraid the doctor can't see you **this week**.
Is next week OK?

4 You use the expression *these days* to talk about the present time in general, and *in those days* to talk about a past period:

It's difficult to find good quality products **these days**.
These days every office has a fax, a photocopier and its own computer.

In **those days** people had quite big families.

5 Numbers and adjectives come after *this, that, these* and *those* and before the noun:

I bought **these two books** second hand for just £1.   My mother doesn't like **these plastic cups**.
How much are **those new CD players**?

A Match the sentences to the pictures:

1 How much is this plate, please?

2 Can you pass me that plate, please, Tom?

3 This bird is called 'Geronimo'. It's an owl.

4 What is that bird over there? Is it an owl?

5 Excuse me, are these shoes yours?

6 Excuse me, where did you buy those shoes?

7 I saw that film last week.

8 This film is great, isn't it?

B Complete the sentences with *this*, *that*, *these* or *those*:

1 He's so busy that I don't see much of him _____ days.

2 We haven't got enough money to go on holiday _____ year.

3 What's the name of _____ man we met _____ morning?

4 Have you been in _____ new supermarket in the centre?

5 The price of petrol _____ days is incredible!

6 Who are _____ people over there?

7 Listen! Do you know _____ song?

8 _____ exercise is very easy!

9 When I was a child, I played a lot of sport.

In _____ days I was very active.

C Change the sentences following the model and making any necessary changes:

e.g. This is my favourite hat   *This hat is my favourite.*

1 This is my mother's favourite song. _____

2 That was a terrible joke! _____

3 This is a delicious cake. _____

4 These are comfortable shoes. _____

5 That is a fashionable colour. _____

6 Those are my best trousers. _____

7 These are very popular books. _____

8 That was a great party. _____

9 Those are beautiful paintings. _____

UNIT 24 Personal pronouns

1 **There are two sets of personal pronouns. Can you match the subject pronouns to the correct object pronouns?**

Object pronouns: us, me, you, them, her, it, him

Subject pronouns	Object pronouns		Subject pronouns	Object pronouns
I	_____		it	_____
you	_____		we	_____
he	_____		they	_____
she	_____			

2 **You use subject pronouns as the subject of a verb:**

I like your hat.   **You live** near here, do you?   **He's** my boss.
She's on holiday.   **We were** in London yesterday.   **They come** from Nigeria.

3 **You use object pronouns:**

a as the object of a verb:
Could you **help us** with this, please? She **gave me** £5.
I **told them** to be here at 6 o'clock. She **saw him** in town.

b after a preposition:
She was waiting **for us**. I talked **to him** yesterday.
Can you take me **with you**?

I don't know anything **about him**.

c after the verb *to be*:

This **is us** in Greece, and this **is us** in Italy last year, and this **is me** in Paris.

Hello, John, it's **me**.

4 **You can use *you* or *they* to talk about people in general, and *we* to talk about a group including the speaker:**

They have good food in this restaurant.   **You** can buy this book anywhere.   **We** drink a lot of tea in England.

5 **You use pronouns after you have talked about someone or something for the first time, to avoid repetition:**

I spoke to Mary this morning. **She** said **she** was very busy.
Patrick lives near the coast. **He** has a lovely house.

A Underline all the subject pronouns in these sentences:

1 I can't forget the last time we went to that restaurant. The food made me ill, and it wasn't cheap, either.

2 Do you know where we can buy an English newspaper? Someone told us there was a shop near here. Can you help?

3 I got a letter from Simon today. I hadn't heard from him for ages. He's working in Milan now, apparently.

4 Val invited me to her party, but I'm not sure if I can go. She lives miles away, and I've got a million things to do.

B Now look at the sentences again. There is an object pronoun in every sentence. Can you find them?

C Match the parts of the following dialogues:

1 Do you know Mr and Mrs James?   It's in Africa, I think.

2 Where's Timbuctoo?   He's in hospital now.

3 Mike had an accident on Sunday.   It's boring.

4 That's a brilliant film.   They eat a lot of pasta.

5 I'm not interested in football.   We met them last week.

6 Where did you buy those shoes?   I've seen it three times.

7 What's the food like in Italy?   Paul gave them to me.

D Look at the picture, add the personal pronouns to the sentences, then match the sentences to the right speakers by putting the correct letter in the brackets after each sentence:

1 Do you know Sue? _____'s a top model. (   )

2 I made her dress. Do you like _____ ? (   )

3 I think I'm in love with _____ , but _____'s not very interested in _____   (   )

4 We are her assistants. _____ are always very busy. She travels everywhere with _____ . (   )

5 Don't bring flowers in here. Sue doesn't like _____ . (   )

6 I'm her manager. _____ have to talk to _____ if _____ want an interview with _____ . (   )

7 _____ gave us these photographs of _____ ! (   )

This, that, these, those, one, ones

Cycle 1

1 **You use *this* (singular) and *these* (plural):**

a **to introduce or identify people:**
Mary, **this** is John.
These are my neighbours, Mr and Mrs Baxter.

This is the BBC
World Service ...

b **to talk about people or things near you:**
This is really good coffee.
These are the books I bought from Jane.

c **to start a conversation on the phone:**
Hello. **This** is Sally; can I speak to Jane, please?
Tom, **this** is Barbara. How are you?

2 **You use *that* (singular) and *those* (plural):**

Those are expensive
shoes. Buy these,
they're cheaper.

a **to talk about people or things not so near you:**
This is my house, and **that** is John's over there.
Is **that** a bird or a plane up there?

b **to check the identity of someone you cannot see:**
Is **that** you, David?
Hi, is **that** Sally?

3 **You use *this*, *that*, *these* and *those* to reply to something someone has said. *That* is most common:**

'Coffee?' '**That**'s a good idea.'
'Is **that** the London train?' 'Yes, **that**'s right.'
'I've got a new job in the city.' '**That**'s fantastic!'

4 **You use *one* (singular) and *ones* (plural) to avoid repeating a noun:**

a **after an adjective:**
My car is the **blue one**. (= the blue car)
Your question is a **difficult one**. (= a difficult question)

b **after 'the':**
Our house is **the one** in the middle.
She gave me a lot of books. **The ones** I really enjoyed
were love stories. (= the books I enjoyed)

I need
batteries for my
personal stereo. Which ones
are best ?

c **after 'which' in questions:**
We've got lots of tapes. **Which one** do you want to listen to?

UNIT 25 Practice

A Rewrite these sentences using *one/ones* to avoid repetition:

1 I love cakes, especially the cakes my mother makes!
2 Our car is the black car at the end of the road.
3 I'm not sure if I need a big bottle or a small bottle.
4 He lost his umbrella, so he wants to buy a new umbrella.
5 The hotel is a modern hotel on the coast.
6 The books I bought are the books on the table.
7 I always have two pens with me, a blue pen and a red pen.

NASAL APPLIANCES FROM THE HITTITES TO THE MEDICI →

8 Is this museum the museum you were talking about?

B Match the questions and answers:

1 'Would you like a coffee?'   'The brown ones on the desk.'
2 'Which gloves are yours?'   'Sure. Which one?'
3 'Which shirt should I wear to the party?'   'Thanks, I'd love one.'
4 'Have you seen my new photos?'   'Your new cotton one.'
5 'Can I borrow a book?'   'The ones of Spain? Yes.'

C Complete the short dialogues with these sentences:

That's a lot.   That's all right.   That's why you're tired.   That's great.

1 a I'm sorry I broke your cup.
  b _____

2 a These boots cost £90.
  b _____

3 a We're getting married!
  b _____

4 a We danced all night.
  b _____

D Complete the dialogue using *this*, *that*, *these* or *those*:

1 a Bill, _____ is Wolfgang.
  b Oh! Are you German?
  a Yes, _____ 's right.

3 a Is _____ Jane?
  b Yes, speaking. Who's _____ ?
  a _____ is Tom from next door.

Bill, _____ is Wolfgang.

Is _____ Jane?

2 a I'm going to Greece on holiday.
  b _____ 's nice.

4 a Where are my shoes?
  b Are _____ yours over there?

Cycle 1

UNIT 26 Possessive pronouns

1 These are the possessive pronouns:

I like your car. **Mine** is very old; **yours** looks very fast.

The red umbrella is **hers**.

Thanks for your address. Let me give you **ours**, too.

This isn't my shirt, it's **his**.

Note: There is no possessive form for 'it'.
'Yours' is both singular and plural.

'Which team won?' '**Theirs**.'

2 You use the possessive pronoun to avoid repetition:

e.g. That book is my book. (= that book is mine)

That book is **mine**, and the pictures are **mine**, too.
The jazz records are **hers**, the rock records are **his**.
All the new furniture is **ours**.

'Excuse me, is this newspaper **yours**?'

3 You can use the possessive pronouns after *of*:

He was an old friend of **mine** (not: 'of me').
The teacher was talking to a student of **his**.
Listening to music is a hobby of **ours**.

Can I borrow that map of **yours**?
Are the Smiths friends of **hers**?
I think the dog is one of **theirs**.

4 You can use possessive pronouns in short answers after questions with *whose ...?*

54

UNIT 26 Practice

A Complete the sentences following the model:

e.g. Have you got a blue pen? No, _____*mine is red.*_____ (red)

1 'Has David got a new car?' 'No, _____ (very old).'

2 'Did Sheila say she has a Japanese camera?' 'No _____ (German).'

3 'Is this your coffee?' 'No, _____ (over there).'

4 'Is your house bigger than this one?' 'No, _____ (smaller).'

5 'Do they have a colour TV?' 'No, _____ (black and white).'

6 'Will we have first class tickets?' 'No, _____ (second class).'

B Rewrite these sentences using *a ... of ...* to replace the underlined words following the model:

e.g. This is one of his paintings. _*This is a painting of his.*_____

1 Susan is one of our friends. _____

2 The small man is one of our neighbours. _____

3 Is singing one of your hobbies? _____

4 Hamid is one of my students. _____

5 Pink is one of her favourite colours. _____

6 I am one of their fans. _____

7 Roast beef is one of my favourite meals. _____

C Complete these sentences:

'Whose car is that?' 'It's ___his___.'
(deel) pro.p.

'Whose is this?' 'It's ___his___.'
(deel) pro.p.

'Excuse me, is this ___yours___ ?'

'I haven't got a pen on me.'
'Here, you can borrow ___mine___.'

UNIT 27 | Adverbials of time

1 The following expressions are used to say when something happens or happened:

the day before yesterday   the week before last   yesterday
last week   today   this week   tomorrow   next week
the day after tomorrow   the week after next

I have an important meeting **the day after tomorrow**.

With *month* or *year* you use the same expressions
as with *week*, for example:

the month before last   last year
this month   the year after next

2 You use *ago* with the past simple tense to show
how long before the time of speaking something
happened:

I'll be leaving school **the year after next**.

The game **started ten minutes ago**. The bus **went an hour ago**.

When you use *ago* you use expressions of time like *five minutes, an hour, three weeks, four months, a few years* and so on. The following expressions are also very common:

ages ago   a long time ago   some time ago   not long ago   a short time ago

⚠ WARNING: You do not use *ago* with the present perfect tense. You cannot say:
I have seen him two minutes ago.

3 You use adverbials of frequency to say how
often something happens:

always	frequently	occasionally
never	hardly ever	normally
often	sometimes	usually
rarely		

We don't **often** swim in the sea.

I'm **always** sick when I travel by sea.

Adverbials of frequency usually come before the main verb:
I **hardly ever watch** TV.   You can **sometimes waste** a lot of time.

But they come <u>after</u> the verbs *am, is, are, was, were* when these are used as main verbs:
She **is usually** very late.   You **are probably** right.

Some adverbials of frequency (*sometimes, occasionally, normally, usually*) can come at the beginning of
the sentence:
Sometimes I go swimming at the weekend.
Normally I go swimming on Thursday night.

A **Answer these questions about yourself:**

1 When did you last go swimming? *I last went swimming three months ago.*

2 When did you last go to the cinema? _____

3 When did you start school? _____

4 When were you born? _____

5 When was your mother born? _____

6 When did you have breakfast today? _____

7 When were you last ill? _____

8 When did you start learning English? _____

B **Answer these questions:**

1 What is the date the day after tomorrow?   _____

2 What day was it the day before yesterday?   _____

3 What month was it the month before last?   _____

4 How old will you be the year after next?   _____

5 How old were you the year before last?   _____

C **Use adverbials of frequency to make true sentences:**

1 I am late for lessons. *I am often late for lessons.* _____

2 I get up late on Sunday. _____

3 I watch TV in the evening. _____

4 I play tennis in the summer. _____

5 In my country it is cold in winter. _____

6 I read in bed before I go to sleep. _____

Now write three true sentences about a friend:

7 _____

8 _____

9 _____

D **Say whether these statements are true (T) or false (F):**

1 Adverbials of frequency never come at the beginning of a sentence. (*F*)

2 'Sometimes' can come at the beginning of a sentence. (   )

3 'Always' often comes at the beginning of a sentence. (   )

4 Adverbials of frequency usually come before the main verb. (   )

5 You always use the present perfect tense with 'ago'. (   )

6 In conversations we often use short questions. (   )

UNIT 28 Adverbials of probability and degree

Cycle 1

1 You use adverbials of probability to say how sure you are about something:

certainly   definitely   probably   perhaps   possibly   maybe

I **definitely** saw her yesterday.   The driver **probably** knows the quickest way.

All adverbials of probability (except *maybe*) come before the main verb:
He can **probably answer** your question.   They will **certainly help** you.

OR: after the verbs *am, is, are, was, were* when these are used as main verbs:
I **am certainly** very tired.   You **are probably** right.

Some adverbials of probability can come at the beginning of the sentence:

perhaps   maybe   probably   possibly

Maybe Annette can tell you. **Perhaps** he has forgotten.
Probably they'll come later. **Possibly** she didn't understand.

2 Common adverbials of degree/frequency: *a lot; (not) much; very much*

Sometimes these words are used as adverbials of frequency:
The baby cries **a lot**. (a lot = very often)   We don't go out **much**. (not much = not often)

Sometimes they are adverbs of degree:
Did it rain **very much** last night? (very much = very heavily)

a lot, (not) much and *very much* usually come at the end of their clause:

Things haven't changed **much**. They always shout **a lot**.
We enjoyed the film **very much**. Do you play football **very much**?

but they are sometimes followed by an expression of time or place:

We enjoyed the film **very much last night**. Things haven't changed **much here**.

⚠ WARNING: *much* is not used in positive sentences. You do not say:
I liked it much.
You say:
I liked it **a lot**, OR I liked it **very much**.

58

UNIT 28 Practice

A Use adverbs of probability to write true sentences (you may need to add the word *not* as well):

1 The USA will win the next football World Cup.
   The USA will definitely not win the next football World Cup.

2 My country will win the next football World Cup. _____

3 I am the oldest person in my class. _____

4 I will go away for a holiday this summer. _____

5 It will rain tomorrow. _____

6 The next leader of my country will be a woman. _____

7 I will get married next year. _____

8 I will get most of these sentences right. _____

B Six of these sentences are correct and five have mistakes. Find the sentences which are wrong and write them out correctly underneath.

1 Nearly I have finished this exercise. ✗ *I have nearly finished this exercise.*

2 I cut myself this morning, and it hurt a lot. _____

3 I like a lot your new dress. _____

4 We don't work very much at the weekend. _____

5 This is a very good book. I enjoyed it much. _____

6 He is very lazy. He doesn't help very much his parents. _____

7 I have almost finished this exercise. _____

8 People say that it rains a lot in England. _____

9 I always enjoy very much the weekend. _____

10 I don't work much at the weekend. _____

11 They are very noisy children. They shout a lot. _____

29 Adverbials of duration

1 You use *for* to say how long something lasts:

I've been working here **for fifteen years**. I hadn't eaten **for ten hours**.
I will be away **for three weeks**. We stayed in Paris **for a couple of days**.

Notice that *for* is followed by a period of time which tells *how long* something lasts:

fifteen years   ten hours   three weeks   a couple of days

2 You use *since* to give the time when an action started:

I've been working here **since 1980**. I hadn't eaten **since eight o'clock**.

Notice that *since* is followed by a time:
1980   eight o'clock   this morning   yesterday   last week

or an event:

I've been working here **since the war**. I hadn't eaten **since breakfast**.

or a clause:

I've been working here **since I left school**.
I hadn't seen him **since I was a child**.

Since is usually found with the present perfect or the past perfect tense.

You use *since* with the present perfect when you are talking about a period of time up to the present:
We **have lived** here **since we were children**. (=and we still live here.)

You use *since* with the past perfect when you are talking about a period of time up to a given time in the past:
It was 1973. Elizabeth **had been** queen **since 1953**. (=and in 1973 she was still queen.)

We also have the common expressions: *It's ..... since + past simple* and *It was .... since + past perfect*:
It's a long time **since I saw** Jeff.   It was five years **since we had last met**.

3 You use *from ... to* or *from ... till/until* to say when something started and finished:

The shops will be open **from nine until five thirty**.
The winter season lasts **from December to March**.
We worked non-stop **from six in the morning till nine at night**.

Till and *until* can be followed by a clause:
We can watch television **till Dad gets home**.
I lived in Manchester **until I went to university in 1987**.

UNIT 29 Practice

A Complete these sentences using the *since* clauses:

1 He hasn't played football
2 We have been good friends
3 She hasn't written to us
4 He has been out at work
5 She has been learning English
6 I have been feeling hungry

a ever since we first met.
b since she started secondary school.
c since seven o'clock this morning.
d ever since supper time.
e since he hurt his leg last week.
f since she sent that letter on your birthday.

B Complete the following sentences by adding *for, since, from* or *until*:

1 There has been a university in Oxford ____*for*____ more than eight hundred years.

2 They have been married _____ 1966.

3 The First World War lasted   1914 _____ 1918.

4 _____ 1992 _____ last year we had a flat in the centre of town.

5 Can you wait for a few minutes _____ I'm ready?

6 I haven't spoken to Bill _____ we were at school.

7 We usually stop for lunch _____ one

_____ two thirty.

8 It has been raining _____ early this morning.

9 It's nearly five years _____ Jenny left school.

10 She was at college _____ two years and she's been working here _____ almost three years.

C Complete these to make true sentences:

1 I have been learning English since _____

2 I have lived in _____ for _____

3 I have an English lesson today from _____ until _____

4 I usually sleep from about _____ to about _____ in the morning.

5 It's _____ since I had my breakfast.

6 I haven't been to the cinema since _____

UNIT 30 | *In/on/at* (time)

1 You use *at* with:

a clock times   at ten o'clock, at midnight
b meals   at breakfast
c religious festivals: at Christmas, at Easter

And notice these special expressions:

at the weekend   **at** the moment   **at** that time   **at** night   **at** the end of the month

2 You use *in* with:

a months   in January, in September
b years   in 1988, in the year 2001
c centuries   in the fourteenth century, in the last century
d parts of the day   in the morning, in the evening
e seasons   in the spring, in winter

It often snows in winter.

3 You use *on* with:

a days   on Monday, on Sunday
b parts of specific days   on Tuesday evening
c special days   on New Year's Day, on Christmas Eve
d dates   on Friday 13th, on the ninth of May
e special occasions   on my birthday, on our anniversary

... on my birthday.

4 You also use *in* to talk about when something will happen in the future:

I'm busy now, so I'll talk to you **in** ten minutes.
They say he will be an important person **in** a few years.

The London train leaves **in** two minutes.

⚠ **Be careful! We do not use *at*, *in* or *on* before words like *this*, *next*, *last*, or *every*, or before *today* and *tomorrow*:**

We'll see you next week sometime.
What are you doing this weekend, John?

We go camping almost every summer.

UNIT
30 Practice

A **Look at the following lists. Each one has a word or expression which does not belong in the group because it takes a different preposition. Can you find which one?**

e.g. ... night, Tuesday, Christmas, the end of the morning.

We say *at night*, *at Christmas* and *at the end of the morning*, so Tuesday is the odd one out.

1 the morning, July, 1999, nine o'clock

2 May 31st, Friday morning, the weekend, Sunday

3 my sister's birthday, eight fifteen, the weekend, lunch

4 the twentieth of August, winter, Wednesday evening, Friday

5 December, the late afternoon, 1956, five o'clock

B **Complete these sentences with *at*, *in*, or *on*:**

1 I was born _____ 1975.

2 My birthday is _____ September.

3 My mother's birthday is _____ the seventeenth of January.

4 I wake up most mornings _____ half-past seven.

5 Last year we went on holiday _____ July.

6 I work best _____ the morning.

7 Yesterday I went to bed _____ midnight.

C **Now write sentences like those in B with information about yourself.**

D **Complete the sentences using the most logical of these words or expressions:**

at the moment   at the end of the month   at dinner   on my birthday   on the first of April
on Monday morning   in the morning   in the next century   in August

1 Do you think life will be very different _____ ?

2 I was given this watch _____

3 It's traditional to play jokes on people _____ .

4 My grandmother would always wear her best clothes _____ .

5 It's very hot here _____ so most people go away on holiday.

6 Jeff slept badly so he felt very tired _____ .

7 I'm afraid Mr Markham is busy _____ . Can you wait a few minutes?

Review: Cycle 1 – Units 1–30

This is the first of the review units.

If you have studied units 1 – 30,

a it will help you see how much progress you have made.

b it will remind you of what you have learnt.

c it will help you see if there are some units you should look at again.

If you have not studied units 1 – 30,

a it will show you how much you know already.

b it will help you decide which units are most useful to you.

The exercises can be done in any order. If you are not sure of the answers, you can check the grammar explanations by looking at the unit in question.

GOOD LUCK!

Mixed tenses

Unit 3: Present simple

A Complete the sentences:

1 January _____ one of the coldest winter months.

2 Hi, my name _____ Carlos. I _____ from Peru.

3 Where _____ you from?

4 My father _____ a doctor.

5 What _____ your father _____ ?

6 I _____ two brothers and a sister.

7 _____ you _____ any brothers or sisters?

8 My hobbies _____ reading, swimming and going to the cinema.

B Make questions using these words:

e.g. you/like/spaghetti?   *Do you like spaghetti?*

1 you/want/go/cinema? _____

2 your father/work/an office? _____

3 your friend/speak/English? _____

4 you/know/that man? _____

5 your mother/have/job? _____

6 you/want/travel abroad? _____

Review: Cycle 1 – Units 1–30

Unit 2: Present continuous

C Complete these questions using the present continuous:

e.g. what/you/think?   *What are you thinking?*

1 What/you/wear/today? _____

2 Where/you/go/tonight? _____

3 What/you/do/now? _____

4 Where/you/sit/at the moment? _____

5 you/listen/music/now? _____

6 you/go on holiday/with your family/this year ? _____

7 you/wear/a watch? _____

8 you/have/lunch/now? _____

Now write your real answers to the questions.

Units 5, 6: Present perfect

D Complete the questions using the verbs in (brackets):

Have you ever ...?

1 (visit) Bath? _____

2 (break) your arm or leg? _____

3 (cook) for more than 5 people? _____

4 (see) a crocodile? _____

5 (take) a photograph? _____

6 (meet) a famous person? _____

Now write your real answers to the questions.

E Look at these activities. Then write if you have done them today, or if you haven't done them yet:

have breakfast	have a shower	read a newspaper	do your homework
eat lunch	finish work	watch TV	speak English
do the washing-up	talk to a friend		

1 I have ...   2 I haven't ... yet.

_____   _____

_____   _____

_____   _____

_____   _____

F **What have they been doing? Complete the dialogues using these verbs:**

revise for my exams   cut onions   wait for two hours   play football

1 Why are you crying? _____

2 Why are you so tired? _____

3 Why are you angry? _____ _____

4 Why are you so dirty? _____

Unit 7: Was/were

G **Complete the text with *was* or *were*:**

We 1 ___*were*___ in a hurry because we 2 _____ late. Our flight 3 _____ at 7.30,

and Steve 4 _____ worried that we might miss the plane. It 5 _____ not easy to find

a taxi at that time of the morning. We eventually got one, and because there 6 _____n't

a lot of traffic, the drive 7 _____ quite quick. It 8 _____ 7.15 when we finally arrived

at the airport. There 9 _____ only 15 minutes left before take-off! We 10 _____

the last people on the plane, of course.

H **Multiple choice. Complete the sentence with the appropriate tense:**

1 We _____ our cousins this weekend.
  a visit   b are visiting   c have visited

2 My dog _____ five years old.
  a has   b are   c is

3 Patrick is very active. He _____ sport every day.
  a is playing   b plays   c play

4 'Have you heard the new record by Madonna?' '_____'
  a Yes, I did.   b No, I didn't.   c No, I haven't.

5 I'll telephone you as soon as I _____ home.
  a get   b will have got   c am getting

6 Where _____ you yesterday?
  a were   b did   c was

Review: Cycle 1 – Units 1–30

7 _____ you go abroad on holiday last year?
   a Did   b Do   c Were

8 I _____ hot food.
   a am liking   b like   c liking

9 Tomorrow _____ the thirty-first of May.
   a is   b are   c is going to be

10 Do you think it _____ tomorrow?
   a rains   b will rain   c is raining

11 There _____ a man, a woman and some children in the garden.
   a was   b were   c are

12 What _____ this sign means?
   a you think   b think you   c do you think

13 Why _____ that?
   a said you   b did you say   c you said

14 'We've got a new teacher' 'Really? _____ ?'
   a How is he   b What's he like   c How is he like

Units 8, 9: Past simple and past continuous

I Complete the text using these verbs in the past simple or past continuous:

shop need find out be surprise know come wear see play walk be

The other day I (1) _found out_ something that (2) _surprised_ me while I (3) _was shopping_ in the city centre. I (4) _was walking_ down the High Street when someone I (5) _knew_ (6) _came out_ out of a very expensive clothes shop. The surprising thing (7) _was_ that she (8) _was wearing_ terrible old jeans and a dirty T-shirt. Later on I (9) _saw_ that those were the clothes she (10) _needed_ for her job: she (11) _played/was_ an actress who (12) _was playing_ the part of a punk in a new film!

J Complete these questions using:

buy speak pay do go understand

1 '_did you go_ to a restaurant yesterday?' 'No, we went last week.'
2 'Where _did you buy_ your sunglasses?' 'I didn't. They were a present.'
3 'How much _did you pay_ for your camera, Sandra?'
4 'What _were you doing_ at ten o'clock last night?' 'We were talking with some friends.'
5 '_did you understand_ what he said?' 'No, he _was speaking_ Italian, I think.

Review: Cycle 1 – Units 1–30

Unit 11: Present tenses used for the future

K Complete the sentences using the present simple or present continuous:

1 Today is Monday 21st, so the day after tomorrow ___is___ the 23rd.
2 This morning I got up at 5 a.m. Tomorrow _I get_ at 7 a.m.
3 Today I flew to Paris. On Friday _I'm flying_ to Acapulco.
4 Last night we had a pizza. Tonight _we are having_ fish and chips.
5 We went to a disco last month, and we _are going_ to another one next week.
6 The first train left at 8.30; the next train _leaves_ at 11.25.
7 The film I saw last night began at 6. Tonight the film _begins_ at 8.15.

Unit 12: Will and going to

L Choose the correct answer:

1 'There's someone at the door.' 'OK, _I go/I'll go._'
2 My neighbours _will have/are having_ a barbecue tonight.
3 I _am going to/will_ help you if you want.
4 Look at those clouds. I think it _will/is going to_ rain soon.
5 According to the timetable, the next bus _goes/will go_ at 6.
6 We _will meet/are going to meet_ Bill and Patty tomorrow.

M Look at the pictures and complete the sentences using *will* or *going to*:

1 He _is going to_ have a shower.
2 They _are going to_ see a play.
3 They _are going to_ have a crash.

4 'I think I _will_ have the omelette.'
5 'We _will_ see you on Sunday, then.'

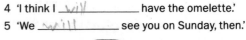

Units 13, 14, 15: There, what and wh- questions

N Complete the dialogues:

1 '_what_'s the matter? You look worried.'
'_there_'s a spider on my desk !'
'_where_ is it exactly? I can't see it.'
'It's on my books'.
'Well, it isn't _there_ now.'

2 'Excuse me. _where_ can I buy a
newspaper near here?'
'_there_'s a newsagents on Park Street.'
'_where_'s that?'
'Just round the corner.

Review: Cycle 1 – Units 1–30

3 'Hi, Mark! _____*how*_____ are you?'

'Fine. _____*where*_____ are you going?'

'We're off to the centre.'

'Sorry, _____*what*_____

did you say?'

'I said we're going to the centre.'

'_____*why*_____?'

_____*what*_____'s happening?'

'_____*there*_____'s a sale on at Debenhams.'

Units 16, 17, 18: Nouns

O Choose the correct answer:

1 How many *brother/brothers* and *sister/sisters* do you have?
2 *Man/men* and *woman/women* can do the same jobs.
3 I like your jeans. *Is it/Are they* new?
4 Sheila's having her *hairs/hair* cut this afternoon.
5 Don't worry. The police *is/are* coming.
6 There aren't so many *bus/buses* after 8 p.m.
7 They say that eating *carrot/carrots* will help you see well in *dark/the dark*.

Units 19, 20, 21: A/an/some and the

P Add *the, a, an* or *some* where necessary:

1 Would you like _____*a*_____ piece of _____ cake I made yesterday?

2 Yes, that'd be nice. But just _____*a*_____ small piece.

3 A lot of people think that New York is _____*a*_____ capital of _____ United States.

4 You're working too hard. You need _____*a*_____ holiday.

5 Do you drive on _____ left or on _____ right-hand side of _____ road in your country?

6 You often have to wait for _____ hour or more before you can see _____*a*_____ doctor.

7 'I'm going to _____ supermarket. Do you want anything?' 'Yes, can you get me _____*a*_____ can of soup

and _____*some*_____ eggs, please?'

8 'What time are you going to _____*a*_____ match tomorrow?' 'I've told you _____*a*_____ hundred times,

at two o'clock.'

Review: Cycle 1 – Units 1–30

Units 22 – 26: Possessives, demonstratives and pronouns

Q **Fill in the missing words in these sentences:**

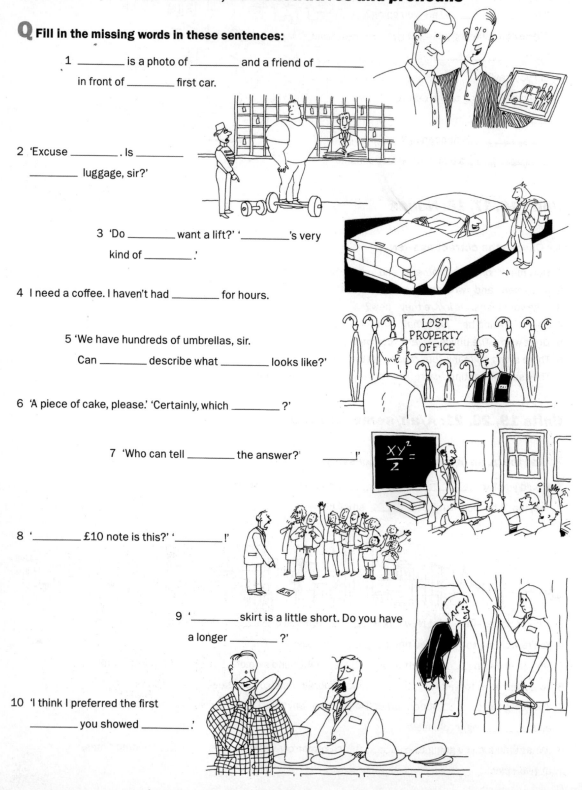

1 _____ is a photo of _____ and a friend of _____ in front of _____ first car.

2 'Excuse _____ . Is _____ _____ luggage, sir?'

3 'Do _____ want a lift?' '_____'s very kind of _____.'

4 I need a coffee. I haven't had _____ for hours.

5 'We have hundreds of umbrellas, sir. Can _____ describe what _____ looks like?'

6 'A piece of cake, please.' 'Certainly, which _____ ?'

7 'Who can tell _____ the answer?' '_____!'

8 '_____ £10 note is this?' '_____!'

9 '_____ skirt is a little short. Do you have a longer _____ ?'

10 'I think I preferred the first _____ you showed _____.'

Cycle 1

Review: Cycle 1 – Units 1–30

Units 27, 28, 29: Adverbials

R Choose which adverbial best completes these sentences:

1 What was the weather like *next week/last week*?

2 They eat fish and chips *always/a lot* in England.

3 We enjoyed the party *much/a lot*.

4 It's ages *until/since* the holidays start.

5 It's ages *until/since* we last went to the sea.

6 They are *probably/maybe* going to get married in May.

7 If you phone them now they'll *possibly/probably* be there.

8 This park is so popular you can *occasionally/hardly ever* find a place to sit down.

Unit 30: In/on/at (time)

S Fill the gaps with *in/on/at* where necessary:

1 We're having our holiday _____ the autumn this year.

2 What did you do _____ the weekend?

3 It snowed _____ Christmas Eve last year.

4 Our first lesson is _____ the morning.

5 School finishes _____ 3.30 in England.

6 A lot of people are too worried to go out _____ night.

7 The announcement said our plane will take off _____ half an hour.

8 Do you want to come with us _____ next week?

9 Can you imagine what life was like _____ the seventeenth century?

10 I've felt sick _____ every morning this week.

71

May/might (possibility)

1 **You use *may* or *might* to talk about something which is possible, but we are not sure of:**

a in the present:

'Where is Sue?' 'She **might** be at the office.'

'Is Chris Sutton a football player?' 'He **might** be, I'm not sure.'

'I'm sure his wife's name is Elise.' 'You **may** be right.'

b in the future:

'What are you doing tonight, John?' 'I **might** go to the pub.'

'Is it going to rain tomorrow?' 'It **may**. I haven't seen the weather forecast.'

'Valerie **might** not come to school tomorrow. She's a bit ill today.'

2 **Note that *may* and *might*, like all modal verbs, have only one form. There is no -s ending for *he/she/it*:**

I **might** go to the party tonight.

You **might** meet my mother if you come tomorrow.

He **might** be French. I don't know.

Ask that woman where the post office is. She **might** know.

It **might** rain later, so take an umbrella.

Be careful: you use an infinitive without *to* after *may/might*:

They **might be** angry if we are late. (not: *might to be*)

It **may be** true, I don't know. (not: *may to be true*)

3 **The negative of *might* is *might not* or *mightn't*; the negative of *may* is *may not* (there is no short form):**

'We **might not** be able to sell these chairs.'

'The traffic is bad, so I **mightn't** be back before 10 or 11.'

4 **There is no important difference in meaning between *may* and *might*, but *might* is a little less sure than *may*:**

Take some paper and pens. They **might** be useful.

Take some paper and pens. They **may** be useful.

A Read these sentences and decide if they are future (F) or present (P):

1 I might be able to visit you this Friday. _____

2 John may be back home now. Give him a ring. _____

3 You may know the answer to this question already. _____

4 They might be politicians, it's hard to say. _____

5 We might be going to France this year. _____

6 You may be wrong about her age. She doesn't look 50. _____

7 Try this cheese. You might like it! _____

8 Chinese may be the most important language next century. _____

B Change the sentences using *may/might*:

e.g. Perhaps he is at the party.   *He might be at the party.* _____

1 Perhaps the shops are closed now. _____

2 Perhaps they are on holiday. _____

3 Perhaps the weather will be good tomorrow. _____

4 Perhaps I will get married before I am 30. _____

5 Perhaps they will go to the disco tonight. _____

6 It's nice here. Perhaps I'll stay an extra week. _____

7 Perhaps we will go to see the new play at the theatre. _____

8 They've trained a lot. Perhaps they will win the match. _____

C What do you think? Write your opinions about the statements:

e.g. It'll rain tomorrow.   *Yes, I think it will.* _____
  No, I don't think it will. _____
  I'm not sure. It might. _____

1 The next leader of your country will be a woman. _____

2 You will go to the cinema this month. _____

3 You will receive a letter this week. _____

4 The price of your favourite drink will go up this year. _____

5 Someone will ask you a difficult question today. _____

6 You will eat in a restaurant next week. _____

7 There will be some very good news tomorrow. _____

8 You will go to a party this weekend. _____

9 The weather will be better next month than it is now. _____

10 You will listen to music this evening. _____

Cycle 2

Can/could/be able to (possibility and ability)

1 You use *can* (negative *cannot* or *can't*):

a to say that something is possible:
Swimming after eating **can** be dangerous.
Making mistakes **can** be a good way of learning.
Smoking **cannot** be good for you!

goes
She ~~gos~~ to the
~~Sinema~~ with her friends
cinema

I **can't** spell very well.

b to say that someone knows how to do something:
My brother **can** drive.
Can you speak French?

c to say that someone has the ability to do something:
She's a great driver: she **can** drive almost any car.
I **can't** eat fish.
Anyone **can** become a qualified teacher.

d with verbs like *see, hear, feel, smell, remember, recognise* and *imagine*:
She **can't** remember the name of the book.
I **can't** see the reason for doing that.
Can you imagine living in a palace?

'Don't shout! We **can** all hear you.'

You can use *be able to* instead of *can* except in category a, but *can* is more common, and less formal:

My brother **is able** to drive. I **am not able** to eat fish.
She **isn't able** to remember the name of the book.

2 You use *could* (negative *could not* or *couldn't*):

a to talk about someone's ability in the past:
He **could** run faster than any of us.   She **could** tell the most incredible jokes.
A lot of them **couldn't** read or write.

b with verbs like *see, hear, smell, feel, remember, recognise* and *imagine* in the past:
You **could** see they weren't happy.   The policeman **could** smell gas.
He **couldn't** see them, but he **could** hear them in the dark.

c to say you are not completely sure if something is possible:
There's a lot of traffic. That **could** explain why he's late.
There **could** be a storm tonight: look at the clouds!

3 You use *be able to* instead of *can*:

a after another modal verb (*will/must/might* etc):
I **might be able to** help you later on.   You **should be able to** buy some cheese in that shop.
b if you want to use an *-ing* form or a *to-infinitive*:
It's nice **to be able to** get some exercise.   He complained about not **being able to** go to London
I enjoy **being able to** get up late at the weekend.
c to talk about something someone managed to do in a particular situation in the past (negative *wasn't/weren't able to* OR *couldn't*):
Were you **able to** buy everything on the list?   They **were able to** save enough money to buy a car.
I **wasn't able to** finish the meal. (=I couldn't finish it)

A Rewrite these questions replacing *know how to* with *can* or *can't*:

1 Do you know how to drive? _____

2 Do you know how to play the piano? _____

3 Where could we find someone who knows how to repair clocks? _____

4 Do any of your friends know how to use a word processor? _____

Now give your real answers to these questions.

B

1 Look at the picture, then use the verbs in the box to write sentences about what Jack can do, like this:

Jack can drive. I don't know if he can cook.

drive cook play chess sing play the guitar paint ski speak Spanish play tennis type skate ride a horse

2 Now write sentences about the activities you can and can't do, like this:

I can ski, but I can't cook.

3 Now write sentences about when you learnt to do these things, like this:

I can drive now, but I couldn't two years ago.

C Complete the sentences using:

can could can't couldn't were able to will be able to won't be able to

1. I don't think we _____ travel to Mars before 2010.

2 Luckily the weather was great, so we _____ have a picnic.

3 My cousin _____ swim when he was three, but I still _____ .

4 The music was so loud that I _____ hear what you were saying.

5 If we don't finish early, we _____ see the programme on TV.

6 Anyone _____ do that!

Which sentence has more than one possible answer?

D Rewrite these sentences using *be able to*, like this:

I can get up late. I enjoy being able to get up late.

The reasons I enjoy holidays ...

1 I can wear casual clothes. *I enjoy* _____

2 I can watch TV when I want. _____

3 I can see my friends. _____

4 I can travel abroad. _____

5 I can stay up late. _____

Cycle 2

Can/could/will/would (offers and requests)

1 You use *can I* or, to be more polite, *can I possibly* or *could I (possibly)*:

a when you offer to do something for someone:

Can I help you, sir?

Could I carry your suitcase for you, sir?

b when you ask if it is OK to do something:
Can I take the last biscuit?
Could I borrow £10 from you, Sam? I'll pay you back soon.

2 You can use *I'll* to offer to do something. It is more informal than *can I* or *could I*:

I'll take you into town if you want.
I'll answer the door for you.

3 You use *can you* or, to be more polite *could you* to make a request:

Can you help me with the washing-up, Harry, please?

'**Could you** come here, please? I need some help.'

You can also use *would you mind + -ing* to make a request, and *would you mind not + -ing* to ask someone to stop doing something:

Would you mind answering a few questions, please?

Would you mind not smoking?

Would you mind not talking during the examination, please?

4 You use *would you* or *will you* to make a polite request to someone when you are more important than them. *Would you* is more polite than *will you*:

Jane, **would you** open the letters on my desk, please?
Will you be quiet for a moment, please?

5 You use *would you like* to offer someone something:

Hugh, **would you like** another drink?
Would you like to come to Scotland with us?

Cycle 2

A Change these statements into polite questions, using *could*:

1 I want to have another cup of coffee. _____ ?
2 Give me a cigarette. _____ ?
3 Tell me when the train leaves. _____ ?
4 We want to have a table near the window. _____ ?
5 I want to have a ticket to London. _____ ?
6 I want to go home early today. _____ ?

B Do the same with these questions, using *would you like* to make them into polite offers:

1 Do you want to watch TV now? _____ ?
2 Do you want soup with your meal? _____ ?
3 Do you want to go home now or later? _____ ?
4 Do you want sugar in your tea? _____ ?
5 Do you want me to type these letters? _____ ?
6 Do you want us to help you plan the meeting? _____ ?
7 Do you want a single or a double room? _____ ?
8 Do you want me to start work early tomorrow? _____ ?

C Complete the requests using *Would you mind ...?* following the model:

e.g. I'm hot. (open the window) _Would you mind opening the window?_

1 It's cold in here. (close the door) _____ ?
2 I can't concentrate. (turn the music down) _____ ?

3 I've got a cough. (not smoke) _____
_____ ?

4 We can't understand you. (not speak French)
_____ ?

5 The manager is busy at the moment. (wait a minute) _____ ?
6 I'm sorry, Simon's not here now. (leave a message) _____ ?

Cycle 2

Would like/want (wants and wishes)

1 **You use *would like* to talk about something you want:**

a *would like to + infinitive*:
I **would like to be able** to speak several languages.
They **would like to know** what time we'll be back home.

b *would like + noun*:
They **would like seats** in the non-smoking section.
We **would like an English-German dictionary**, please.

2 **You can use the short form *'d* for *would* after a pronoun:**

We**'d like** to go now, please.
He**'d like** to see you again on Thursday, if possible.
I**'d like** you to do this for homework, please.

3 **The negative is *would not like* or *wouldn't like*:**

Don't be late. The boss **wouldn't like** that.

'I **wouldn't like** to meet him on a dark night.'

4 **Stronger forms: *would like – would love / wouldn't like – would hate***

I**'d love** another ice-cream!
You know what I**'d love**? I**'d love** to travel around the world.
We**'d hate** to live somewhere cold.

5 **You use *want to* to talk about something you need or desire:**

a *want to + infinitive*; negative *don't want to + infinitive*:
I **wanted to be** a pilot when I was young.
We **don't want to go** shopping this afternoon.
Do you **want to come** with us?

b *want + noun*; negative *don't want + noun*:
Do you **want a cup of tea**?
Who **wants another piece of cake**?
I **don't want dogs** in my house.

Careful! You don't normally use *I want* when you are asking for something.
It is not polite. In a shop you don't say:
'I want a packet of chewing gum.'

It is better to say:
'**Can/could I have** a packet of chewing gum?' OR
'I**'d like** a packet of chewing gum, please.'

'I **'d like** a packet of chewing gum, please.'

A What do they want? Using the pictures, match the requests and the reasons:

1 'Can I have a packet of cigarettes and a box of matches?'
2 'How much does it cost to stay in that hotel in France?'
3 'Where is Park Street, please?'
4 'Can I be excused, please?'
5 'I need flour, eggs, sugar, butter, milk and apples.'
6 'Please be quiet.'
7 'Could I ask you a few questions, Prime Minister?'
8 'Is this seat free?'

a He wants to leave the room.
b She wants to sit down.
c She wants to make a cake.
d They want to go to a party.
e She wants to get some information.
f They want a holiday.
g He wants to study.
h He wants to smoke.

B Look at this list. Give your reactions to some of the ideas using *I'd like to ...* or *I'd love to ...* or *I wouldn't like to ...* or *I'd hate to ...* :

e.g. I'd love to learn how to fly.
      I wouldn't like to wake up at 4 a.m. every day.

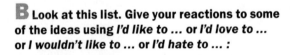
'I'd _____ to find a spider in my bed.'

speak English fluently
speak several languages well
be able to cook
meet your favourite singer
be famous
go to New York next week
be very rich
have a sports car
find a spider in my bed
be 100 years old
be in hospital
live in a haunted house
live in another country
work in a noisy factory
be a teacher/politician/stuntman
wake up at 11 a.m. every day

C Now find out three things your friend would like to do, and three things he/she wouldn't like to do.

Cycle 2

Have to/have got to/must/mustn't (obligation)

1 **You use *must* to say that it is necessary or important for someone to do something; the negative is *mustn't*:**

a in the present:

I **must** go now, I don't want to be late.

b in the future:

I **must** talk to him tomorrow afternoon.
You **mustn't** forget to phone me.

2 **You use *must* when you are giving your opinion about something that is very important, when you want to make a strong suggestion, or when you are giving someone an invitation:**

You **must** go and see the new Spielberg film. It's great.
This is a book that you really **must** read.
You **must** visit us.

3 **You use *must not* or *mustn't* to say that it is important NOT to do something:**

You **mustn't** take photos in the gallery, it's bad for the paintings.
I **mustn't** forget to write a cheque for the rent today.

4 **You use *has to/have to* when you talk about something that must happen, such as when a law or someone else says that something is necessary or important:**

Because Sandra is an au-pair, she **has to** get up early and help with the children's breakfast.
Val won't be in work today. She **has to** see the doctor.

5 **You use *don't have to* to say that something is not necessary:**

You **don't have to** do the whole exercise.
Tomorrow is Sunday, so I **don't have to** get up early.

6 **You use *had to* or *didn't have to* for the past of both *must* and *have to*:**

I **had to** go to London yesterday for a meeting.
The doctor told me I **had to** stop smoking.
'**Did** you **have to** wait long for the bus?'

7 **You use *do, does* and *did* to make questions with *have to* and *not have to*:**

'When **does** Dave **have to** go back to work?'
'**Do** you **have to** book a table in that restaurant?'
'**Did** everyone **have to** wear a uniform before?'

8 **In informal English, you can use *have got to* instead of *have to*:**

It's late. We've **got to** go.
Where **have you got to** send that letter?

UNIT 35 Practice

A You are the manager of a company talking to a new employee. Put a tick (✔) next to the things you think are very important for people who work for you:

work hard   speak good English   be smart   know how to type

have long hair   be polite   arrive early   be punctual   be organized

Now tell the new employee about the job, using *must*:

1 _____ 3 _____

2 _____ 4 _____

B Look at these signs. They all give information about what you must or mustn't do. Complete the sentences using 'must' or 'mustn't':

e.g. This sign means you mustn't drive over 30 mph.

1 This sign means you _____ .
2 This sign means you _____ .
3 This sign means you _____ .
4 This sign means you _____ .
5 This sign means you _____ .
6 This sign means you _____ .
7 This sign means you _____ .
8 This sign means you _____ .

C What was life at school like when you were young? Complete the sentences using *had to* or *didn't have to*:

1 _____ stand up when the teacher came into the room.
2 _____ wear a uniform.
3 _____ do a lot of homework.
4 _____ have short hair.
5 _____ study languages.
6 _____ eat at school.
7 _____ take a lot of exams.

D Complete the sentences using *has to* or *have to*:

1 Because Jill is a student she _____ read a lot of books.

2 Frank's a sportsman. He _____ keep very fit.

3 If you want to be a pilot you _____ have good eyesight.

4 Before you can drive a car you _____ take a test.

5 You _____ be 18 or over to see some films.

6 If you break something in a shop you _____ pay for it.

Now rewrite the sentences using *has got to* or *have got to*.

81

Should/ought/had better (advice)

UNIT
36

1 **You use *should* or *ought to* to talk about the right thing to do in a situation:**

Jane's in hospital. We **should** visit her.

You **should** go and see that film. It's great.

We **ought to** leave now, it's getting late.

You **ought to** be polite to people you don't know.

You use *should not* (or *shouldn't*), and *ought not to* when it is not the right thing to do:

Children **shouldn't** go to bed late.

You **shouldn't** eat too much chocolate, it's bad for you.

If you don't like people, you **ought not to** be a teacher.

2 **You can use *should* or *ought to* when you are giving someone advice about what to do:**

You **should** see a doctor if you are in pain.

You **ought to** buy a new car. Yours is dangerous.

You **should** spend your money carefully.

For advice about what not to do, you use *shouldn't* or *ought not to*:

You **shouldn't** drink and drive.

You **ought not to** smoke so much.

3 **You can also use *I think ... should* and *I think ... ought to* to give your opinion. The negative is *I don't think ... should/ought to ...*:**

I think we **ought to** go now.

Do you think I **should** buy the red or the blue dress?

My friends don't think I **should** go to Britain next year.

4 **You can also use *had better* + infinitive or *'d better* (negative *had better not* + infinitive) to give your opinion or some advice:**

We'd better leave now, or we'll be late.

You'd better not go out. It's raining.

A Match the sentence parts:

1 If you feel hot	you should put the heating on.
2 If you are cold	you ought to see a doctor.
3 If you feel hungry	you should see a dentist.
4 If you feel sleepy	you should go to bed now.
5 If you don't feel well	you ought to open the window.
6 If your teeth hurt	you should have something to eat.
7 If you don't understand something	you should ask for help.

B Write one piece of positive advice and one piece of negative advice using *should* or *shouldn't* for these situations:

1 In a hospital   (be calm)   (make a lot of noise)

_____   _____

2 At work   (arrive late)   (work hard)

_____   _____

3 On the motorway   (drive carefully)   (drive close to the car in front)

_____   _____

4 In the library   (play music)   (work in silence)

_____   _____

Now rewrite your answers using *ought to* and *ought not to*.

C Look at the pictures, then give your friend advice using *I think you should ...* or *I don't think you should ...* :

1 I've got an exam tomorrow morning. What should I do?

3 I found a small sum of money on the ground this morning. What should I do?

5 I've been invited to a party by a group of people I don't really know. But my favourite film is on tv. What should I do?

2 I saw someone driving dangerously in town. What should I do?

4 The person next to me in the exam was cheating. What should I do?

6 I need a holiday. I have enough money for either a weekend in New York, or a week in Scotland. I can't decide. Where should I go?

Cycle 2

UNIT 37 | Impersonal *it*

1 You use *it* to talk about the time or the date:

What time is it?　　It's one o'clock.　It's nearly two o'clock.
What day is it today?　It's Monday.　It's the first of January.

2 You use *it* + *since* to say how long ago something happened:

It's two weeks **since** I washed the car.　It's nearly a year **since** our last holiday.
It's a long time **since** you last wrote to me.

3 You use *it* to talk about the weather:

It's very cold.　It'll be nice and warm.　It was very hot in Brazil.
I think it's going to rain.　It's often very windy in autumn.

4 You use *it* + *adjective* + *...ing* or *it* + *to - infinitive...* to express a general opinion:

It's **great living** in London.　It's **dangerous driving** fast at night.
It's difficult **to** learn a foreign language.　It's not safe **to** go out at night.

You can say *It is/was ... of you/ him/ her to ... :*
It was clever **of you to** remember my name.　It is kind **of you to** write to me.

You can say *It is/was ... for ... to ... :*
It's easy **for** anyone **to** make a mistake.　It's hard **for** me **to** get up early in the morning.

5 You use *It* + *(that) ...* to express an opinion.

It's **great that** she has passed her exams.　It's surprising Alan didn't send you a birthday card.

Six more very common expressions:

It"s lucky ...　It's nice ...　It's a good thing ...　It's a pity ...　It's possible ...　It's funny ...

It's lucky it's not raining.　**It's a pity** it's so cold.　**It's possible** that we'll get a letter tomorrow.
It's funny we haven't met before.　**It's a good thing** you can speak English.

6 You use *I like/don't like/hate it ....* to express an opinion:

I like **it** here.　I hate **it** when you leave .

7 You use *Who is it?* to ask who someone is. You use *It's* to identify someone:

A Who's that over there?　B It's Bill.

8 Some more common expressions with *it*:

It doesn't matter ...　It takes ages ...　It takes a week ...

A I'm afraid I'll be a bit late.
B Don't worry. **It doesn't matter.**

A How long does it take to get to London?
B **It takes** about an hour by train.

Now do the practice exercises and say whether each answer belongs to number 1, 2, 3, 4, 5, 6, or 7 above.

A Complete these sentences by writing *It's a pity ... / It's lucky ... / It's a good thing ...* :

1 _It's a pity_ English is such a difficult language.

2 Everything's very expensive. _____ we brought plenty of money with us.

3 There's nothing to eat. _____ we had a big breakfast.

4 It's nice to see you, but _____ Ian isn't here too.

5 It's awfully cold in here. _____ we are wearing warm clothes.

6 It's very crowded in here. _____ we didn't come earlier.

7 He's a very clever boy. _____ he's so lazy.

B Use these expressions to complete the dialogue:

> Oh, it's great being in London.   Hello, it's me, Angela.   it's ages since I saw you.   Who is it?
> It's nice to talk to you.   Well, it's a bit cold, but it's not too bad.

A: Hello. _Who is it?_ _____ B: _____

A: Oh, hi! What's it like in England? B: _____

A: What about the weather? B: _____

_____

A: _____ B: Well, _____

Continue the dialogue with these expressions:

> I didn't like it very much on the plane.   it was a very long journey.   it's four o'clock in the morning.
> Was it very uncomfortable?   Eight o'clock.   I didn't know it was so late.   It's really nice to hear from you.

A: Did you have a good journey? B: Not really. _____

_____

A: Why not? _____ B: No, it was comfortable, but _____

_____

A: What time is it over there? B: _____ Why?

A: Well _____

_____ here in Singapore. B: Oh, I'm sorry. _____

A: Don't worry. _____ _____

Cycle 2

38 Verbs with two objects

1 Some verbs often have two objects – an *indirect* object and a *direct* object:

I'll buy **some chocolate** (direct object) **for the children** (indirect object).
I'll buy **the children** (indirect object) **some chocolate** (direct object).

She wrote **a long letter** (direct object) **to her mother** (indirect object)
She wrote **her mother** (indirect object) **a long letter** (direct object)

2 With these verbs you normally use *for* for the indirect object:

book	get	buy	keep	bring	make
cook	pour	cut	prepare	find	save

They kept a place **for Jack**.

Will you bring something **for the children**?

Could you pour a cup of coffee **for your mother**?

I'll book a room in the hotel **for you**.

She cooked a great meal **for us**.

I bought some flowers **for her**.

3 With these verbs you normally use *to* for the indirect object:

give	post	tell	lend	promise	write	pay
hand	read	offer	sell	pass	show	teach

They say they posted the letter **to you** last week. He promised it **to me**.
Show it **to Bill** when you've seen it. Do you think you could lend it **to us**?

4 When the indirect object is very short you can put it right after the verb:

Give **Mary** my love. She sent **her sister** a birthday card.
He cooked **them** a wonderful meal. Ken bought **his teacher** a present.

A Rewrite these sentences changing the indirect object to *him, her* or *them*:

1 He cooked a nice meal for all his friends. *He cooked them a nice meal.*

2 She lent some money to her grandmother. _____

3 Hand that plate to your brother. _____

4 Who'll read a story to the children? _____

5 I've made some coffee for father. _____

6 Jack's gone to get some water for his mother. _____

7 He offered the job to a young girl. _____

B Rewrite these sentences using an indirect object with *to* or *for*:

1 I have booked them seats. (the children) *I have booked seats for the children.*

2 Can you make them a cup of tea? (everyone) _____

3 I've written her a letter. (my sister) _____

4 Who's going to cook them supper? (the family) _____

5 We can show them our photographs. (all the visitors) _____

6 Could you cut them some bread? (your brothers and sisters) _____

7 I sold her my old skis. (your friend) _____

C Complete these sentences to show what presents Diana gave her family:

1 She bought a bicycle *for her little brother, Simon.*

2 She gave Helen _____ .

3 She bought a pipe _____ .

4 She sent some flowers _____ .

5 She bought _____ a box of chocolates.

6 She gave a dictionary _____ .

7 She bought a nice new teapot _____ .

8 She gave _____ a pullover.

Close your books and see how many of Diana's presents you can remember.

39 *Make and do*

1 You use *make* with nouns referring to:

Plans: appointment arrangement choice decision plan
Travel: journey tour trip visit
Talking and sounds: comment noise point promise sound speech suggestion
Food and drink: breakfast a cup of tea some coffee a meal a sandwich

I think I **made the wrong decision.**   Let's **make a plan.**
In 1978 she **made a trip** to America.   We'll **make a short visit** if we have time.
If you **make a promise** you have to keep it. Don't **make too much noise.**

2 If you *make* something you produce something new:

Sheila **makes** all her own clothes. You can **make** petrol from coal.

3 Some common expressions with *make*:

make friends (with) – **make** a mistake – **make** some money
make a difference – two and two **make** four – I think Pedro would **make** a good teacher

4 You use *do* with *-ing* forms and with words to do with work:

Who's going to **do the cleaning?**   He **does** all **the shopping** and I **do the washing.**
I have **a lot of work** to **do.**   He gets up early and **does a hard day's work.**

5 You often use *do* with a noun instead of another verb if the meaning is clear from the noun:

You must **do your teeth** before you go to bed.   Have you **done the dishes** yet?
I'll **do the kitchen** if you **do the flowers.**   Do I need to **do my hair?**

6 Some common expressions with *do*:

do well **do** badly **do** your homework **do** an exercise

A Complete these sentences using *make* or *do*:

1 Don't forget to _____ your homework.

2 Read your book carefully and _____ the exercise on page 52.

3 If you want to see Mr. Brown you must _____ an appointment .

4 I have to _____ a speech at the meeting tomorrow.

5 The baby is going to sleep. Try not to _____ a noise.

6 I'll _____ the garden if you _____ the house.

7 We have to _____ a long journey. We should try to leave early.

8 Some pop stars and sports stars _____ a lot of money.

9 'Don't be frightened. He just wants to _____ friends.'

B Complete these questions, then tell a friend your answers:

1 Have you ever had to _____ a speech?

2 Who _____ most of the washing-up in your house?

3 If you _____ a promise , do you always keep it?

4 Do you _____ friends easily?

5 Was it easy to _____ this exercise?

10 'Just be careful and try not to _____ a mistake.'

Close your books and see how many questions you can remember.

C Complete these dialogues using *make* or *do*:

1   A: What work do you want to _____ when you leave school?

B: If I _____ well in my exams I'd like to be a doctor.

A: Then you would _____ a lot of money.

B: I don't mind about the money. I just want to _____ an interesting job.

2

A: Are you going to _____ a cup of coffee?

B: I have to _____ the dishes first.

A: OK then. I'll _____ the coffee, while you _____ the washing up.

B: Right. While we have coffee we can _____ plans for our holiday this year.

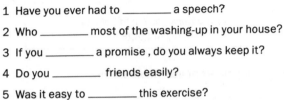

Cycle 2

UNIT 40 Uncount nouns (2)

(See Unit 18 for patterns with uncount nouns)

1 Review of Unit 18:

Uncount nouns do not have a plural form. You do not use *a/an* with uncount nouns. You can use *some* with uncount nouns.

I bought **some rice** and **some milk**.

2 Some nouns which are uncount nouns in English have plurals in other languages:

advice	homework	machinery
baggage	information	money
equipment	knowledge	news
furniture	luggage	traffic

She gave me a **lot of useful advice.**
There's **not much traffic** in town at midday.

How many of the words above have plurals in your language?
Mark them and remember that they are uncount in English.

'Do you think you could help me with my **luggage**?'

3 If you want to use these words with a plural meaning you often use these words:

bit: She gave me a few **bits of advice.**   I have a couple of **bits of news** for you.
piece: They had only a few **pieces of furniture.**

You can say a *piece of* or *a bit of* if you want to show that you are talking about a single item:
A calculator is **a useful piece of equipment.**   That's **a heavy bit of luggage.**

4 Nouns ending in *-ing* are uncount:

Living at home is much cheaper.   **Skiing** is an expensive hobby.

5 Many abstract nouns are uncount. Here are some of the commonest ones:

time trouble weather love fun travel work happiness music

We had lovely **weather** in Spain and Greece.

Travel by train isn't always comfortable.

6 Some nouns have two meanings – one count and one uncount:

Hurry up. We haven't **much time.**   I've been to Athens **three times.**

90

Cycle 2

A Use these words to complete the sentences below:

advice information news homework money traffic furniture equipment

1 I want to buy some stereo equipment. I wonder if you could give me some _____.

2 Did you hear the _____ on the radio this morning?

3 I can't go out tonight. I have too much _____ .

4 They bought a lot of new _____ for the dining room.

5 He has two computers and lots of other electronic _____ .

6 I'd like some _____ about trains to Oxford please.

7 How much _____ will we need for the journey?

8 There's always a lot of _____ in the rush hour.

B Rewrite these sentences using the words given in brackets:

1 Let me give you some advice. (a piece)
  Let me give you a piece of advice.

2 There was some old furniture in the room. (a few bits of)
_____

3 I have some homework to do. (a couple of bits)
_____

4 The fire destroyed some expensive machinery. (a piece)
_____

5 I wonder if you could help me with some information. (a bit)
_____

6 I have some good news for you and some bad news. (a piece; a bit)
_____

7 A computer is very expensive equipment. (a piece of)
_____

8 They had a lot of luggage. (more than a dozen pieces)
_____

C Use these words to complete the sentences below:

fun music trouble happiness weather travel work

1 If you behave badly you will get into a lot of _____ .

2 We have lovely _____ in summer and autumn.

3 I've got a lot of _____ to do before I can go home tonight.

4 We had a lot of _____ when we went out last night.

5 That piano sonata is one of my favourite pieces of _____ .

6 Money doesn't always bring _____ .

7 I enjoy foreign _____ .

Quantifiers (1) – patterns with *of*

1 **When you are talking about a particular group of people or things you can use these patterns:**

All of the children enjoyed the party.   **All of** us enjoyed the party.
They didn't eat **all of** the cakes.   They didn't eat **all of** them.
We picked **some of** the flowers.   We picked **some of** them.

2 **When you are talking about two people or things you use *both*:**

Both of the girls stayed at home.   **Both of** them stayed at home.

You use *neither* for the negative:
Neither of the boys stayed at home.   **Neither of** you stayed at home

3 **You can use numbers and fractions with these patterns:**

'I've broken **one of** the glasses.'

'I've read about **a quarter of** it.'

About half of the pupils are girls.   **Two of** them were very big, and one was quite small.

4 **You can also use these expressions:**

For a large number or amount: a lot of   lots of   many of   plenty of
I've read **lots of** the books in the library.   I've read **lots of** them.

For more than half: I know **most of** the people in your class.

For a small number or amount: I've got some new magazines. Would you like to borrow **a few of** them?

For none: none of   not ... any of

None of us enjoyed the programme.

She didn't like **any of** them.

5 **You can use all these words with a possessive :**

I'm going to invite **all of my** friends.   I've read **most of your** books.

A Complete these sentences to make true statements:

1 _two of_ the people in my country speak English.
2 _neither of_ the children in my country must go to school until they are _____ .
3 _both of_ the young people in my country go to university.
4 _one of_ the people in my country live in large towns or cities.
5 _none of_ the people in my country live in villages.
6 _most of_ my classmates are men/boys.
7 _none of_ the TV programmes at the weekend are interesting.
8 _both of_ my friends live in my town/village.

B Complete these sentences using *one, two, all, both, some, most, none, neither*:

1 _Two of_ the men are wearing suits.
2 _neither of_ the boys are playing.
3 _both of_ the boys are reading.
4 _one of_ the women is sitting down.
5 _none of_ the men are sitting down.
6 _most of_ the adults are standing up.
7 _none of_ the children are reading.

8 _both of_ the women are wearing suits.
9 _both of_ the girls are playing.
10 _neither of_ the girls are reading.
11 _two of the_ the women are standing up.
12 _two of the_ the women are wearing dresses.
13 _both of the_ the children are playing.
14 _one of the_ the men is wearing a pullover.

Write six sentences about the picture. Write three that are true and three that are not true:

1 _____
2 _____
3 _____
4 _____
5 _____
6 _____

Give your sentences to a friend. See if he/she can say which are true and which are not true.
Close your books and see how much you can remember about the picture.

Cycle 2

Quantifiers (2)

(Review the patterns in Unit 41. All the examples there are with count nouns.)

1 You can use these words with uncount nouns:

all of   some of   a lot of   lots of   plenty of   most of   none of   a bit of

'Don't hurry, we have **plenty of time**.

He earns **a lot of money**.

We've finished **most of** the bread. Could you buy some more?

2 You can say   they/them all ... you all ... we/us all ... they/them both ... you both ... we/us both ... :

After the game **they both** went home together.   I know them and I like **them both**.

We all live in a yellow submarine.   There is plenty of room for **us all**.

all and *both* come before the main verb:

We will **all miss** the train.   They have **both missed** the bus.

or after *is, was, were*:

We missed the train and we **were all** late.   They **were both** tired.

3 In Unit 41 you looked at patterns for talking about a particular group:

If you are making a general statement you use these patterns without *of the*:

All children enjoy a good party.   We picked **some** flowers.
Most children start school quite young.   **Many** people all over the world learn English.

4 You can also use   a lot of ...   lots of ...   plenty of ... :

A lot of children start school at the age of five.
Lots of people all over the world learn English.

A Use these words to complete the sentences below. Sometimes you will need a singular form and sometimes you will need a plural form:

traffic shop bread car luggage advice subject house help
animal building furniture country idea friend weather rice

1 Would you like some ___bread___ and butter?

2 There were a lot of ___cars___ on the road. pl

3 I have left most of my ___luggage___ in the car.

4 Most of the University ___building___ in Cambridge seem to be quite old.

5 We saw some interesting ___animals___ in the zoo.

6 My grandfather gave me a lot of good ___advice___ when I was a child.

7 We visited a lot of different ___countries___ last year. pl

8 We had a lot of really bad ___weather___ last winter.

9 They have built a lot of new ___houses___ in the last few years. pl

10 Would you like some more ___rice / bread___ with your meat?

11 Plenty of my ___friends___ live near London. pl

12 I enjoyed most of the ___subjects___ I studied at school. pl

13 Most of the ___shops___ will be closed for the holiday. pl

14 We need to buy some new ___furniture___ for the bedroom.

15 She's very clever. She has lots of good ___ideas___. pl

16 There is a lot of ___traffic___ in town around lunch time.

17 Andrew was very kind. He gave us a lot of ___help___.

B Rewrite these sentences using *all of them/us* or *both of them/us*:

1 I like them both. ___I like both of them.___

2 There is room for them all. ___There is room for all of them___

3 They all wanted to come. ___All of them wanted to come___

4 We both stayed at home. ___both of us stayed at home___

5 They wanted to see us both. ___they wanted to see both of us___

6 They all live in a yellow submarine. ___all of them lives in a yellow submarine___

7 We both come from Liverpool. ___both of us come from Liverpool___

8 There is room for us both. ___there is room from both of us___

Cycle 2

1 *a few* means the same as *some*:

We were quite tired so **a few** of us went to bed early.

Red Riding Hood picked **a few** flowers for her grandmother

few means the same as *not many*:

They were all very excited. **Few** of them went to bed before midnight.

It was a dreadful accident. **Few** passengers survived.

2 You can use *any* with count or uncount nouns:

You use *any* in positive statements when you mean *any one at all* or when you mean *It doesn't matter which one*:

You can buy it at **any** book shop. You can hire a car at almost **any** airport.

Any ten year-old knows how to use a computer. I'd like **any** book by Jane Austen.

Because it has this meaning it is very **common in negatives and questions**:

There aren't **any** tomatoes left. There's some sugar, but there isn't **any** rice.

'Have you got **any** children?'

Are they in **any** danger?

But you usually use *some* in requests and offers because they are for specific things:

Could you lend me **some** money? Could I have **some** tomatoes please?

Would you like **some** tea? Here, have **some** cake.

A Complete these sentences with *some/a few* or *not many/few* ...:

1 We invited a lot of people to the meeting but ___not many/few___ came.

2 I am going to buy _____ things for supper.

3 There are lots of girls in my class but _____ boys.

4 Nobody wanted to go out in the rain, but _____ people had to.

5 We all wanted to go home early but _____ people had to stay behind and work.

6 We saw lots of interesting animals and _____ birds.

7 Lots of us wanted to go skiing but _____ of us could spare the time.

8 I don't like dangerous sports but _____ of my friends do.

B Fill the blanks with *some* or *any*:

1 Would you like _____*some*_____ coffee?

2 We've got plenty of rice, but we haven't _____*any*_____ potatoes.

3 I'd like _____ apples and _____ oranges please.

4 You can buy stamps at _____ post office.

5 I think _____ child who has a bicycle should have lessons in road safety.

6 No thanks, I don't want _____ coffee, but I'd like _____ tea please.

7 We bought _____ fish but we didn't buy _____ meat.

8 She likes _____ film about animals.

9 I would like to go with you, but I haven't _____ time to spare.

10 You can get your car mended at _____ good garage.

11 It's a very common word. You will find it in _____ dictionary.

12 A: Can you lend me _____ money?

   B: I'm sorry. I haven't _____ .

13 Almost _____ bank will change traveller's cheques.

14 _____ children are quite dangerous on their bicycles.

Nouns to describe other nouns

1 In English, you often put a noun in front of another noun to tell you more about it:

A What sort of dress was she wearing?
B It was a beautiful **silk dress**.

A Did you leave it in the dining room?
B No. It's on the **kitchen table**.

2 You do this:

a to show what something is made of:

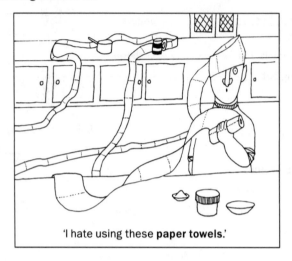

'I hate using these **paper towels**.'

They were kept in a **glass case**. He put it in a **cardboard box**. She wore an expensive **silk dress**.

Note: For something made of wood you usually say *wooden*:
He put it in a **wooden box**. There was an old **wooden table** in the corner.

b to say where something is:
Put these flowers on the **dining-room table**. It's in the **kitchen cupboard**.
London hotels are very expensive.

c to say when it happens:
Are you going to the **six o'clock class**? Let's have a **Christmas party**.

d to say what size or how heavy it is:
She bought some milk in a **one litre carton**. There was a **ten foot wall** round the house.

e to say how expensive it is:
He wore a **fifteen hundred dollar suit**. She bought a **five dollar ticket**.

f to say what it is about:
Where's my **history book**? I'm listening to the **sports news**.

3 You often use a noun which has been formed from the verb by adding *-er*:

He got a job as a **window cleaner**. She's a **good language learner**.

⚠ WARNING: The first noun is almost never found in the plural. A man who cleans windows is a window cleaner. A cheque for a hundred pounds is a hundred pound cheque. An exception is *sports*. We talk about a *sports field* for example.

A Write down what these things are. Put in brackets the point they relate to on the previous page:

1 a belt made of leather   *a leather belt (2a)*

2 a handkerchief made out of paper

3 a table made of wood

4 a bag made out of plastic

5 a chair in the kitchen

6 furniture used in the garden

7 seats found in an aeroplane

8 a meeting on Thursday

9 a party on someone's birthday

10 an appointment at two o'clock

11 a traveller's cheque for fifty pounds

12 a note worth ten pounds

13 a bag weighing one hundred kilos

14 a baby weighing three kilos

15 a book about cookery

16 a magazine about fashion

17 the page about sports

18 someone who sells newspapers

19 someone who teaches languages

20 someone who plays cards

Note: Using nouns to describe other nouns is so common in English that it is impossible to list all the ways this happens. Sometimes the two nouns are used together so often that they have become one word. (You dry your hair with a hairdryer)

Can you find the following?

1 a story teller   2 a dishwasher   3 a tin opener   4 an ice cube   5 a cigarette lighter
6 an egg-timer   7 a petrol station   8 a dog kennel   9 a carpet sweeper   10 a hairdryer

Cycle 2

1 **You use prepositions of place to say where something is. Very common prepositions of place are:**

above behind below beside between in near on opposite over under

There's a poster **on** the wall **above** the bed.
You can see some shoes **under** the bed.
The lamp is **on** the small table **beside** the bed.
The table is **between** the bed and the door.
The boy's clothes are **in** the wardrobe.
There is a tennis racket **behind** the wardrobe.
The wardrobe is **near** the window.
The window is **opposite** the door.
He has put his coat **over** the arm of the chair.
His books are **on** the shelf **below** the window.

2 **Some prepositions are more than one word:**

I was standing **in front of** Jim.
Jim was **next to** Jane.

⚠ Warning: you say *opposite* NOT *opposite to*.

3 **You can also use adverbs and adverb phrases to say where someone or something is:**

abroad away downstairs upstairs here indoors outdoors
there anywhere everywhere somewhere nowhere

Paddy doesn't live in England now. He lives **abroad**.

I'm sorry, you can't talk to Mr Smith. He is **away** just now.

The kitchen is **downstairs**, but the dining-room is **upstairs**.

Sarah was **here**, but now she has gone.

I'd love to visit the United States.
I've never been **there**.

'Mummy, I can't find my shirt **anywhere**!'
'I've looked **everywhere**.'
'Well, it must be **somewhere**.
Shirts don't just disappear.'
'It's **nowhere** I can think of.'

I want a job where I can work **outdoors**. I need fresh air,
and I don't want to stay **indoors** all day.

Practice

A Look at the two pictures (A, B), then read the sentences and write whether they describe A or B:

1 The TV is on a table in the corner. _____

2 There is a video below the TV. _____

3 There are books on the shelf above the table. _____

4 The flowers are in a vase on the table next to _____ the window.

5 The painting is opposite the sofa. _____

6 There is a cat under the table. _____

7 There is a poster of Paris on the wall. _____

8 The flowers are between two photographs. _____

9 The light switch is next to the door. _____

10 The TV is between the window and the door. _____

11 The cat is on the rug between the table and _____ the sofa.

12 There are some books behind the sofa. _____

13 The light is above the sofa. _____

14 There is a crack in the ceiling above the TV. _____

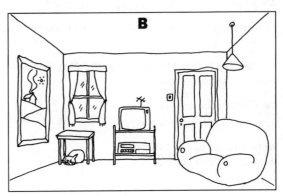

Cycle 2

B Complete the sentences using the words in brackets:

1 I haven't always lived _____ you know. I've also lived _____ , in France, Germany and Thailand. (abroad/here)

2 It's very difficult to buy Italian ice-cream _____ , that's why I always eat lots of it when I am _____ on holiday. (there/here)

3 I am going to be _____ in the office for a few hours now, but you won't be able to see me tomorrow, because I shall be _____ at a conference. (away/here)

4 Frances and Jonathan live _____ , on the ground floor; my flat is on the first floor, and Mr Jones lives _____ , on the second floor. (downstairs/upstairs)

5 I enjoy working _____ , except when it is raining. Then I prefer to be _____ . (indoors/outdoors)

C Do the same for these sentences, using these pairs:

under/beside   on/under   behind/next to

1 Keep your shoes _____ the bed, not _____ it!

2 If you want to see, put the desk _____ the light, not _____ it.

3 I prefer to sit _____ my friends not _____ them.

101

Expressions of time

1 You use *during* (or *in*):

a to say something happened in a certain period of time:
  The phone rang **during** the interview.
  I went out once **during** the morning.

b often to say something happened from the
  beginning to the end of a period, or for a certain
  time in that period:
  We put the radiators on **during** the winter.
  We were very busy **during** the holidays.

⚠ WARNING: You do not use *during* to say how long something lasts.
  It tells you when something happened, not the duration of something:

We were very busy
during the holidays.

My parents were in Dublin ~~during~~ for two weeks.

Note: *During* is followed by a noun, not a number or a preposition.

2 You use *before* to say that something happens earlier than a certain time or event, and *after*
to say it happens later:

We will finish **before** six o'clock.
Turn the light off **before** you leave.

*Can I talk
to you after the
lesson?*

Note: You can use *before/after*
with a noun or a phrase.

3 You use *from ... until* or *from ... till* or *from ... to* to say that something began at one time and
finished at a certain time:

I waited for you **from** 4 **to** 6 o'clock!   The shops are open **from** 9 **until** 5.

4 You use *by* to say that something will happen at or before a certain time:

I must be home **by** seven tonight. (= not later than 7)
Give me your work **by** Friday lunch-time. (=Wednesday or Thursday would be better, but Friday morning is
possible)

5 You use *about* or *around* to give a general or approximate time:

*I'll see you
at about eleven.*

*Someone
called at around
half-past six.*

A **Complete the sentences using the following:**

by six   during the holidays   by now   during the storm   by 2020   during the morning
by the end of the week   during the demonstration   by bedtime   during the lesson

1 All the lights went out _____ .

2 Give him a ring. He should be home _____ .

3 I had a lazy time. I didn't do much _____ .

4 The forecast said that the weather will get better _____ .

5 If we catch the next train we can be in Cardiff _____ .

6 Colin fell asleep _____ .

7 The population of England will probably reach 65 million _____ .

8 The police said that no-one was arrested _____ .

9 Please call after 12.30, because we are always busy _____ .

10 I'm staying in a Youth Hostel and I have to be in _____ .

B **Complete the sentences:**

1 The postman comes *at around/from* eight in the
   morning.

2 It rained *after/during* the night.

3 *Before/By* the end of the week the group had visited
   all the most important sights of the capital.

4 I think the film starts *at about/from* 6.45 tonight.

5 Eva could speak quite well *during/after*
   two weeks in the country.

6 Put your boots on *before/after* you go out!

C **Complete the sentences using *from, before, after, until*:**

1 What are you going to do _____ school today?

2 The skiing season is _____ October _____ April.

3 Have I got time for a bath _____ we go out?

4 The coach leaves at 5.20, so get to the station _____ that.

5 The banks are only open _____ Monday _____ Friday.

6 You should always wash your hands _____ you eat.

7 My grandparents often have a short sleep _____ lunch.

8 Most people feel a little nervous _____ an examination.

D **Write sentences saying which of these activities you normally do a) before breakfast b) after
breakfast c) during the evening:**

read a paper   have a shower   get dressed   watch TV   go out with friends
go to work/school   write letters   brush your teeth   polish your shoes   relax

UNIT 47 Adverbs of manner

1 **Most adverbs of manner are formed by adding *-ly* to an adjective:**

bad – **badly**   quick – **quickly**   beautiful – **beautifully**   slow – **slowly**   careful – **carefully**

2 **Sometimes there is a small change in spelling:**

-le changes to -ly: gentle – **gently**
-y changes to -ily: easy – **easily**
-ic changes to -ically: automatic – **automatically**
-ue changes to -uly: true – **truly**
-ll changes to -lly: full – **fully**

3 **Adjectives like *friendly* and *lonely* that already end in *-ly* have no adverb form. Instead you can say *in a friendly way* or *in a friendly manner*:**

He smiled at me **in a friendly way.**

4 **You use adverbs of manner to say how someone does something, or how something happens:**

I'm afraid I sing very **badly.**
The children sat and waited **quietly** for the dentist.
Read these instructions **carefully.**

Sarah drives very **slowly.**

5 **Note: adjectives give information about a noun, and adverbs give information about a verb:**

There was heavy rain all day: It rained **heavily** all day.
He's a quick reader : He reads **quickly.**

6 **The adverb of manner for the adjective *good* is *well*:**

Luke is a good tennis player. He played **well** in the match.
I'm not a good skier: I don't ski very **well.**

7 **Some adverbs of manner have the same form as adjectives.**
The most common are: *fast, hard, late, loud, early*:

They drove down the motorway **fast.**

The class started **late** and finished **early.**

Cycle 2

A Put the adverbs from these adjectives in the right category:

1 -ly	2 -ily	3 -ically	4 -lly
_____	_____	_____	_____
_____	_____	_____	_____
_____	_____	_____	_____
_____	_____	_____	_____

polite   happy   soft   angry   comfortable   helpful   fluent
nice   sudden   sad   frantic   reasonable   dramatic   dull

B Now use adverbs from above to complete these sentences:

1 I know someone who can speak three languages _____ .

2 This is a very popular shop because everything is _____ priced.

3 Classical music was playing _____ in the background in the restaurant.

4 'Get out of my office!' the manager shouted _____ .

5 'Do you mind if I smoke?' he asked _____ .

6 The train stopped _____ and I nearly fell out of my seat.

7 'Did you find the money you lost?' I asked. Jim shook his head _____ and said no.

8 The teacher waited until we were sitting _____ , and then began her lesson.

C Answer these questions following the model:

e.g. Do you know anyone who is a good tennis player?
    Yes, my brother (father, friend). He plays very well.
    OR
    No, I don't know anyone who plays well.

Do you know anyone who ...

1 is a quick reader?   4 is a dangerous driver?

2 is a good dancer?   5 is a good singer?

3 is a slow eater?   6 is a fast talker?

And what about you? Which of those activities do you do well/badly?

D Complete the sentences by choosing between the words given:

1 Unemployment is a *serious/seriously* problem now.

2 The train went *slow/slowly* through the mountains.

3 I didn't realize that you were *good/well* friends with Jack.

4 It rained *heavy/heavily* all day.

5 We heard some *loud/loudly* noises upstairs.

6 The countryside here is *beautiful/beautifully*.

Cycle 2

1 You use *at* to talk about:

a **a specific place:**
I was **at my friend's house.**
We waited **at the bus stop** for ages.
Neil wasn't **at work.** I think he's ill.
Let's stay **at home** tonight.

b **an exact address:**
She lives **at 5, Regent Street.**

c **public places or institutions:**
I'll be **at the station** at nine.
We met **at university** in 1985.

d **shops or workplaces:**
He's **at the doctor's** now.

e **organised social events:**
Were you **at Steve's party**?
He spoke **at the conference** last year.
We were **at the theatre** last night.

They arrested him **at the airport.**

f **a place on a journey:**
Does this bus stop **at Sainsbury's**?
The London train calls **at Bath and Reading.**
We stopped **at Oxford** on the way home.

g **parts of a place, with words like** *back, front, top, bottom* **and** *end*:
The Smiths live **at the end of the road.**
The bathroom is **at the top of the house.**
The answers are **at the back of the book.**

2 You use *in* to talk about:

a **a country or geographical region:**
They're **in Spain** now.
We took these photos **in the mountains.**

b **a city, town, village or large space:**
My parents used to live **in Bath.**
They were walking **in the park.**
The college is **in Brighton.**
What shops are **in the area**?
The group are playing **in Leicester** tonight.

c **a road or street:**
They live **in Kingsdown Road.**
There are lots of shoe shops **in that street.**

d **being inside a room or a building:**
It was very cold **in the school.**
I thought I heard a noise **in the kitchen.**

e **Containers or liquids:**

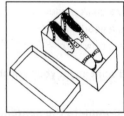

There's a fly **in my coffee.**

The shoes were **in a box.**

We spent the afternoon swimming **in the sea.**

A Complete the sentences by matching the two parts:

1 The title of the story was	in the corridor.
2 I bought the souvenir when I was	at the top of the page.
3 The train stops	in bed.
4 I keep my money	in the garden.
5 You'll find the telephone	at Exeter and Plymouth.
6 I spend about 38 hours a week	in a box in my room.
7 The weather's so lovely, let's eat	in Paris last year.
8 Pauline's not feeling well. She's	at work.

B Here is a description of my house. Fill in the gaps using *in* or *at*:

We live (1) _____ an old house (2) _____ the end of a

quiet street (3) _____ Birmingham. There are four

rooms downstairs. I have my study on the left

(4) _____ the front of the house. There are a few chairs

(5) _____ the room and (6) _____ one corner there is

a table with a computer – that's where I do most of my

work. The sitting room is also (7) _____ the front of the

house, on the right as you come in. The kitchen is

(8) _____ the back. It looks out over the garden. There

is another small sitting room (9) _____ the back of the

house. There are four bedrooms upstairs, two

(10) _____ the front and two (11) _____ the back.

There's a bathroom (12) _____ the end of the corridor.

C Now describe where you live:

1 Which rooms are at the front? _____

2 Which rooms are at the back? _____

Do you have any of these objects? TV, phone, computer, washing machine. **Where are they in your house?**

D Complete the sentences with *at/in*:

1 Hamid works _____ a restaurant _____ Oxford.

2 We live _____ number 32 Redland Road now.

3 We had a wonderful week _____ Madrid.

4 The accident happened because the driver didn't stop _____ the traffic lights.

5 There's a supermarket _____ the end of the street.

6 We had great fun last night _____ Mick's party.

7 Are there any fish _____ this river?

8 It's too cold to go out. I'm staying _____ home tonight.

Prepositions with forms of transport

1 You can use *by* with most forms of transport when talking in general:

I always go to work **by car**.
It's quicker to go to Birmingham **by train**, you know.
When the weather's good, more people travel **by bike**.

2 You use *in + my/your ...* or *in + the ...* to talk about a specific car, van, lorry, taxi or ambulance:

We all went to the party **in Jim's car**.
You haven't been **in my new car**, have you?
They went to hospital **in the ambulance**. I followed **in the car**.

3 You use *on + my/your ...* or *on + the ...* with a specific bike, horse, coach, bus, ship, train or plane:

You can buy something to drink **on the train**.

I met an interesting man **on the bus** this morning.

'Excuse me, is there somewhere I can lie down **on the ship**?'

4 If you walk somewhere, you say *on foot*:

Take a taxi – it's too far to go **on foot**.

5 At the start and end of a journey, you talk about getting *in* or *into* and *out of* cars, vans, lorries, taxis and ambulances:

We paid the driver and got **out of the taxi**.

It was difficult for Chris to get **into the car**.

6 At the start and end of a journey by plane, bus, coach, train and ship you talk about getting *on* or *onto* and *off* the type of transport:

Everyone wanted to get **off the ship** as soon as possible.   Please do not smoke until you have got **off the plane**.
We got **onto the train** and looked for a seat.

A Complete the sentences in a logical way by matching the phrases:

1 Everyone	by car	felt very nervous.
2 I first travelled	on the coach	when I was 14.
3 It's cheaper	by coach	than by train.
4 The nurse	by bicycle	gave me an injection.
5 We watched a video	on the plane	on the way to the airport.
6 If more people went	by plane	there'd be less pollution.
7 I'll take the shopping	in our car	if it's not too heavy.
8 We can take 5 people	on my bicycle	if necessary.
9 When I go	in the ambulance	I take a map.

COACH
London to Birmingham
£12.50

TRAIN
London
to
Birmingham £42.50

B Complete the sentences with *in, into, out of, on, onto, off*:

1 We all got _____ the train and walked out of the station.

2 Sally parked and got _____ the car quickly.

3 We can get _____ the bus here and walk to my house. It's not far.

4 The Prime Minister got _____ the Rolls Royce and returned to Downing Street.

5 There was a queue of people in the rain patiently waiting to get _____ the coach.

6 The driver jumped _____ the lorry and ran to see if he could help the people who had been injured in the crash.

7 Mike put the shopping _____ the car and drove home.

C Change these sentences using an expression with *go* and a form of transport:

e.g. I drove to London. *I went to London by car.* _____

1 Tom is flying to Mexico tomorrow. _____

2 Ian walked home after the party. _____

3 We caught the train to Bristol. _____

4 How much does it cost to take the coach to Paris? _____

5 I used to cycle to school every day. _____

6 Last year we drove to Scotland. _____

7 Sarah always feels seasick when she goes on a ship. _____

8 They took a taxi into the city. _____

Review: Cycle 2 – Units 31–49

Cycle 2

Units 31 – 36: Modal verbs

A Use the right modal verbs to complete the dialogues below:

can can might will will would would

A (1) _____ I help you?

B I (2) _____ like to speak to Dr. Jones please.

A I'm afraid he's out. (3) _____ you mind waiting?

B Not at all. How long will he be?

A I don't know. I'm afraid he (4) _____ be quite a
long time. I (5) _____ try to telephone him if
you like.

B No, don't do that. (6) _____ I leave a message?

A Yes, of course. I (7) _____ give it to him when
he gets back.

Unit 37: Impersonal It

B Complete the sentences below using these phrases with *it*:

It's very expensive It looks like It was silly of me It was kind of you
It's nice to meet you It's a pity It gets very cold

1 _____ to forget my keys.

2 _____ . My husband
has told me a lot about you.

Who's that over there?

3 _____ Bridget.

4 _____ to remember my birthday.

5 _____ it's so late. I'm afraid we have to go home.

6 _____ travelling first class.

7 _____ in December and January.

Unit 38: Verbs with two objects

C **Complete these sentences using the words in brackets:**

1 She invited her friends round and cooked a nice meal. (them)
   She invited all her friends round and cooked them a nice meal.

2 I posted the letter this morning. (to the bank)
_____

3 Can you get a newspaper when you go to do the shopping? (for your father)
_____

4 Karen showed her new dress. (me)
_____

5 Her aunt is going to make clothes when it is born. (for the baby)
_____

6 Will you keep some food if I'm too late for supper? (me)
_____

7 I usually read a story before they go to sleep. (the children)
_____

8 James handed the papers when he had finished writing. (to his teacher)
_____

9 Mr. Wilson teaches English every Tuesday. (us)
_____

10 I've lent my bicycle so he can cycle to school. (to my brother)
_____

Unit 39: Make and do

D **Complete the following sentences using *make* or *do*:**

1 Mary has to _____ some work in the house before she goes to school.

2 Will you _____ a promise?

3 Twenty pounds and fifteen pounds – that will _____ thirty-five pounds altogether.

4 The sitting room is very untidy. Can you _____ a bit of cleaning up before you go out?

5 We are hoping to _____ a trip to Italy later this year.

6 Did you _____ any skiing over the holidays?

7 It was a dreadful match. Our team didn't _____ very well.

8 I promise I'll be very quiet. I won't _____ a sound.

9 Write very carefully and try not to _____ any mistakes.

10 Have you any toothpaste? I want to _____ my teeth before I go to bed.

Review: Cycle 2 – Units 31–49

Unit 40: Uncount nouns

E **Complete these sentences changing the words in brackets to plural where necessary:**

1 Ken and Sylvia both had a lot of _____*luggage*_____ . (luggage)

2 Harry is very bright.. He has a lot of good _____*ideas*_____ . (idea)

3 My parents both gave me useful _____ . (advice)

4 Most big towns are full of _____ at the weekend. (traffic)

5 We are going on holiday next week. I hope we have plenty of good _____ . (weather)

6 We played lots of _____ when we were kids. (game)

7 Let's go out and have some _____ after school. (fun)

8 It was hard work. We had a lot of _____ . (problem)

9 They bought some expensive new _____ . (furniture)

10 They played some lovely _____ on the radio last night. (music)

Units 41, 42: Quantifiers

F **Choose the right words to complete these sentences:**

1 My father went out and bought *lot of/lots of* books.
2 I telephoned my two friends but *both them/both of them* were out.
3 *All/All of* students have to learn English.
4 There are two good films on but I've seen *both them/them both*.
5 Someone has opened my drawer and stolen *all my/my all* money.
6 There's *plenty/plenty of* milk. I've only drunk *half it/half of it*.

7 *Most /Most of* children in the class were girls.

8 *Neither/Neither of* my parents was at home.
9 *Some/Some of* my friends left school last year.
10 *A few/A few of* our friends are coming to see us tomorrow.

Unit 43: Few and a few

G **Complete these sentences using *few* or *a few*:**

1 We went out for a drive to visit _____ friends.

2 I bought some presents to take home and _____ things for myself.

3 It was very cold so _____ people came to the meeting.

4 I drank a glass of orange juice and ate _____ sandwiches.

5 A lot of us watched the programme, but _____ of us enjoyed it very much.

Review: Cycle 2 – Units 31–49

Unit 43: Some and any

H **Complete these sentences using *some* or *any*:**

1 I'd like _____ biscuits please.

2 I bought _____ rice but I didn't buy _____ potatoes.

3 You could put an advertisement in _____ newspaper.

4 I'd like _____ sugar, but I don't take _____ milk in my coffee, thanks.

5 _____ taxi will take you to the University.

6 Can I have _____ more bread and butter please?

7 There's _____ water in the fridge, but there isn't _____ milk.

8 You can buy it at _____ good book shop.

9 I wanted _____ bananas, but our local shop didn't have _____ .

10 Here you are. Have _____ grapes.

Unit 44: Nouns to describe other nouns

I **Look at Unit 44 – Practice. See if you can remember how these things are described:**

1 a cookery book *a book about cookery* _____

2 a two o'clock appointment _____

3 a language teacher _____

4 a kitchen chair _____

5 a Thursday meeting _____

6 a newspaper seller _____

7 a leather belt _____

8 aeroplane seats _____

9 a fashion magazine _____

10 a ten pound note _____

Review: Cycle 2 – Units 31–49

Unit 45: Expressions of place

J Look at the pictures and complete the sentences below:

1 Dad is standing _____ Mum and Richard.

2 Mum is _____ Penny.

3 Sue is standing _____ Richard.

4 Dad is standing _____ Joe.

5 Richard is _____ Sue.

6 There is a _____ beside the computer.

7 The _____ is under the desk.

8 The book is _____ the desk.

9 There is a _____ in front of the computer.

10 Next to the desk there is a _____ .

Unit 46: Expressions of time

K Look at the timetable and complete these sentences giving the right numbers and using *about, by, during, from, at, after, to* or *until*:

Monday	
0900 — 1030	History
1030 — 1100	Break
1100 — 1230	Maths
1230 — 1400	Lunch
1400 — 1530	English
1530 — 1700	Geography
1700 — 1830	French

1 We have maths _____*from eleven to*_____ _____*twelve thirty.*_____

2 We have history_____ o'clock _____ .

3 We can meet _____ the break _____ forty-five.

4 We have to be back in class _____ lunch _____ o'clock.

5 I asked permission to leave at six _____ the last lesson.

6 All our lessons last _____ an hour and a half.

7 We have _____ and a half hours of lessons every day.

L Complete these dialogues using *by* in one part and *until* in the other:

1 A The meeting will probably go on _____ nearly five o'clock.

   B Oh dear. I have to be home _____ five thirty.

2 A John and Jean will be here from the fifth _____ the twelfth.

   B Can they get here _____ ten o'clock on the fifth?

Review: Cycle 2 – Units 31–49

Unit 47: Adverbs of manner

M **Make adverbs from these adjectives and use them to complete the sentences:**

bad careful fast good hard happy sad sleepy slow

1 You should always drive _____ , especially on wet roads.

2 Kim won the first game easily, but he played very _____ in the second.

3 The children were playing _____ together.

4 I'm very sorry, he said _____ .

5 I'm sorry I can't understand when you speak _____ . Could you speak more _____ ?

6 I'm tired. I had to work _____ all day, and I slept very _____ last night.

7 I tried hard, but I'm afraid I didn't do very _____ .

8 Andrew woke up late and got out of bed _____ .

Unit 48: At/in (place)

N **Complete these sentences using *in* or *at*:**

1 I'll meet you _____ the bus stop.

2 We went to the Louvre while we were _____ Paris.

3 We couldn't find a supermarket _____ the main street.

4 I don't want to go out. I'd much rather stay _____ home.

5 There's a great film on _____ our local cinema.

6 There were hundreds of beautiful flowers _____ the garden.

7 Pisa is _____ northern Italy.

8 It's really cold _____ our house at this time of year.

9 Ron has finished school. He's _____ Art College now.

Unit 49: Prepositions with forms of transport

O **Complete these sentences using the right preposition:**

1 It's too far for me go to school _____ foot. I usually go _____ my bike, unless it's wet. Then I go _____ bus.

2 It was very hot when we got _____ the plane in Singapore.

3 I can't afford to go _____ taxi. I'll just have to go _____ the bus.

4 I had a bad leg so it was difficult getting _____ the car.

5 We got _____ the coach ready for the trip to Stratford.

6 There was a man with a really fierce dog _____ the train this evening.

7 If you are very ill they will take you to the hospital _____ ambulance. If not you will have to go _____ bus

   or _____ the car.

8 I got _____ the train at Northfield and did the rest of the journey _____ foot.

9 There's a video _____ the coach to help passengers pass the time.

General review A: Cycles 1 and 2

A Make questions to go with these answers (Units 1 – 14):

1 A _How old are you?_   B I'm twenty-three.

2 A _____? B We live in Bromley, near London.

3 A How long _____? B We've lived there nearly six years.

4 A _____ in Bromley? B Yes, I like it very much.

5 A _____ in Bromley? B No, I work in London.

6 A _____? B No, I don't drive to work. I go by train.

B Complete these sentences by putting the verb in the right tense (Units 1 – 12):

1 I got very wet while I (wait) _____ for the bus.

2 We live in Birmingham. We (live) _____ here for five years.

3 You should take your umbrella. It (rain) _____ quite heavily.

4 It was my first visit to New York. I (never be) _____ to America before.

5 I'm sorry I can't come out. I (do) _____ my homework.

6 We were very tired. We (work) _____ for over three hours.

7 Mary (wave) _____ when she saw me.

8 We (prepare) _____ the salad when the telephone rang.

9 It's nearly ten o'clock. I (work) _____ since six o'clock this morning.

10 The next train (leave) _____ in half an hour.

C Complete these sentences by adding a preposition where necessary (Units 45, 46, 48, 49):

1 We have an extra English class _at_ two o'clock _____ tomorrow.

2 We can go to the cinema either _____ the evening or _____ Friday.

3 Are you going to town _____ bus or _____ your bike?

4 A Is your father _____ home?
  B No, I'm sorry. He's _____ work.

5 We stayed _____ a flat _____ the centre of Paris.

6 We will be _____ home _____ Christmas, but we'll be away _____ January.

7 Let's go _____ my car. It's too far to go _____ foot.

8 Are the Niagara Falls _____ Canada or the USA?

9 Part of Turkey is _____ Europe and part of it is _____ Asia.

10 George left home _____ half past six this morning.

11 I'll see you _____ next week _____ Friday.

12 Did you enjoy yourselves _____ the cinema?

13 I have to get _____ the bus _____ the next stop.

14 Can you hold the door so I can get _____ the car?

15 It's usually very cold _____ winter, but it was quite warm _____ this year.

General review A: Cycles 1 and 2

D Rewrite these sentences with the adverbial in the right place:

1 I have been to Portugal but I have been to Spain. (twice; never)

_____

2 I enjoyed his first book, but I didn't like his second. (a lot; very much)

_____

3 He was driving and that saved his life. (quite slowly; certainly)

_____

4 You have to work if you want to do. (hard; well)

_____

5 We play football but we play hockey. (sometimes; never)

_____

E Choose the words and phrases to complete these dialogues:

A Good morning. (1) *Will/ Could* I have two kilos of (2) *potato/ potatoes* and half a kilo of (3) *rice/ rices* ?

B Here you are. (4) *Do/ Would* you like anything else?

A Yes please. (5) *Will/ Can* you give me (6) *any/ some* apricots – about half a kilo.

B I'm sorry. We haven't (7) *some/any* apricots left. We have (8) *few/ a few* peaches though.

A Thank you. I'll take one kilo please.

A Hello. Where (9) *will you go/are you going*?

B We are off to Italy.

A (10) *Did you go/Have you been* before?

B Yes, we (11) *have gone/went* last year.

A How long (12) *you will be/ will you be* away?

B Two weeks. We'll be back (13) *in/on/at* the second of August.

A I hope you have (14) *good weathers/ a good weather/ good weather*.

B Oh yes. (15) *It/There* is always fine in Italy.

Should/ought/must/can't (probability)

1 **When you want to say that something is probably true or that it will probably happen you can use *should* or *ought to*:**

> The road is very good. It should be an easy journey.

The sun is shining. It **ought to** be a nice warm day.

I think I can do that for you. It **shouldn't** be any problem.

It's eight o'clock. Father **ought to** be home soon.

⚠ WARNING: You only use these forms for things you want to happen. You don't say:

We've missed our bus. We ought to be late.

2 **When you are fairly sure that something is true you can use *must*:**

There's someone at the door. It **must** be the postman.

Hello. Nice to meet you. You **must** be Sylvia's husband.

3 **If you are sure that something is not the case you use *cannot* or *can't*:**

He **can't** be very old. He's not more than forty is he?

> That can't be true.

> But we've just started. You can't be tired already.

⚠ WARNING: You do not use *must not* or *mustn't* with this meaning. You can't say:

That mustn't be true.   You mustn't be tired already.

'But we've just started. You (mustn't) be tired already.' ✗

'You've just had lunch. You can't be hungry again.' ✓

A Use *should be* or *ought to be* with one of these phrases to complete these dialogues:

nice and quiet   very comfortable   a good game   an exciting trip   a nice day   really funny

1 A We're thinking of going to New York this summer.

   B Wow! That *ought to be an exciting trip.*

2 A Mum has just bought some nice new armchairs.

   B That's nice. They _____ .

3 A I think the weather's going to be fine tomorrow.

   B Yes. It _____ .

4 A I'm looking forward to the football match this weekend.

   B So am I. It _____ .

5 A We are going to have a holiday in the mountains.

   B That sounds great. It _____ .

6 A There's a good film with Robin Williams. He always makes me laugh.

   B Yes. It _____ .

B Complete these sentences using *must be* or *can't be*:

1 It's still early. Surely you *can't be* tired already.

2 The dog is barking. There _____ someone at the door.

3 I hear your daughter's got a really good job. You _____ very proud of her.

4 It's not very expensive. It _____ more than twenty dollars.

5 There's no answer. They _____ out.

6 'You have just had lunch.
   You _____ hungry again.'

7 She's very short. She _____ taller than five feet.

8 It's getting dark. It _____ getting late.

9 But you look so young. You _____ Rebecca's father!

10 I'm sorry to hear your wife's in hospital. You _____ very worried.

11 Bob has been off work for six weeks. He _____ very ill.

12 I've eaten most of them. There _____ many left.

13 It's really freezing cold. It _____ the worst winter we've ever had.

Cycle 3

UNIT 51 Can/could/may/need (requests and permission)

1 You use *can* to say someone is allowed to do something. You use *cannot* or *can't* to say that they are not allowed to do it:

You **can** leave your coat here if you like. You **can** go now.

'We **can't** go in there. It's private.'

'You **can't** drive a car until you are seventeen.'

If you are making a general statement you can say *You're allowed to ...* or *You're not allowed to ...*

In Britain **you're not allowed to** drive a car until you're seventeen, but in some countries **you're allowed to** drive when you're only sixteen.

2 You can use *may* or *may not* to say that someone is allowed or not allowed to do something:

You **may** leave your coat here if you like. You **may** go now.

We **may not** go in there. It's private. You **may not** drive a car until you are seventeen.

NOTE: Nowadays the use of *may* is rather formal.

3 When you are making a request or asking permission you use *can*:

Can I ask a question, please? **Can** I use your telephone, please?

If you want to be formal or very polite you use *could*:
Could I ask a question, please? **Could** I use your telephone, please?

May is also used to ask for permission, but this is very formal:
May I come in now, please? **May we** leave these things here?

4 You use *needn't, don't need to,* or *don't have to* when you are giving someone permission or advice **not** to do something, or saying that something is not necessary:

You **don't need to** cook your own supper. You **don't need to** shout.

'You **don't have to** say anything if you don't want to.'

'You **don't have to** pay now.
You can send a cheque later.'

NOTE: *don't need* and *don't have* are followed by *to*. *Needn't* is just followed by the verb:
You **needn't** come to work today. You **needn't** write it out in full.

A Here are some people making requests or asking for permission. Write under the pictures what the people are saying. Use *can* or *could*:

a

b

c

d

e

f

g

h

Here are some words to help you: borrow your pen;   have another biscuit;   play with you;
go home early tonight;   ask a question;   have a kilo of bananas;   take this chair;   have a lift home.

Close your books and see how many of the sentences you can remember.

B Here are some things you *don't need to do* or *don't have to do* if you are staying in a hotel. Write under the pictures:

1

2

3

4

5

6

7

8

Here are some words to help you: clean the windows; make your bed;   clean the furniture;
cook your own meals;   lay the table;   wash the dishes;   tidy your room;   clean the bath.

Close your books and see how many of these sentences you can remember.

UNIT 52 Likes/dislikes/invitations

1 **To talk about liking or disliking something, you use *verb* + -*ing* with:**

enjoy like love feel like fancy dislike detest hate mind

Do you **enjoy skiing**?

My cousin **loves watching** football on TV.

It's raining. I don't **feel like going** out, thanks.

I **hated cooking** when I was younger, but I **liked ea**ting out.

I **fancy having** a night out tonight. What about you?

Do you **feel like coming** to the cinema with us, Dave?

2 **To invite someone to do something you can use:**

a *How about + -ing*:
  How about coming with us to the cinema?
  How about having a meal with us later on in the week?

Note: You can use this structure with a noun:
How about another drink? How about a trip to London?

b *Would you like + to - infinitive*:
  Would you like to have something to eat?
  Would you like to come to the party?

c *You must + infinitive* without *to*:
  You really **must have** some more ice-cream.

You **must visit** us when you're in Hong Kong.

d To make an informal invitation to a friend, you can also use an imperative sentence, or, for extra emphasis, an imperative with *do* before the main verb:

A '**Have** a sandwich.'   B 'I shouldn't.'
A 'Oh, **do take** one.'

A '**Come** any time you like.'   B 'We'll try.'
A 'Yes, **do come**.'

A Rewrite these sentences using the right form of *feel like* + *ing* :

e.g. Do you want to go out? *Do you feel like going out?*

1 Do you want to see that new film? _____

2 Don't you want to drive to the mountains this weekend? _____

3 They wanted to get a video. _____

4 It was a hot day and everybody wanted to go to the beach. _____

5 I really don't want to go home now. It's early. _____

6 Is there anything you particularly want to do? _____

Now rewrite the sentences using *fancy.*

B Look at the pictures of the people and the activities, then complete the sentences:

1 I think the old man probably enjoys _____ .

2 It looks like the children don't like _____ .

3 The teenagers love _____ .

4 The old man probably dislikes _____ .

5 The teenagers hate _____ .

6 Frank and June love _____ .

7 The children like _____ .

Now use the same verbs to say how you feel about the same activities.

C Rewrite these sentences using *do:*

e.g. Please have some more coffee. *Do have some more coffee.*

1 You must come in and relax for a moment. _____

2 You must let me buy you that picture. _____

3 You must spend the weekend with us. _____

4 Please write to me with your news. _____

5 Please tell me when you're bored. _____

Now rewrite the sentences using *How about ...+ -ing.*

Saying and thinking + *to-infinitive*

1 You use a *verb + to-infinitive* with some common verbs of saying and thinking:

agree choose decide expect hope learn plan promise

She agreed to go to the cinema with me.

'My son **hopes to study** medicine at university next September.'

They **promised to give** the books back on Friday.
We are **planning to have** a party next week.
I **learnt to drive** in a week. It was easy!

To make a negative, you add *not* before *to*:
It was late so we **decided not to go out**.

I **agreed not to play** the guitar after midnight.

2 You use *verb + object + to-infinitive* with some verbs:

advise tell ask remind order expect

My teacher **advised me to buy** a dictionary.
'I **expect you to be** here at 9 o'clock,' his mother said.
The officer **ordered the soldiers to go back.**
They **told us to be** at the train station at 6 o'clock.

3 You can use *verb + wh-word + to-infinitive* with some verbs:

ask explain learn understand decide forget know remember

I can't **explain how to do** it, I'm sorry.
We can't **decide what to eat.**
I didn't **know what to do.**
I can never **remember how to spell** that word.

When did you **learn how to ski**?

53 Practice

A Complete the sentences:

1 'I'll have the red shirt, please.'   He decided _____ .

2 I started swimming when I was 9.   I learnt _____ .

3 We're going to visit Moscow this year.   We plan _____ .

4 I'll never be late again.   He promised never _____ .

5 She's sure she will be home at ten.   She expects _____ .

6 He's not going to swim after all.   He decided _____ .

B Complete the sentences using one of these verbs:

remind   advised   asked   want   asked   told

1 The teacher _____ me to take the exam.

2 Who _____ you to come to the party?

3 A policeman _____ us not to park the car on the corner because it was dangerous.

4 'The train leaves at ten, so I _____ you all to be ready at half-past nine'.

5 We were lost so we stopped and _____ someone to show us the way to the hotel.

6 Please _____ me to buy some milk on the way home.

C Complete the sentences with the following:

understand what   know how   remember what   forget how   decided when   explained how
understand how   know what   remember where   forgotten what   decide what   explained where

1 This exercise is difficult. I don't _____ to do.

2 Could you repeat that, please? I've _____ you said.

3 When I was young I didn't _____ to ski. Now I'm an expert.

4 We got lost because we couldn't _____ to turn off the motorway.

5 I went to the supermarket, but I couldn't _____ to buy for the cake.

6 Some people find it difficult to _____ to wear to parties.

7 A: Have you _____ to go on holiday? B: Yes, in April.

8 The situation was so embarrassing. I didn't _____ to do!

9 They say you never _____ to ride a bicycle.

10 The guide _____ to go to buy the best souvenirs.

11 It was difficult finding your flat. Fortunately, we met someone who _____ to get there.

12 A lot of people use computers nowdays, but very few actually _____ they work.

Make/let/help + **bare infinitive**

1 **You use** *make* **with the** *bare infinitive* **(the** *infinitive* **without** *to***) to:**

a talk about how you feel because of someone or something:

The film was so sad. It **made** me **cry**. (= I cried because of the film)

You always **make** me **feel** happy. (= I am happy because of you)

I had to wait an hour to see the doctor. That **made** me **want** to complain.

(= I wanted to complain because of the wait)

b talk about doing something because someone tells or forces you:

He **made** me **sit down**.   You can't **make** me **eat it**.   They **made** me **wait** for hours.   I didn't want to see the film, but they **made** me **go**.

2 **You use** *let* **with the** *bare infinitive*:

a to say that someone allows someone to do something:

He **let** me **go** home early.

Shut up and **let** me **talk**!

'**Let** me **help** you'.

When I was young, my parents never **let** me **go out** alone.

b to make a suggestion about doing something:

Let's go to the theatre tonight.

Let's have an ice-cream.

Let's not walk, **let's take** a taxi.

3 **You use** *help* **with the** *bare infinitive*:

Thanks for **helping** me **clean** the car, John.   Your explanation **helped** me **understand** the problem.

You can also use *help* **with the** *to*-infinitive:

She **helped** me **to choose** a shirt.   'Thanks for **helping** me **to clean** the car.'

A What did your parents let you do when you were young?

Write 'They let me ...' or 'They didn't let me ...':

1 go to bed after 10 p.m. _____

2 eat chocolate when I wanted _____

3 visit my friends' homes _____

4 buy my own clothes _____

5 ride my bike on the road _____

6 go shopping alone _____

7 travel alone _____

B Now think about school. What did your teachers make you do?

Write 'They made us ...' or 'They didn't make us ...':

1 play sport _____

2 wear a uniform _____

3 do a lot of homework _____

4 stand up when they came into the classroom _____

5 sing songs _____

6 read newspapers and magazines _____

7 speak English _____

C Use the words below to complete the sentences by making suggestions with *Let's*:

have a rest   go for a drink   go and see it   go inside   do another exercise   ask someone for help

1 I'm thirsty. *Let's* _____

2 It's very hot. _____

3 There's a good film on at the cinema. _____

4 I need more practice. _____

5 I'm tired. _____

6 We're lost. _____

D Complete the sentences by matching the two columns:

1 The bad news	made us go inside.
2 The medicine	made me happy.
3 The bad food	made the cars stop.
4 Meeting you last weekend	made me depressed.
5 The policeman	made my father ill.
6 The rain	made my brother feel better.

E Complete the sentences by matching the two columns:

1 A dictionary can help you	find your way.
2 A map can help you	find what you want.
3 These pills will help you	understand a new word.
4 The shop assistant will help you	go to sleep.

Verbs of perception + object + infinitive/-ing

1 You use an *-ing* clause with an object after these verbs:

see   hear   watch   notice   observe   smell   listen to   find   feel   look at

to talk about someone doing something:

| We **saw him crossing** the road. | They **heard someone playing** the guitar upstairs. | I **found an old man lying** on the floor, and called an ambulance. |

She lay in bed, **listening to the rain falling**.   The children **looked at the monkeys playing** in the zoo.

NOTE: with this structure, the activity started <u>before</u> you first observed it, so you only observe a part of the activity.

2 You use the *infinitive* without *to* with an object with these verbs of perception:

see   hear   watch   notice   observe   smell   listen to   feel   (BUT NOT: find   look at)

to talk about a completed action:

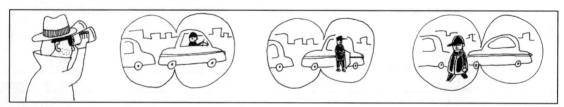

I **saw him park** the car, **open** the door, **get out** and **cross** the road. (= I saw the start and finish of each activity)

The audience **listened to the group play** their latest hits. (= they heard the whole show)

She **watched them steal** the car, and then she phoned the police. (= she saw everything)

A Decide whether these sentences describe finished (F) or unfinished (U) actions:

1 Did you see the police arrest the robber? _____

2 I heard the birds making their nest in the roof. _____

3 Everyone watched the plane land. _____

4 Mrs Jameson noticed someone hiding in the lounge. _____

5 We listened to the group play a few songs, then left. _____

6 Noriko felt something touch her leg when she was swimming. _____

B Look at the pictures, which tell a story, and try to put the sentences below in the correct sequence:

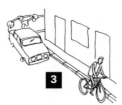

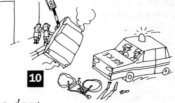

1 A tall man was getting onto his bicycle. I saw him. __1__

2 Then the car crashed into the traffic lights. We heard it. _____

3 A police car was coming to the scene of the accident.
We heard it. _____

4 The children screamed. Everybody heard them. _____

5 The car tried to overtake the cyclist. We watched it. _____

6 A blue car turned into the street. My friend noticed it. _____

7 Some children were standing near the traffic lights.
My friend noticed them. _____

8 He rode down the street. I watched him. _____

9 The car was driving very fast. We heard it. _____

10 The car knocked the man off his bike. We saw it. _____

Now change the sentences following the models:

e.g. He opened the door. I heard him: *I heard him open the door.*
He was opening the door. I heard him: *I heard him opening the door.*

Cycle 3

UNIT 56 Delexical verbs (*give/take/have/go*)

1 You use *have* with some nouns to talk about common activities:

a meals: **breakfast, lunch, dinner, tea, meal, snack**:
We **have breakfast** at 8.30, all right?
When would you like to **have dinner**?

b food and drink: **a drink, a coffee, a taste, a sip etc**:
I think I'll **have a cheese salad**, please.
Can I **have a quick taste** of your ice-cream, Pat?

c talking: **a chat, a discussion, an argument, a conversation**:
Let's **have a chat**. Did you **have an argument** about work?
I was **having a conversation** with Sue when the phone rang

d washing: **a wash, a bath, a shower**:
I want to **have a shower**.

'**Have you had a bath** today?'

e relaxation: **a rest, a break, a holiday, a day off**:
Can I **have some time off** this week? I **haven't had a break** for ages. I think we all need to **have a rest**.

2 These are some of the common nouns used with *give*. Put them in the right categories:

cry   information   kiss   laugh   warning   kick   whistle   shout   punch   example
speech   hug   report   caress   interview   answer   push   scream   news

talking and telling:
other noises:
actions:

3 You use *take* with: *care, a chance, a decision, a photograph, responsibility, a risk, time*:

I'll lend you my camera, but **take care** of it.
The tourists **took some photographs** of the city's sights.
The children **took a long time** to finish the exercise.

4 You use *go* with many common activities:

a *go + -ing*
I'm **going shopping** this afternoon.
Let's **go camping**.
Yesterday I **went swimming**.

b *go for a + noun*:
I want to **go for a walk**.

They **went for a ride** on their bikes.

A Rewrite the following sentences with an expression using *have* from section 1 opposite and making any necessary changes:

e.g. They argued angrily. *They had an angry argument.*

1 We discussed it seriously. _____

2 They were chatting quietly in the reception room. _____

3 They eat dinner very late in Spain. _____

4 I washed quickly then went to school. _____

5 Paula ate a hamburger for lunch. _____

6 Most people prefer to go on holiday in the summer. _____

7 I need to talk with you about Simon. _____

8 Mark enjoys lying in the bath for a long time after playing sport. _____

B Complete these sentences using *give* or *take*:

1 Check the oil, the petrol and the brakes before driving off on holiday. We don't want to _____ any chances of things going wrong.

2 Every time I see the woman who works in the newagent's she _____ me a big smile.

3 The President _____ the journalists a quick interview.

4 Let me _____ you an example of what I mean.

5 The terrorist group said it _____ responsibility for the bombing of the airport.

6 It will _____ a long time to finish repairing these houses.

7 When the home team scored, the spectators _____ a terrific shout.

8 The doctor _____ us a warning about the dangers of smoking.

C Change the sentences to expressions using *go + -ing*:

1 They decided to go for a swim in the river.

_____

2 If you feel hot why don't you go for a swim?

_____

3 When was the last time you went for a walk across the moor?

_____

4 I think I'll go for a jog.

_____

5 The lake is a great place to fish.

_____

1 Many verbs consist of more than one word in English. Generally these verbs are *verb + particle (in/on/out/off* etc). These are called phrasal verbs. A phrasal verb does not have the same meaning as the normal verb:

Normal meaning

Normal meaning, with emphasis

Phrasal verb

2 A common structure is *verb + particle:*

get by   go on   go away   grow up   keep on   meet up   watch out

I can speak a little French. I can **get by.**
I'm sorry I interrupted your story. Please **go on.**
The music was so bad we paid the musicians to **go away.**
We **grew up** in the countryside, but now we live in the city.
It's hard to succeed, but you must **keep on** trying.
They visited different shops, then **met up** at the library.

There's a policeman coming. **Watch out!**

Sometimes phrasal verbs have the same meaning as one-word verbs. Which examples above mean: continue/ manage/ leave?

3 Another structure is *verb + particle + object.* Can you underline the phrasal verbs in these examples?

Someone broke into my flat and stole my tv and video.
We've got an au-pair to look after the children.
I bumped into Chris and Annie in the centre.
The police are looking into the crime.

Which examples above mean: investigate/ meet?

4 Some phrasal verbs have three parts, with two words after the verb. Can you underline the phrasal verbs in these examples?

Mary left before me, but my car is faster, so I caught up with her very soon.

Parts of this cathedral date back to the tenth century.

We were so busy we didn't get round to watching the video until midnight!

Cycle 3

A Underline the phrasal verbs in these sentences:

1 Sue was so busy she stayed up all night to finish her work.
2 Laurence is so rude. How can you put up with him?
3 He took up skiing when he was 4. He was a champion at 16.
4 I'm like my mother, but my sister Sarah takes after our father.
5 If we start out now, we'll be there by nine o'clock.
6 Hurry up! I don't want to be late.
7 'Could you find out what time the train leaves, please?'
8 The soldiers carried out a dangerous raid.
9 If you are hot, take off your coat.

10 The car broke down on the motorway. We had to get help.

B Now put the phrasal verbs from A into categories:

Verb + particle	Verb + particle + obj	Three part Verbs
She stayed up.	*He took up skiing.*	*How can you put up with him?*

C Complete the sentences using these phrasal verbs:

got by   grew up   stay up   watch out   hold on   play around

1 My parents _____ in Bulgaria, but they went to live in London when they were married.

2 They broke the window when they were _____ with a football.

3 Last night we _____ to watch the late film on TV.

4 'Can you speak Chinese?' 'No, when we were there we _____ with a few words and some sign language!'

5 'Can I speak to Paul, please?' '_____, I'll just go and get him.'

6 _____ ! Don't touch the paint, it's wet!

D Rewrite these sentences, replacing the verbs underlined with one of these phrasal verbs:

keep on   find out   got away   bumped into

1 The police followed the robbers, but they escaped.

_____

2 I'm trying to discover whose car this is.

_____

3 Most of the students said they wanted to continue studying.

_____

4 I met an old friend on the ferry. What a surprise!

_____

Cycle 3

Phrasal verbs (2)

1 Some phrasal verbs are used in the structure *verb + object + particle:*

> answer back   ask in   call back   catch out   hand over   invite in
> order about   point out   ring up   take out   take up   tell apart

Paula was out when I rang her up, so I'll **call her back** later.

We'd like to **invite you out** to a restaurant.

'The house is a dreadful mess. We can't **invite anyone in.**'

'The twins look exactly the same.
No one can **tell them apart.**'

2 Many phrasal verbs take an object. With some phrasal verbs the object can go before or after the particle:

> add on   bring up   call up   fold up   hand over   hand in   knock over   point out   put down
> put away   put up   rub out   sort out   take up   tear up   throw away   try out   write out

She had to **bring up** the children on her own.	She had to **bring** the children **up** on her own.
He **folded up** his newspaper.	He **folded** his newspaper **up**.
I'll try to **sort out** the problem.	I'll try to **sort** the problem **out** for you.
He **took off** his shirt and lay in the sun.	He **took** his shirt **off** and lay in the sun.
He **rubbed out** all the mistakes.	He **rubbed** all the mistakes **out**.

⚠ WARNING: **When the object is a pronoun it must go in front of the particle:**

He **knocked over** a little girl and her brother.	He **knocked** them **over**.
He **tore up** the letter and **threw** the pieces **away**.	He **tore** it **up** and **threw** it **away**.

'**Take out** the money and **hand** it **over**.'

'**Put down** your gun and **put up** your hands.'

A Arrange the following to make sentences:

1 the people in the bank / told / the robbers / all their money / to hand over.

_____

2 were you / when you / how old / skiing / took up.

_____

3 a couple / he / pointed out / of mistakes.

_____

4 their papers / handed in / the students / of the exam / at the end.

_____

5 the shop assistant / in the bag / folded up / and put them / the clothes.

_____

B Replace the underlined words with pronouns. Change the word order where necessary:

1 I was very surprised when they invited Pascal out to lunch.

_____

2 The student quickly rubbed out the mistakes and wrote the sentence out again.

_____

3 Please help me put away the plates and cups.

_____

4 I'm going to ring up the Carters and ask Angela round to dinner.

_____

5 George brought up all three children and kept his job at the same time.

_____

6 My doctor advised me to give up smoking.

_____

C Complete these sentences using the following phrasal verbs:

clean up   take up   knock over   point out   fold up   call back   tell apart   write out

1 I'm not very fit. I think I'll _____ jogging.

2 I can't talk to you now I'm afraid. Can you _____ later?

3 The guide will _____ all the interesting places on the route.

4 This is a great tent. It will _____ and fit into this tiny bag.

5 Parties are great. But it's no fun when you have to _____ afterwards.

6 Be careful you don't _____ the bottle.

7 They look almost the same. They are very difficult to _____ .

8 Give me some paper and I'll _____ my address.

Cycle 3

1 Many verbs often go with a certain preposition. Some verbs have different meanings with different prepositions:

VERB + TO

Belong to: The house **belongs to** the Smiths.
Listen to: The audience **listened to** the music in silence.
Speak to: I haven't **spoken to** anyone about this.
Talk to: Could I **talk to** you for a minute, Sam?

Write to: Please **write to** us when you have time.

VERB + ABOUT

Care about: I don't **care about** the cost. I want a new car.
Complain about: They **complained about** the terrible weather.
Dream about: I **dreamed about** you last night, Eva.
Speak about: They were **speaking about** their holidays.
Talk about: I'm going to **talk about** our new product.
Think about: What are you **thinking about**?

Write about: You should **write about** your travels.

VERB + AT

Laugh at: Nobody **laughs at** my jokes.
Look at: **Look at** me!
Shout at: He was angry, so he **shouted at** me to go away.

Smile at: She's so friendly. She **smiles at** everyone.

VERB + FOR

Apologize for: I must **apologize for** being so late.
Apply for: I'd like to **apply for** the job you advertised.
Ask for: We finished the meal and **asked for** the bill.
Look for: 'What are you **looking for**?' 'My pen. I lost it'
Pay for: I'll **pay for** the food, you can pay for the drink.

Wait for: Do you want me to **wait for** you?

VERB + ON

Count on: You can **count on** me. I'll help you.
Depend on: I might go out. It **depends on** the weather.
Rely on: He's never late. You can **rely on** him.

VERB + INTO

Bump into: I spilled the wine because someone **bumped into** me.
Crash into: The car **crashed into** the tree.

Drive into: The mechanic **drove** the car **into** the garage.

Cycle 3

A Complete these sentences using a verb with *to* or *about*:

1 _____ me when I'm talking to you!

2 They asked the explorer to _____ his experience in the jungle.

3 'Is this your flat?' 'No, it _____ my sister.'

4 Because the service was so terrible, we _____ the manager.

5 The visitors wanted to see the manager to _____ the uncomfortable beds.

6 A lot of children _____ Father Christmas with a list of presents.

7 Today I want to _____ you _____ our business plans.

8 Biographers are writers who _____ famous people.

9 They went to sleep and _____ winning a lot of money.

10 We must _____ where to go on holiday this summer.

11 'Do you mind if I _____ the radio?'

12 'Who do these _____ ?'

B Complete these sentences using a verb with *at* or *for*:

1 Everyone _____ the comedian when he fell over. It was funny.

2 Simon _____ his watch and saw that he was late.

3 I hate _____ the bus in the rain.

4 When he lost his keys, Mark _____ them for an hour.

5 My secretary _____ me _____ a week off work to visit her sick mother.

C Complete these sentences using a verb with *on*:

1 If someone is reliable, it means you can _____ them.

2 People who are not dependable are people you can't _____ .

3 We want to have a picnic tomorrow, but it _____ the weather.

4 I'd like to buy your painting, but it _____ the price.

Cycle 3

1 Look at these examples:

I hurt the cat by accident.

Bill fell and hurt himself.

You can use a reflexive pronoun to show that you did something to or for yourself:
I bought the car **for myself**. (= not for you. I will use it)
He was talking **to himself**. (=not to anyone)

2 The singular form of the reflexive pronoun is -*self*, and the plural is -*selves*. Match the reflexive pronouns to the right subject pronouns:

I ...	It ...	yourselves	itself
You ...	We ...	himself	herself
He ...	You ...	ourselves	myself
She ...	They ...	yourself	themselves

3 Verbs like *wash* and *shave* do not normally take reflexive pronouns in English. You can use reflexive pronouns for special emphasis:

I **washed** very quickly and went downstairs.
We taught Harry to **wash himself** when he was two.
It was cold so we **undressed** quickly and got into bed.   It's very difficult to **undress yourself** with a broken arm.

4 You often use reflexive pronouns with these verbs:

blame cut dry enjoy help hurt introduce teach

Helen **taught herself** Japanese from a book.
You mustn't **blame yourself** for the bad result: it wasn't your fault.
'Can I have a drink of water?' '**Help yourself.**'

The man **introduced himself** as 'Little John.'

5 You can also use the reflexive pronoun to emphasise that you did something without help:

I made the table **myself**! (=I didn't buy it)
I'm not going to pay anyone to paint the house, I'll do it **myself**! (=I will paint the house)
'What a lovely card! Did you make it **yourself**?'

If you do something *by yourself*, you do it alone:
Paul was sitting **by himself** in a corner.

A **Complete the sentences using the words in brackets:**

1 Everyone looked at _____ when I fell over and hurt _____ . (myself/me)

2 John often sings to _____ . I think I'll ask _____ why he does it. (him/himself)

3 Unfortunately a lot of young people kill _____ because they think no-one loves

_____ . (them/themselves)

4 Because nobody introduced _____ to the other people at the party, we had to introduce

_____ . (us/ourselves)

5 My daughter was four when I showed _____ how to dress _____ . (herself/her)

6 This computer will program _____ when you switch _____ on . (it/itself)

7 I hope _____ will enjoy _____ tonight . (yourselves/you)

8 Help _____ to anything _____ want in the kitchen. (yourself/you)

B **Match the two parts of these short dialogues:**

1 Can I borrow a pen and some paper?   No, I made it myself.

2 Where did you learn to paint?   Enjoy yourselves.

3 We're off to the party now.   Sure, help yourself.

4 What did you say? I didn't hear.   Let me introduce myself.

5 Sorry, who are you?   I taught myself, actually.

6 Did you buy that table?   I was talking to myself.

7 Why is he wearing a bandage on his finger?   I think they did it themselves.

8 Who cut their hair?   He burnt himself.

C **Complete the sentences using** *by myself/ for yourself/ to himself* **etc:**

1 Can I help you with that?   No thanks, I want to do it _____ .

2 Did Jim go with Paul?   No, he went _____ .

3 Do you like holidays with friends?   No, we prefer holidays _____ .

4 Who bought the books for him?   Actually, he bought them _____ .

5 Are you self-employed?   That's right, we work _____ .

6 Does she live with her parents?   No, she lives _____ .

7 Will you order something for me, please?   No, you should order _____ .

8 Let me buy you something.   No, keep your money _____ .

-ing and *-ed* adjectives

Jill is **bored**. She has a very **boring** job.

Children can be very **annoying**. Mr. Brown is **annoyed**.

Mary is very **frightened**. It's a **frightening** film.

1 The commonest *-ing* adjectives are:

amusing   interesting   worrying   annoying   shocking   disappointing
boring   surprising   exciting   terrifying   frightening   tiring

If something interests you, you can describe it as *interesting*. If something frightens you, you can describe it as *frightening*, and so on.

I got some **interesting** news this morning.   There was a **frightening** film on tv last night.

There was a **shocking** story in the newspaper this morning.   I'm going to bed early. I've had a **tiring** day.

2 The commonest *-ed* adjectives are:

annoyed   finished   tired   bored   frightened   worried   closed   interested
broken   delighted   pleased   disappointed   excited   surprised

If something annoys you, you can say you feel *annoyed*. If something interests you, you can say you feel *interested* and so on.

If you break something it is *broken*. If you finish something it is *finished*.

Usually these *-ed* words come after part of the verb *be* or a few other verbs like *feel, look, seem* and *sound*.

The wolf **looked delighted** to see Little Red Riding Hood.

'I think it's **broken**.'

A Use -*ing* words to say what you think of these things:

1 Horror films *frightening* _____   2 Computer games _____

3 English lessons _____   4 Football _____

5 Small children _____   6 Road accidents _____

7 Jogging _____   8 Pop music _____

B Use -*ed* words to say how you would feel if these things happened:

1 If you were driving a car and you were stopped by the police _____

2 If you got an unexpected parcel in the post _____

3 If you heard that you had won a lot of money in a competition _____

4 If you broke your leg and were in hospital for three weeks _____

5 If you woke up in the night and heard burglars in the house _____

C Complete these sentences using an -*ing* or -*ed* adjective formed from the verb in brackets. Use the -*ed* form in one sentence in each pair and the -*ing* form in the other:

1 a Annette was _____*bored*_____ She had nothing to do. (bore)

   b She had a book to read but it was very _____*boring.*_____

2 a I enjoyed our visit to the museum. It was really _____. (interest)

   b I like swimming but I'm not _____ in jogging.

3 a I didn't enjoy the film very much. The dinosaurs were too _____ . (terrify)

   b The whole house was on fire. We were all _____ .

4 a There are far too many accidents on the roads. It's very _____ . (worry)

   b I thought we were lost. I was really _____ .

5 a My brother always laughs at me. He's very _____ . (annoy)

   b He wasted a lot of money. His father was extremely _____ .

6 a We were all _____ to hear that the president had been killed. (shock)

   b I don't feel at all well. I've got a _____ cold.

7 a The first half was good but the second half wasn't very _____ . (excite)

   b We were all very _____ when we heard the news.

8 a I knew what would happen. It wasn't at all _____ . (surprise)

   b I was _____ to hear that Anna had failed her exam.

9 a It was _____ that there weren't more people at the concert. (disappoint)

   b There weren't many people at the theatre. The actors were very _____ .

10 a He told a few funny stories but they weren't very _____ . (amuse)

   b I don't think that's very funny. I am not _____ .

Cycle 3

1 The indefinite pronouns are:

anybody anyone anything everybody everyone everything
nobody no one nothing somebody someone something

2 The indefinite pronouns always take a singular verb:

Everybody knows that. **Everything was** fine.

'Is **anybody** there?'

'There's **somebody** at the door.'

3 When you refer back to indefinite pronouns you use a plural form
if you are not sure whether to say *he* or *she, him* or *her, his* or *her(s)*:

Somebody's been eating my porridge and **they**'ve eaten it all up.

Has **everyone** had as much as **they** want? **Anyone** will tell you if you ask **them**.

But you can use the singular form after *someone* or *somebody*
if you know whether you are referring to a man or a woman:
Somebody called. **She** left a message.

4 If you use the indefinite pronouns *nobody, no one* or *nothing* you must not
normally use another negative word in the same sentence.

You do not say: There wasn't nobody there. I didn't do nothing. Nobody didn't come.
You say: There was **nobody** there. I did**n't** do **anything**. **Nobody** came.

5 There are also indefinite adverb forms: *anywhere, everywhere, somewhere, nowhere:*

There was **nowhere** to hide. I can't find Barbara **anywhere**.

6 You can use the word *else* after indefinite pronouns to refer to other people or other places.

Everyone else is downstairs. I don't like it here. Let's go **somewhere else**.

7 You can add apostrophe *'s* to the word *else*:

He was wearing **someone else's** jacket. This isn't mine. It's **somebody else's**.

Cycle 3

A **Complete these sentences putting the indefinite pronouns or adverbs in the right place:**

1 Shop at Binn's! There's ___*something*___ for ___*everybody*___ . (everybody / something).

2 Get a free prize! _____ likes
to get _____ for _____ .
(everybody / nothing / something)

3 _____ knows _____ but
_____ knows _____ .
(everybody / everything / nobody / something)

4 _____ should do _____ ,
but _____ ever does _____ .
(anything / nobody / something / somebody)

5 I know _____ , because _____ ever tells me _____ .
(anything / nobody / nothing)

6 I've looked _____ , but I can't find it. I've probably left it _____ else.
(everywhere / somewhere)

B **Complete these sentences using an indefinite pronoun or adverb with *else* or *else's*:**

1 I spoke to Janet but I didn't talk to ___*anyone else*___ .

2 He's not at home. He must have gone _____ .

3 I saw three people. There was Ken and Sylvia and _____ .

4 I was the only one there. There was _____ .

5 I'm sorry we haven't any lemonade. Would you like _____ ?

6 Let's go to the cinema. There's _____ to do.

7 I'm really hungry. I'd like _____ to eat.

8 We stayed all the time in Athens. We didn't go _____ .

9 That doesn't belong to me. It must be _____ .

10 I had to borrow Stephen's jacket. _____ was big enough.

11 'It's not here. You must have

left it _____ !'

12 'You must get better. That's the most important

thing. _____ matters.'

1 You add *-er* for the comparative form and *-est* for the superlative form of one syllable words:

cheap → **cheaper** → **cheapest** hard → **harder** → **hardest**
These shoes are much **cheaper** than those. He works **harder** than most people.

If the word ends in *-e* you add *-r* and *-st*:
safe → **safer** → **safest** large → **larger** → **largest**
This is the **safest** place. You need something much **larger**.

If they end in a single vowel and a consonant you double the consonant:
big → **bigger** → **biggest** hot → **hotter** → **hottest**
It gets **bigger** every day. It's much **hotter** in summer.

2 With two syllable adjectives ending in a consonant followed by *-y* you change the *-y* to *-i* and add *-er* or *est*:

busy → **busier** → **busiest** happy → **happier** → **happiest**
Friday is the **busiest** day of the week. You would be **happier** at home.

3 You use *more* for the comparative and *most* for the superlative of most two syllable adjectives, all longer adjectives and all adverbs ending in *-ly*:

careful → **more careful** → **most careful** seriously → **more seriously** → **most seriously**
You should be **more careful**. You could have been **more seriously** injured.

4 With these common two syllable adjectives and adverbs you can either add *-er* and *-est*, or use *more* and *most*:

common cruel gentle handsome likely narrow pleasant polite simple stupid

You should try to be **gentler**. You should try to be **more gentle**.

Note that two common adjectives - *quiet* and *clever* - usually only add *-er* and *-est*.
You do not generally use *more* and *most* with these words.
It's much **quieter** living here. She's **cleverer** than her brother.

5 A few common adjectives and adverbs have irregular comparative and superlative forms:

good/well	better	best
bad/badly	worse	worst
far	farther/further	farthest/furthest

You can ask him when you know him **better**. I feel much **worse** today.

6 The comparative form is used:

With *than* to compare two things or people directly (see Unit 64):
These shoes are much **cheaper than** those. She's **cleverer than** her brother.

To show a change of some kind:
It's much **quieter** living here. It gets **bigger** every day.

To compare something with a standard:
Bigger cars generally use a lot of petrol. The new computer games are **more exciting**.

A Put the adjectives below into two groups:

certain; careful; cheap, cold; dark; expensive; famous; full; great; green;
hard; high; important; interested; interesting; kind; often; small; useful.

Group A: One syllable words with comparative in -er and superlative in -est:	Group B: Longer words using more and most:

Write down the comparative and superlative of four words from each group:

Group A: cheaper, cheapest	Group B: more famous, most famous

B Write down the comparative and superlatives of these words:

nice _____   busy _____

clever _____   late _____

happy _____   good _____

quiet _____   bad _____

big _____   hot _____

C Make the comparatives of these adjectives and use them in the sentences below:

young easy important expensive useful bad heavy

1 It's only a cheap bike. I couldn't afford anything _____ .

2 That small dictionary is all right, but a big one would be _____ .

3 I used to enjoy all kinds of sports when I was _____ .

4 Let me help you with your bag. It's much _____ than mine.

5 Luckily this year's exam is much _____ than last year's.

6 I know the children often behave badly, but they were much _____ a few years ago
   when they were _____ .

7 Last winter was very cold but it seems this year will be even _____ .

8 Which is _____ , grammar or vocabulary?

9 My sister is three years _____ than me.

10 The weather has been awful - and it's getting _____ .

11 Petrol is much _____ nowadays.

Cycle 3

1 You use *the* with a superlative adjective and a noun:

It's **the best film** I've ever seen.   Which is **the biggest city** in the world?   I was **the youngest child** in my family.

You often use the expression *one of the ... –est ... :*
Liverpool is **one of the biggest cities** in Britain.

You often use a possessive with the superlative:
Jack is **one of my oldest friends**.   This is **London's oldest theatre.**

2 When you are comparing two things you can use a comparative adjective with *than*:

English is **more useful than** Latin.   Tokyo is **bigger than** London.

3 You can use adverbs of degree with comparative adjectives:

slightly   a bit   not much   a lot   far   much

This pullover is **much nicer** than that one, and it's **a bit cheaper too.**
I'm coming home soon. I won't be **much longer.**

4 You can use *as ... as ...* to show that two things or people are similar in some way:

Their house is **as small as** ours.   I'm **as tired as** you are.

You can use *not as ... as ...* **to show that two things or people are different in some way:**

'I'm **not as young as** I used to be.'

'It's **not as easy as** you think.'

5 When two things are alike in some way you say one is *the same as* the other:

Your car is quite old. It's **the same as** ours.   This book is **the same as** mine.
He's very funny – just **the same as** his brother.

6 When two things are the same you can use the words *just* or *exactly*:

I'm **just as pleased as** you are.   They are **just as bad as** when they were children.

7 When two things are almost the same you can use the words *nearly, almost,* or *not quite*:

It's **nearly as hot as** it was yesterday.   This one is **not quite as good as** that.

Cycle 3

A Look at the pictures and complete sentences about Tom, Helen, Anne and Bill:

1 Bill is as tall as _____*Helen*_____ , but he isn't as
tall as _____*Tom*_____ .

2 Tom is a bit taller than _____ and
_____ , and much taller than
_____ .

3 Helen is just as tall as _____ , but she
isn't as heavy as he is.

4 Bill is a bit younger than _____ and
much younger than _____ and
_____ .

5 Both _____ and _____
are younger than Helen.

6 _____ is the oldest and
_____ is the youngest.

7 _____ isn't quite as old as _____ .

8 _____ is as tall as _____ , but she isn't as tall as _____ .

9 _____ is just a bit older than _____ but he's much heavier than she is.

10 _____ is the youngest but _____ is the lightest.

Tom	Helen	Anne	Bill
20	19	14	12

B Rewrite these sentences using a superlative adjective:

1 I have never seen such a big dog before. _It's the biggest dog I have ever seen._

2 I have never met such a nice person. _She's_ _____

3 They had never heard such a funny story. _It was_ _____

4 Mary had never read such a good book. _It was_ _____

C Write sentences like these about people and places you know:

1 London is a much bigger city than Leeds.   1 _____

2 Peter is a bit taller than Fred.   2 _____

3 Oxford is an older city than Birmingham.   3 _____

4 Emma is much older than her sister.   4 _____

D Can you answer these questions?

1 What is the commonest word in English? _____

2 What is the highest mountain in the world? _____

3 What is the longest river in the world? _____

4 What is the biggest city in your country? _____

Close your books and ask a friend these questions.

1 You use *so* and *such* to emphasise something that you are talking about :

You are kind.

You are **so** kind. (= very kind)

Jim's tall.

He's **such** a tall person!

2 These patterns are common:

so + adjective:

I feel **so good** today.   The weather's **so nice**.   He's **so young**.

so + adverb:

Everything happened **so quickly**.   Why are you leaving **so soon**?

so many   so much   so few   so little:

There are **so many** wonderful shops here!   We had **so little** time.
I know **so few** people.   There's **so much** to do!

3 The patterns with *such* are different:

a *such + a/an* (+ adjective) + singular noun:
   Henry is **such a sweet person**. The dog made **such a mess**!

b *such* (+ adjective) + uncountable noun:
   I've never had **such good advice**. This is **such boring homework**.

c *such* (+ adjective) + plural noun:
   He paints **such beautiful pictures**.

4 You use *so ... + that* or *such ... + that* to talk about a result:

It was **so cold that** we stayed at home.
It is **such a long book that** I couldn't finish it.

The train was **so crowded that** we couldn't move.

A Change the sentences using *such* and the word in brackets making any necessary changes:

e.g. I didn't know their house was so big. (place) *I didn't know their house was such a big place.*

1 Why were you in the shop for so long? (time) _____

2 I really like Sue. She's so nice. (person) _____

3 I can never hear him. He speaks so quietly. (in ... voice) _____

4 We saw you driving your BMW yesterday. It looks so powerful. (car) _____

5 Have you heard the new REM album? It's so good. (CD) _____

B Match the parts of the sentences with the logical results:

1 The food was so delicious ...   that all the hotels were full.

2 We had such good weather ...   that I couldn't stop to talk.

3 I was in such a hurry ...   that I didn't recognise it.

4 The town has changed so much ...   that we talked for hours.

5 The dog was barking so loudly ...   that we came back with tans.

6 It was such a long time since I'd seen him ... that we cried.

7 There were so many tourists ...   that I helped myself to more.

8 The film was so sad ...   that we couldn't hear the TV.

C Check if these sentences are correct or wrong. Correct any mistakes:

1 The Smiths are so nice people. _____

2 You look so young in those clothes. _____

3 Thanks for the party. We had such good time. _____

4 It was such a boring film that we fell asleep.

_____

5 He was driving so fast that he didn't notice the police car. _____

_____

6 Bob's an expert. He knows such much about computers. _____

Cycle 3

Review: Cycle 3 – Units 50–65

Unit 50: Probability

A Use these modal verbs to complete the sentences:

should   must   can't   ought to   must   can't

1 'You've been driving for 8 hours. You _____ be tired'.

2 It's not far to Bristol, so we _____ be there by 4 o'clock.

3 Finish all that work in one hour! You _____ be serious!

4 No-one is answering the phone. They _____ all be out.

5 We did this exercise yesterday so it _____ be easy.

6 £25 for one coffee! That _____ be right!'

Complete these sentences so they have the same meaning as numbers 2, 3, 4, 5, and 6 above:

7 We're nearly there now. It _____ take much longer.

8 You _____ be joking!

9 They _____ be at home.

10 We _____ be able to finish it quickly.

11 That _____ be a mistake!

Unit 51: Requests and permission

B Rewrite these statements as polite questions using *may* or *could*:

1 I want to have another drink.

_____ ?

2 I want you to give me directions to the nearest bank.

_____ ?

3 Tell me when I can see Mr Smart.

_____ ?

4 I'd love some more chocolate cake.

_____ ?

5 The man wants you to tell him what time the film starts.

_____ ?

6 We'd like to leave now.

_____ ?

7 Janet wants to have a quick talk with the manager.

_____ ?

8 It's very hot. They want to take their jackets and ties off.

_____ ?

C **Complete the sentences using** *can't, doesn't need to, needn't, don't need to,* *are not allowed to:*

1 You _____ leave your suitcase there. It's dangerous.

2 You _____ smoke on the Underground now. It's illegal.

3 They _____ do the whole exercise. Five questions is enough.

4 'Your father _____ worry. I'm a very careful driver.'

5 We _____ get up early tomorrow. It's Saturday.

6 'They _____ park their car there! It's my garden.

Unit 52: Likes, dislikes and invitations

D **Complete these sentences using the correct form of the verb:**

1 My father /dislike/do/ the washing-up.

_____ .

2 How about /go/ to the beach this weekend?

_____ ?

3 Young children normally /enjoy/watch/ adventure films.

_____ .

4 Nature-lovers often /enjoy/go/ camping.

_____ .

5 You must /tell/ us about your holiday.

_____ .

6 How about /let me/do/ the cooking this evening?

_____ ?

7 I don't mind /listen/ classical music.

_____ .

8 I /hate/sleep/ in the dark when I was a child.

_____ .

9 Do you /fancy/come/ with us to the disco?

_____ ?

Cycle 3

Review: Cycle 3 – Units 50–65

Unit 53: Saying and thinking

E Complete the sentences using the words in brackets:

1 'I'll buy you a present.'

He _promised to buy his wife_ _____ a present. (promise/wife)

2 'OK, I won't smoke in the house.'

My father _____ in the house. (agree)

3 'If we're lucky we'll get there before the match starts.'

The fans _____ before the start of the match. (hope)

4 Could you give me a hand with the shopping?

Sheila _____ with the shopping. (ask/husband)

5 We're not going abroad after all. It's too expensive.

We _____ go abroad after all. (decide)

6 You can't leave until the room is clean.

The officer _____ the room. (order/soldiers)

7 Use a dictionary to check new words.

The teacher _____ new words. (advise/students)

8 Don't show anyone your work.

He _____ his work. (tell/artist)

9 Can you ski?

Someone_____ . (ask/me/know)

Unit 54: Make/let/help

F Complete the sentences using the correct form of *make*, *let* or *help*:

1 'Could you _____ me clean the house, please?'

2 'What shall we do tonight?' 'I know, _____'s go out.'

3 I don't think parents should _____ their children stay up late every night.

4 I'm afraid the pills didn't _____ me. I've still got a headache.

5 'When does the play start?' _____ me see ... At 8, I think.'

6 The heavy traffic _____ me miss my train.

7 Father: 'Go to bed!'

Son: 'You can't _____ me!'

8 The robbers _____ the bank clerk give them all the money.

Review: Cycle 3 – Units 50–65

Unit 55: Verbs of perception

G Choose the correct form of the verb:

1 Listen! You can hear the birds *singing/sing*.
2 Are you coming to watch the team *playing/play*?
3 We saw them *getting/get* into the car and drive off.
4 They saw hundreds of people *swimming/swim* as they drove along the coast.
5 I thought I heard you *coming/come* in at two o'clock.
6 If you notice someone *acting/act* suspiciously, phone the police.

Unit 56: Delexical verbs

H Complete the sentences with a correct form of *give, take, have* or *go*:

1 Your salad looks delicious. Can I _____ *take* _____ a mouthful?
2 Let me _____ you an example of what I mean.
3 There's no hurry, so _____ your time.
4 The referee _____ the player a warning for playing dangerously.
5 When do you _____ breakfast here?
6 We _____ a wonderful holiday last year.
7 They decided to _____ for a ride in the country.
8 _____ care not to break anything!
9 They were _____ an interesting chat about their holidays.
10 Most sensible people don't like _____ risks.

Units 57, 58: Phrasal verbs

I Match the particles to the verbs, then complete the sentences below using the correct form of the phrasal verbs:

    find hurry look take stay keep go look   up out on on after up up up

1 You're so slow. _____ *Hurry up.* _____
2 Can I _____ to watch the end of the film on TV?
3 Henry agreed to _____ the children while his wife was away on business.
4 My mother was really angry when she _____ that I hadn't gone to school.
5 I didn't know your phone number so I _____ it _____ in the phone book.
6 Don't let me disturb you. Please _____ with your work.
7 No-one was listening, but he _____ speaking.
8 If you want to get fit, you should _____ a sport.

Review: Cycle 3 – Units 50–65

Unit 59: Verbs with prepositions

J Choose the correct preposition:

1 He said he had dreamt *with/about* me the night before.
2 This house used to belong *on/to* Madonna, you know.
3 You'll never guess who I bumped *on/into* this morning.
4 I might go out tomorrow. It depends *of/on* how I feel.
5 You look worried. What are you thinking *about/on*?
6 If you break anything, you'll have to pay *for/about* it.
7 They had to ask the shop assistant *about/for* help.
8 They promised they would write *to/at* each other every week.

Unit 60: Reflexives

K Complete the sentences with the appropriate reflexive pronoun where necessary:

1 'That's a great dress. Where did you buy it?'
  'Actually, I made it _____.'
2 'We're off to the concert now.' 'Fine.
  Enjoy _____.'
3 'Can I go to the disco in jeans?' 'No, I think
  you should change _____.'

4 Neil was angry because he cut _____ while he was shaving _____ .

5 They say that people who talk to _____ are a little strange.

6 The washing machine will turn _____ off when it has finished. It's very handy.

7 Mrs Banks got up, washed _____ and went to work as normal.

8 I have two uncles who live by _____ .

Unit 61: -ing and -ed adjectives

L Choose the correct form of the adjective:

We found the tour of the city (1) *fascinating/fascinated*. There were so many (2) *interesting/interested* places to see. We were both very (3) *impressing/impressed* by the historic monuments, but the children, of course, began to look (4) *boring/bored* quite quickly. They were more (5) *interesting/interested* in the shops. I wanted to have a (6) *relaxing/relaxed* evening in the hotel, but the children insisted on going out, so we bought a paper to see if there was an (7) *amusing/amused* film on. They were quite (8) *disappointing/disappointed* when they realized they had already seen all the films.

Review: Cycle 3 – Units 50–65

Unit 62: Indefinite pronouns

M **Complete the sentences using one of the words in brackets:**

1 Do you know _____ who lives near here? (nobody/anybody)

2 Keep this a secret. Don't talk to _____ . (nobody/anybody)

3 I want to ask you _____ . (something/anything)

4 Are you sure that we haven't forgotten _____ ? (nothing/anything)

5 If you get lost, ask anyone. _____ will help you. (they/he)

6 He talked so fast that _____ understood what he was saying. (somebody/nobody)

7 There's _____ Ken doesn't understand about electronics. He's a genius. (everything/nothing)

8 You can put the book back _____ on the shelf. It doesn't matter. (everywhere/anywhere)

Unit 63: Comparatives with adverbs of degree

N **Complete these sentences by choosing the appropriate adverbial and adding it in the correct place:**

1 The video we watched last night was the funniest I have seen for a long time. (easily/a bit)

_____

2 It's hotter today than it was yesterday. (far/very)

_____

3 I feel more relaxed now. (quite/a good deal)

_____

4 This is the best book she's written. (slightly/by far)

_____

5 This exercise is more difficult than I thought. (rather/quite)

_____

6 More people went to the exhibition than expected. (a little/a lot)

_____

7 The things they sell in the shops nowadays are more expensive than last year. (much/many)

_____

8 I think it would be a better idea to go on holiday in the spring when there aren't so many tourists. (much/a lot)

_____

Unit 64: The ... est; than; as ... as

0 **Complete the sentences using either the base form, the comparative or superlative form of:**

good big expensive long exciting lucky famous competitive

1 Can you think of anything _____ than
  flying by balloon?

2 All sports are _____ now than they used to be.

3 This is one of the _____ restaurants in the area.

4 'How _____ is that ring, please?'

5 You can keep my dictionary for as _____
  as you like.

6 Brazil is the _____ country in South America.

7 Thieves have stolen two of Picasso's _____
  paintings.

8 Mike is the _____ person I know.
  He escaped unhurt from a plane crash once!

9 'Today is my _____ day.'

10 'How are you?' 'I've never felt _____ :'

11 I'm afraid I can't wait any _____ .

12 One day we will be even _____
  than the Beatles!

Unit 65: So/such

P Complete the sentences using *so* or *such*:

1 It's _____ kind of you to come and help me.

2 I've never stayed in _____ a comfortable hotel.

3 It's _____ a pity you can't come to our party.

4 There were _____ many people in the queue that we decided not to go to the cinema after all.

5 The room was in _____ a mess after the party.

6 No-one had ever seen Mark look _____ worried.

7 Why are you driving _____ fast?

8 Have you ever heard _____ a ridiculous story?

9 We had _____ fantastic weather that we were on the beach every day!

10 'You say _____ wonderful things to me!'

General review B: Cycle 1

A Complete these sentences, putting the verbs in the right tenses (Units 1 – 12):

My friend Helena 1 (move) _____ to our city on the south coast last year. Before she 2 (come) _____ here, she 3 (go) _____ abroad for four months because she 4 (finish) _____ with her boyfriend and 5 (want) _____ to get out of London. She 6 (worry) _____ that there would be nothing to do, but she 7 (be) _____ totally wrong. There 8 (be) _____ a brilliant theatre and lots of restaurants and clubs. Also, she 9 (find) _____ that everything 10 (be) _____ much cheaper, and she 11 (make) _____ a lot of friends here. In fact she 12 (go) _____ on holiday with a group of new friends next month.

B Complete the sentences with the correct tense of these verbs in the negative (Unit 4):

be be finish hear work rain be feel go arrive

1 Chris _____ to the cinema tonight because he's tired.

2 I'm sorry, I _____ what you said.

3 Could you buy some fruit? There _____ any left.

4 Paul _____ well lately, so he called the doctor for an appointment.

5 Boris _____ French, he's from Switzerland.

6 The lesson _____ yet, so stay where you are.

7 Don't put any money in that drinks machine. It _____ at the moment.

8 The flight from Tangiers was delayed, so I'm afraid that it _____ yet.

9 Leave your umbrella, it _____ now.

10 We had a lovely meal out, and it really _____ expensive.

C Complete this conversation adding the appropriate articles and pronouns where necessary (Units 19 – 26):

'Jane, here's 1 __*the*__ recipe for iced coffee 2 __*you*__ asked 3 _____ for after 4 _____ meal 5 _____ had 6 _____ last week.'

'Great. Let 7 _____ just get 8 _____ piece of 9 _____ paper and 10 _____ pen to write everything down. OK. What are 11 _____ ingredients?'

'Well, 12 _____ need 13 _____ coffee, either ground or instant, of course, and 14 _____ sugar to make 15 _____ sweet, then 16 _____ ice and 17 _____ milk. You can use 18 _____ vanilla, too.'

'OK. What do 19 _____ do first?'

General review B: Cycle 1

'Right. Put 20 _____ vanilla and 21 _____ coffee in 22 _____ small saucepan. Add about

half 23 _____ litre of 24 _____ water, and boil 25 _____ all quickly. Then turn off

26 _____ heat and add 27 _____ sugar. Leave 28 _____ for 29 _____ few

minutes. Then pour 30 _____ liquid through 31 _____ coffee filter into 32 _____ jug.'

'That sounds fine. What about 33 _____ ice?'

'Fill 34 _____ couple of 35 _____ glasses with as much of 36 _____ ice as possible, pour

in 37 _____ coffee. When 38 _____ is cool, add 39 _____ milk and enjoy

40 _____ delicious drink.'

D Complete these sentences using possessives, pronouns or adjectives (Units 22 – 26):

1 Where did you buy _____ painting?

2 _____ books are about literature, and _____ are about cooking.

3 Yesterday was one of _____ days when everything went wrong.

4 I need a new handbag. The _____ I've got is too small.

5 'I was talking to Patrizia this morning.' 'Who's _____ ?'

6 'We enjoyed _____ meal. I hope you enjoyed _____ .'

7 This is a photo of Jacky and _____ husband.

8 _____ time tomorrow we'll be on the beach.

E Complete the question forms (Units 14, 15):

1 'We're going to the cinema. Do you _____ with us?'

2 'What _____ see?' 'Blood Castle.'

3 'What sort _____ ?' 'A comedy, I think.'

4 'When _____ ?' 'At half-past seven.'

5 'And how long _____ ?' 'About 2 hours, I think.'

6 'Is _____ expensive?' 'No, not at all.'

7 'So, how much _____ ?' '£3.50.'

8 'Great. Where _____ showing?' 'At the Odeon.'

159

Cycle 3

General review B: Cycle 1

F Complete the sentences using the following (Units 27 – 30):

since in very much ago from hardly ever since recently in until
probably ago since in until until probably very much often hardly ever

1 We've been incredibly busy _____ .

2 The weather turned bad a couple of days _____ .

3 Hurry, the shops close _____ ten minutes.

4 If you see someone looking at a map, they are _____ tourists.

5 'Did you enjoy your holiday?'

   'Yes, _____ .'

6 'The party next door went on _____

   4 o'clock _____ the morning!'

7 I haven't had time to relax _____ I got up this morning.

8 Dinner is served _____ 7.00 _____ 11.30 every evening.

9 I'm _____ ill. I think I've only missed two days' school in my life.

10 It's ages _____ you did the washing-up! You're so lazy.

11 My father re-decorated the bathroom six months _____ .

12 I'm planning to retire _____ eight years.

13 Some of my classmates have been together _____ they were in kindergarten.

14 Children think most things are interesting. They are _____ bored.

15 I enjoy my work _____ .

16 The meeting went on _____ three o'clock in the afternoon.

17 I will _____ be a bit late home tonight.

18 It's good to be honest, but it's _____ better to remain silent.

General review: Cycle 2

A Complete the sentences with a modal verb (Units 31 – 36):

1 £100 for a hamburger! You _____ be joking! You _____ be serious!

2 The accident happened when the driver _____ stop the car. People _____ jump out of the way of the car.

3 The last thing the driver _____ remember is turning the corner.

4 Take an umbrella. It _____ rain.

5 With your new glasses you _____ to read better. (2 modals)

6 _____ you mind staying late and helping me tonight, please?

7 The phone's ringing. That _____ be my mother.

8 You _____ wear a uniform in most schools nowadays.

9 The train leaves at 6 o'clock, so you _____ be late.

10 'I'm sorry I'm late.' 'Oh, you _____ apologize. We've only just started the meeting.'

11 If you _____ choose anywhere in the world, where _____ you most like to live?

12 What _____ you do if you saw a robbery?

B Rewrite these sentences using an impersonal *It* structure (Unit 36):

1 This is my favourite place. I like _____

2 Can you tell me the time? What _____

3 Tomorrow the weather will be stormy. It _____

4 We haven't had a holiday for almost a year. It _____

5 Your sister was very kind. She lent me some money. It _____

6 Is that Joseph? Who _____?

7 What a pity they weren't here with us. It _____

8 Driving in a city can be frightening. It _____

C Complete the sentences by putting the words in brackets in the right order (Unit 40):

1 I'll _____ when they arrive.
(your exam results/post/you)

2 Could you _____ when you go to the shops?
(for me/something/buy)

3 Please _____ now. (that dictionary/to me/bring)

4 Their mother promised _____ . (them/to read/a story)

5 My father is trying _____ .
(a present/to find/for my mother)

6 They spent the morning writing _____ .
(to their friends/postcards)

7 The children told _____ .
(to the policeman/their version/of what had happened)

8 Can I offer _____ ? (another piece of cake/you)

9 I never know _____ .

D Complete the sentences using the correct form of *make/do* (Unit 39):

1 Don't put your dirty boots there! You'll _____ a mess.

2 I haven't had time to _____ my homework.

3 I'm just _____ some coffee. Do you want a cup?

4 We've _____ a decision. We're going to get married.

5 Do you know anyone who enjoys _____ the ironing?

6 You all _____ well to get here so early.

E Rewrite the sentences using the word in brackets and making any necessary changes (Units 40 – 44):

1 There were so many cars on the road that we arrived late. (traffic)

_____

2 Bournemouth is on the coast, so is Brighton. (both)

_____

3 My friends can't speak Japanese. (none)

_____

4 Most of the suitcases were already on the plane. (luggage)

_____

5 We bought one or two souvenirs for family and friends. (a few)

_____

6 You can buy stamps in every post office. (any)

_____

7 I've listened to almost all the records in the school library. (most)

_____

8 Everyone in our class has travelled abroad. (all)

_____

9 Many of the facts you gave me were wrong! (information)

_____

10 He wrote me a cheque for one hundred pounds. (pound)

_____

General review C: Cycle 2

F Choose the correct word to complete the sentences (Units 45 – 48):

1 Meeting you in town was a *really/real* surprise!

2 Someone has put the cups back *in/on* the shelf.

3 The price is written *in/at* the top of the page.

4 It's raining *hard/hardly*.

5 Do you know anyone who lives *at/in* the countryside?

6 The nearest supermarket is *opposite/in front of* the train station.

7 Tim put a pile of books *on/above* his desk.

8 It was only 6 a.m. but the manager was already *in/at* work.

9 A man was asking for money *next to/out of* the theatre.

10 'I don't know anyone,' he said *lonely/in a lonely manner.*

General review D: Cycle 3

A Complete the text by choosing the correct words:

(1) *A/The* American President and (2) *his/her* wife (3) *arrived/have arrived* in London yesterday (4) *at/on* the beginning of (5) *their/theirs* six-day trip (6) *to/in* Europe. They (7) *can meet/are going to meet* (8) *the/a* Prime Minister and other politicians for (9) *dinner/a dinner* this evening (10) *in/on* Downing Street.

B Do the same for this text:

(1) *The/This* acrobat (2) *who/which* survived a 6,000 foot fall (3) *over/in* Shanghai (4) *when/how* his parachute (5) *doesn't/didn't* open (6) *other/the other* day was very lucky. Even (7) *luckier/luckiest* was Vesna Vulovic, (8) *a/an* Czech air hostess who (9) *come/came* down in the broken tail of (10) *a/the* Boeing 747. The plane (11) *explodes/exploded* at an altitude of 33,330 feet (12) *on/over* Czechoslovakia (13) *on/in* 1972. The Guinness Book (14) *of/for* Records says that her fall (15) *is/has been* the (16) *longest/longer* without (17) *the/a* parachute.

C Do the same for this text:

(1) *On/In* October 12th, a woman driver (2) *has/had* her handbag (3) *taking/taken* when she (4) *waits/was waiting* at traffic lights in Birmingham. She (5) *was feeling/felt* very angry, so she (6) *drove/drives* after the man who (7) *had/has* robbed her. Then the man (8) *had dropped/dropped* the handbag (9) *on/in* the middle of the road, and the woman (10) *was getting/got* (11) *out of/off* her car to pick (12) *up it/it up*, and was happy to find (13) *every/all* her money (14) *was/were* still inside it and that the man (15) *took/had taken* (16) *anything/nothing*. Unfortunately, when she (17) *looked/is looking* up, she (18) *has seen/saw* him jump (19) *onto/into* her car and drive away. The police (20) *was/were* unable to find the car.

General review D: Cycle 3

D Look at the pictures then complete these sentences:

1 'Mary, you _____ clean the floor.' 'I did it yesterday.'

2 'That _____ be enough for the weekend.'

3 'You only got up an hour ago. You _____ be tired!'

4 '_____ I make a suggestion?'

5 'How about _____ for a walk now?'

6 '_____ have some more of my home-made lemonade.'

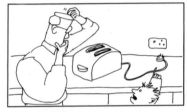

7 'Do you feel like _____ that film?'

8 'I agree _____ you to the beach tomorrow if you promise _____ to bed right now.'

9 '_____ me go! Please, someone, _____ me escape!'

E Complete the text:

I was (1) _____ to a nurse who works
(2) _____ the local hospital. She (3) _____ me a
very (4) _____ story about a man (5) _____ stole
rings, money and other valuables from the nurses' room while he
was waiting (6) _____ the doctor to treat
(7) _____ broken arm. No-one saw him
(8) _____ the objects, but they found
(9) _____ he was a thief when they
(10) _____ the X-ray picture and saw the
things in his pocket!

Verbs not used in continuous tenses

1 **There are some verbs which are not normally used in the continuous tenses. These verbs usually refer to:**

Thoughts: believe know remember think (= believe) understand want wish

I **know** Angela but I **don't know** her brother.   I **think** English is very difficult.

It was very difficult. I **didn't understand** it.   Do you **believe** in fairies?

Likes and dislikes: dislike hate like love prefer

I **like** history but I **don't like** geography.   I quite **liked** hockey, but I **preferred** basketball.

Possession: belong to have own possess

They **own** a big house in the country.   Oh dear! I **don't have** any money with me.

Senses: look seem smell sound taste

The cake **tasted** very good.

'What's that? It **looks** very interesting.'

'Try this milk. It **smells** funny to me.'

2 **Some of these verbs have other meanings. When they are used with these other meanings you can use them in the continuous tenses:**

Have does not mean 'possess' in these sentences:
She's **having** a shower.   I'm **having** a drink.
They're **having** a party.   We're **having** fun.

Think does not mean 'believe':
Be quiet I'm **thinking**.   What are you **thinking** about?

You can say either:
You're **looking** very smart today. OR You **look** very smart today.
She **looked** a bit tired. OR She **was looking** a bit tired.

Look at the use of the verb *taste*:

'I'm **tasting** the milk ... Mm it **tastes** bad.'

3 **You do not normally use the verbs *see* and *hear* in the present continuous tense:**

Normally you use them with *can*:   Please speak a bit louder. I **can't hear** you.
Look over there. I **can see** Peter.

You can use *see* in the continuous tenses when it means *visit*:
Little Red Riding Hood **was seeing** her grandmother.

4 **The verb *be* is not normally used in the present continuous:**

This **is** my friend, Michelle.   **Is** there anyone at home?

A Say whether you think/believe:

1 _____ that some people can tell the future.
2 _____ that there is life on Mars.
3 _____ that some people are born lucky.
4 _____ that thirteen is an unlucky number.
5 _____ that our future is in the stars.
6 _____ that three is a lucky number.
7 _____ that Friday is an unlucky day.
8 _____ that animals have a language.

Say whether you like, dislike, love or hate these things:

9 _____ getting up early in the morning.
10 _____ singing karaoke.
11 _____ cooking.
12 _____ rock and roll music.
13 _____ swimming.
14 _____ dancing.
15 _____ going to the dentist.
16 _____ classical music.

There are eight things in each section above. After each section close your books and see how many you can remember.

Work with a partner. See if you can remember the questions and ask a partner. Can you think of any more questions like these?

B Complete the sentences using the right form of: *look, smell, sound or taste*:

1 Jack is only sixteen, but he _____ much older.

2 I spoke to Mary on the phone. She _____ very happy.

3 I like your perfume. It _____ wonderful.

4 These oranges _____ really sweet.

C Complete these dialogues putting the verbs into the present simple or present continuous:

1 A Hello what (you/do) are you doing?
  B Hi! (I/read) _____ this book.
  A (That/look) _____ interesting.
  B Yes. (It/be) _____ very good.
  A (You/like) _____ reading?
  B Yes, (I/love) _____ it.

2 A Can I borrow your pen?
  B (I/be) _____ sorry. (I/use)
    _____ it.
  A What about this one? Who (this/belong to)
    _____ ?
  B (I/think) _____ it's Carol's.
    (I/know) _____ (she/have)
    _____ one like that. You can ask her.
    (She/work) _____ in the next room.

3 A (You/remember) _____
    Fred Johnson?
  B Yes, (I/know) _____ him well. Why?
  A (I/write) _____ him a letter.
  B Great! Say 'Hello' to him from me.

4 A (That coffee/smell) _____
    great!
  B Would you like some or (you/prefer)
    _____ tea?
  A (You/make) _____ tea as well?
  B I can make some tea if (you/like)
    _____ .
  A Thank you. (I/think) _____
    a cup of tea would be very nice.

1 **-ed adjectives. In Unit 59 we looked at adjectives ending in -ed. These adjectives are formed from verbs:**

annoyed	bored	closed	delighted	excited
finished	frightened	interested	pleased	surprised
tired	worried	broken	disappointed	shut

These adjectives are *passive* in meaning:

We always lock the door:
The door is always **locked**.

We'll finish the job before next week:
The job will be **finished** before next week.

When I was young spiders frightened me:
I was **frightened** of spiders.

2 **Passive verbs are formed from the verb *to be* and the past participle of the verb:**

They were serving lunch when we arrived:
Lunch **was being served** when we arrived.

They are going to build a lot of new roads:
A lot of new roads **are going to be built**.

People learn English all over the world:
English **is learned** all over the world.

3 **The question and negative forms of the passive are formed by making the verb *be* into a question or negative:**

Nobody has sent the letters yet:
The letters **haven't been** sent yet.

They didn't invite Sandra to the party:
Sandra **wasn't invited** to the party.

Will they show that film on TV soon?:
Will that film **be shown** on TV soon?

'Have they delivered the mail yet?:'
'**Has** the mail **been delivered** yet?'

4 **If you want to talk about the person or thing which causes the action, you use *by*:**

A lot of damage **has been caused by the recent storms**.

A Complete the sentences with *is/are/was/were*:

1 We _____ told to be ready at ten o'clock.

2 The police are looking for a man who _____ thought to be dangerous.

3 Guernica _____ painted by Picasso.

4 The 1948 Olympic Games _____ held in London.

5 Rice _____ grown all over Asia.

6 Most people _____ paid at the end of the month.

7 Thousands of gadgets _____ invented every year.

8 The concerts in England and America _____ watched by millions of fans.

B Complete the sentences with *be/being/been*:

1 A new museum has _____ opened in the city centre.

2 Can you drive me to town? My car is _____ repaired.

3 Many changes will have to _____ made to improve our image.

4 Most sportsmen and women hate _____ beaten.

5 Have you ever _____ invited to dinner by a stranger?

6 Our staff have _____ trained to use computers.

C Complete the sentences by putting the verbs in brackets into the passive:

1 The prices of all our products _____ in the sale this year. (reduce)

2 Three people _____ in a road accident yesterday. (kill)

3 I _____ by my grandparents. (bring up)

4 Dogs _____ in the shop. (not allow)

5 E.T. _____ by Steven Spielberg. (direct)

6 Cigarettes _____ in newsagents and supermarkets in Britain. (sell)

7 Today's match _____ because of the weather. (cancel)

8 Tickets for the concerts can _____ from the box office. (buy)

D Look at the two pictures, then use the verbs below to complete the sentences describing what has or hasn't been done:

put away   do   wash   turn off   change   clean   empty

1 The washing-up

2 The radio

3 The dustbin

4 The windows

5 The pots and pans

6 The floor

7 The clock

8 The table

Cycle 4

Reporting the past

1 You use report structures to give information about what people say or think. Common reporting verbs are:

a with *that* clauses:

admit agree answer complain explain promise reply say think

He **agreed that** the exercise was difficult.   They **explained that** they would be late.
Sally **replied that** she was busy.

b with *verb + person object + that* clauses:

convince inform remind tell

We **told them that** the work was important.   I **reminded everyone that** it was Ben's birthday.

2 You normally change the tense of what the speaker says:

Speaker's words:	Reported clause:
I'm so hungry I could eat a horse!	He said that he **was** very hungry.
We've just about finished; just one more page.	They said they **had** nearly **finished.**
The film was absolutely great.	They said the film **was** great.
	They said it **had been** great.
I'll be with you in a couple of minutes.	She said she **would be** here soon.

Note that it is not usually necessary to report every word the speaker says, just the main idea.

3 There are some changes with modal verbs:

Speaker's words:	Reported clause:
Can I help you, sir?	The assistant asked if he **could** help me.
OK, it's time. You must stop now.	The examiner said we **had to** stop.

But be careful: *could, would, should, might* and *ought to* stay the same:

We might need some help.   They said that they **might** need help.

4 You can use the present tenses in the report clauses if:

a You want to say that something is still true:

My name is Henry.   He said that his name **is** Henry. (Or 'was')

b You are talking about a future event:

I'm having a party next Friday.

He told me he **is having** a party next Friday.

A Choose which is the correct reported statement:

1 I really love jazz music.
   a She said she loved jazz music.
   b She said she would love jazz.

2 We were in France for a week.
   a They told us they had been in France for a week.
   b They told us they have been in France.

3 He's working hard.
   a She said he worked hard.
   b She said he was working hard.

4 I'll phone you.
   a You promised you phoned me.
   b You promised you would phone me.

5 But I can't swim!
   a He explained he couldn't swim.
   b He explained he won't swim.

6 She has read the book.
   a He told me she read the book.
   b He told me she had read the book.

7 You should know the answer.
   a She told me I knew the answer.
   b She told me I should know the answer.

B The manager of a busy office asked his staff to work late one Friday. Look at the answers he was given, then complete the sentences:

I'm meeting a client. — Alice

I would normally do it, but I must visit my mother in hospital. — Mary

I can't because I will be in Glasgow. — Mr Jones

I've already arranged something important. — Linda

I stayed late the last time. — Geoff

I don't think I will be able to; I already have too much work. — Peter

1 Alice explained that _____ client.

2 Mary said _____ hospital.

3 Mr Jones told the manager _____ Glasgow.

4 Linda replied that _____ important.

5 Geoff complained that _____ the last time.

6 Peter answered that _____ able to.

C Complete the sentences using *said, told, asked* or *thought*:

1 Someone _____ me the time. I _____ her that I didn't have a watch but _____ that it was about three o'clock.

2 When I was walking in the city, someone _____ me if I was a tourist. I _____ him that I lived here, then _____ him if he wanted some help.

3 'Have I _____ you the story of my first holiday abroad?'

4 The journalist _____ the policeman had _____ him about the murder.

Cycle 4

Short answers

1 You often give short answers to questions in spoken English. Short answers are more polite than just saying *Yes* or *No*:

a When there is a modal in the question, you repeat the modal in your answer:
Would you like some more tea? Yes, **I would**.
Can you come tonight? Yes, **we can**.
                      No, I'm afraid **we can't**.

b When there is an auxiliary in the question,
you repeat it in your answer:
Will your parents be at home tonight? Yes, **they will**.
Do you always work on Saturdays? No, **I don't**.

Have you finished?

Yes, I have.

No, you haven't.

c When *be* is the main verb in the question,
you use *be* in your answer:
Are you married? Yes, **I am**.
              No, **I'm not**.
Is there any more milk in the fridge? Yes, **there is**.

2 For questions about the past, you use the past tense in your short answer:

Had they gone to bed when you got home?	Yes, **they had**.
Were they angry with you?	No, **they weren't**.
Did you have an argument?	No, **we didn't**.
Did I tell you that my father was a policeman?	Yes, **you did**.

3 When you want more information about something, you can use *where?*, *why?*, *when?*, *how?*, or *which? + noun*:

Harry's at university now.	**Which university?** OR **Which one?**
I'm going to town tomorrow.	**When?**
I think they live abroad.	**Where?**
The concert was cancelled.	**Why?**
She put your stuff by the door.	**Which door?**

4 You use *so* with some common verbs and expressions of opinion in short answers:

	POSITIVE	NEGATIVE
Is this where they live?	**I think so.**	**I don't think so.**
Are the banks open now?	**I expect so.**	**I don't expect so.**
Will it rain tomorrow?	**I'm afraid so.**	**I'm afraid not.**
Is Jane coming tonight?	**I hope so.**	**I hope not.**

A Match the questions and short answers:

1 Do you see your friends often?	No, I'm not.
2 Are you new here?	Yes, you can.
3 Have you had breakfast today?	No, I don't.
4 Is the sun shining?	Yes, I do.
5 Are those your friends?	Yes, I have.
6 Do you know London well?	No, they aren't.
7 Can we go home early today?	Yes, it is.
8 Is there anything good on TV?	No, there isn't.

B Write short answers to these questions:

1 Can lions climb trees? _____

2 Is Bonn the capital of Germany? _____

3 Do they speak English in New Zealand? _____

4 Does rice grow in Wales? _____

5 Has the weather been good this week? _____

6 Was Marilyn Monroe an actress? _____

7 Did the Aztecs live in Spain? _____

8 Was the television invented by Einstein? _____

9 Were you born before 1950? _____

10 Are the Rocky Mountains in Europe? _____

C Each of these statements can have TWO different short questions. Match the questions to the statements:

e.g. We met Paul recently.   Where? / When?

Why?   Where?   When?   Which one?

1 I'm going on holiday soon. _____

2 We saw a brilliant video last night. _____

3 She refused to answer one of my questions. _____

4 Did you know that the last time I went abroad I was arrested? _____

5 My parents saw the Prime Minister in a restaurant last night. _____

6 Jack gave away all his books except one. _____

D Answer these questions in the positive using the word in brackets:

1 Is this jacket expensive? (expect) _____

2 Are museums open on Sunday? (think) _____

3 Is the weather going to be the same tomorrow? (hope) _____

4 Was there any food left after the party? (afraid) _____

Now rewrite the same answers in the negative.

Cycle 4

1 You use QUESTION TAGS to make a statement into a question:

You know Bill, **don't you**?
You didn't understand, **did you**?

Generally, you use a negative question tag after a positive statement:
You are foreign, **aren't you**?
They left early, **didn't they**?

After a negative statement, you use a positive tag:
She hasn't been here before, **has she**?
They didn't finish on time, **did they**?

2 There are different types of question tags:

a **After a main clause with a form of the verb be, you make a tag using be:**
  War and Peace wasn't written by an American, **was it**?
  You are going to come to the cinema with us, **aren't you**?

b **After a main clause with an auxiliary or a modal (*has/have/will/would/can/could* etc), you use the same auxiliary or modal in the tag:**
  He will be there tonight, **won't he**?
  They can't drive, **can they**?
  The film hasn't started, **has it**?
  He didn't go to Spain last year, **did he**?

c **After a main clause without an auxiliary or *be*, you use *do/does/did* in the tag:**

'It rains a lot here, **doesn't it**?'

'The war started in 1939, **didn't it**?'

3 You use a question tag:

a **To ask a real question when you do not know the answer. Here, your voice must go up on the tag:**
  You haven't got £5 I could borrow, **have you**?

b **To check that someone agrees with you, or to check that what you say is true. Here your voice must go down:**
  It's Tuesday today, **isn't it**? She is beautiful, **isn't she**?

A Choose the correct tag:

1 'The concert was great, *didn't it/wasn't it?*'

2 'You haven't finished already, *haven't you/have you?*'

3 'No-one telephoned me, *didn't they/did they?*'

4 'Not everyone can drive at eighteen, *can they/can't they?*'

5 'There isn't room for another person, *isn't there/is there?*'

B Look at the following statements, which are all missing tags.

a Underline the verb *be*, modal and auxiliary verbs in the statements:

1 You're not from this country, _____

2 We're going to London tomorrow, _____

3 The weather was wonderful yesterday, _____

4 He was very angry because we were late, _____

5 It snowed last week, _____

6 Inflation used to be a big problem, _____

7 Young people should get as much exercise as possible, _____

8 You shouldn't be rude to people, _____

9 You know you shouldn't shout in restaurants, _____

10 Her friends from NewYork didn't visit you, _____

b Now match the tags below to the sentences with modal and auxiliary verbs:
shouldn't they? should you? aren't we? wasn't it? are you? wasn't he?

c Now add the tags using the right form for *do* for the other statements.

C How sure are you? Look at these questions and write your answers following the model:

e.g. Were Charles Haughey and John Lynch Prime Ministers of Britain or Ireland?

I think they were Prime Ministers of Ireland, weren't they?

1 Is the population of Oslo more or less than a million?

_____ ?

2 Were the 1976 Olympics held in Moscow or Montreal?

_____ ?

3 Did Henry Ford, the pioneer of the Ford automobile, die in 1947 or 1927?

_____ ?

4 Did the group Status Quo start playing in the 1960s or 1970s?

_____ ?

5 Are there 9, 10 or 11 players in a cricket team?

_____ ?

6 Which city is bigger, Istanbul or Berlin?

_____ ?

7 Does 'photophobia' mean that you have a fear of being photographed, or a fear of light?

_____ ?

Cycle 4

1 You use *too* at the end of a clause to say that a statement about one thing or person is also true about another person or thing:

He likes chocolate. I like it **too**. (= I like chocolate)

The Smiths went by train. We did **too**. (= we went by train)

Vincent was absent last week. He'll be away this week **too**.

Be careful: you use *too* in positive statements. In negative statements you use negative verb + *either:*

I didn't understand; my friend **didn't (understand) either**.

She can't come tomorrow, and she **can't come** on Friday **either**.

2 You can also use a structure with *so* after positive statements. Notice the word order is *so* + verb + subject:

a after sentences or clauses with *be*, you use *so* + *be*:

His shirt is new, and **so is his tie**.   My sister is learning Greek; **so am I**.   They were tired; **so was I**.

b after statements with *have* as an auxiliary, you use *so* + *have*:

'I've been to Iceland.' '**So have I**'.

Tania has bought a new car. **So has Steve**.

By ten o'clock the wind had stopped, **so had the rain**.

c after statements with a form of *do*, or statements with no auxiliary verbs, you use *so* + *do*:

I did like his last book; **so did my wife**.

The police came quickly; **so did the ambulance**.

The French produce a lot of wine, and **so do the Italians**.

d after statements with modal verbs, you use *so* + *modal*:

Peter said he would love to go to Japan. **So would I**.

Sandra can cook wonderfully. **So can my friend Eva**.

3 After negative statements, you use *neither* + positive verb + subject:

'I don't feel well'. '**Neither do I**.'

My father didn't go to college; **neither did my mother**.

'The fish isn't fresh, **neither are the vegetables**.'

'I haven't got time to go out tonight' '**Neither have I**.'

A **Match the statements and the right answers:**

1 They've been to Birmingham.	So did we.
2 She'll be away tomorrow.	So do you.
3 My neighbours are on holiday now.	So was I.
4 My sister drives a BMW.	So can I.
5 I was talking to the new Professor.	So are mine.
6 You look very healthy.	So does mine.
7 We worked hard last week.	So have I.
8 Chris can play the guitar.	So will we.

B **Now do the same with these negative statements:**

1 I don't smoke.	Neither can mine.
2 We couldn't hear a thing.	Neither was I.
3 I haven't got a car.	Neither will I.
4 Most of my friends can't cook.	Neither do I.
5 I wasn't in bed early yesterday.	Neither have I.
6 I can't come tomorrow.	Neither can I.
7 We didn't do our homework.	Neither could we.
8 I won't tell anyone.	Neither did we.

C **Change the sentences following the models:**

e.g. I like rock and roll. My sister does too.

I like rock and roll, so does my sister.

'I can't eat any more.' 'I can't either.'

'I can't eat any more.' 'Neither can I.'

1 Greenland is an island. Australia is an island, too. *So is Australia.* _____
2 The whale is an endangered species. The rhino is, too. _____
3 My mother can't ski. My brother can't either. _____
4 Smoking isn't good for you. Eating a lot of chocolate isn't either. _____
5 The Beatles became famous in the 60's. The Rolling Stones did too. _____
6 Paul didn't write to me. Mandy didn't write to me either. _____
7 Mozart was a composer. Beethoven was a composer too. _____
8 Dictionaries aren't allowed in the exam. Computers aren't allowed either. _____

D **Similar or different? Write your real answers to these questions following the models:**

e.g. I live in a port.   EITHER – So do I.   OR – I don't.
    I can't ski.   EITHER – Neither can I. OR – I can.

1 I enjoy meeting people.	6 I don't drink alcohol.
2 I don't live on the coast.	7 I've been to London.
3 I get up early in the morning.	8 I was born in hospital.
4 I didn't speak English yesterday.	9 I want to go home.
5 I wasn't ill last week.	10 I've never been to the US.

Defining relative clauses

1 You use a relative clause to say exactly who or what you are talking about:

a The girl got a three-week holiday in the US.　　b Which girl?
b **The girl who won first prize.**
　(**The girl who won first prize** got a three-week holiday)

a Do you remember the people?　　　　　　　b Which people?
a **The people we met on holiday.**
　(Do you remember **the people we met on holiday?**)

a Can I borrow that book?　　　　　　　　　b Which book?
a **The book you told me about yesterday.**
　(Can I borrow **the book you told me about yesterday?**)

2 Clauses with *who* as subject:

You use clauses with *who* as subject to say which person or people you are talking about. *Who* comes in front of the verb:

The people **who live here** have a funny accent.

You are the only person **who can help us.**

We met someone **who used to work with your father.**

You can also use *that* instead of *who*:

The people **that live here** have a funny accent.

'You are the only person **that can help us.**'

3 Clauses with *that* as subject:

You use clauses with *that* as subject to say which thing or things you are talking about. *That* comes in front of the verb:

The car **that caused the crash** was going much too fast.

I need to catch the train **that leaves at 7.45.**

You can also use *which* instead of *that*:

The car **which caused the crash** was going much too fast.

⚠ Warning: You do not have a second subject in the relative clause. You do **not** say:

　The people who ~~they~~ live next door are friendly. The things which ~~they~~ were stolen were very valuable.

4 Clauses with *that* as object:

You use clauses with *that* as object to talk about people or things. *That* comes in front of the subject of the verb:

The car **that I wanted to buy** was not for sale.

Most of the people **that we met** were very friendly.

You often leave out *that*:

The car **I wanted to buy** was not for sale.

⚠ Warning: You do not have a second object in the relative clause. You do **not** say:

　The car that I wanted to buy ~~it~~ was not for sale. Most of the people that I met ~~them~~ were very friendly.

A Complete the sentences with *who*, *that* or *which*:

1 I don't know the names of the people _____ you talked to.

2 What's the name of the hotel _____ we stayed in last year?

3 I have read everything _____ Agatha Christie wrote.

4 Thanks for the postcard _____ you sent us.

5 Pierre has a brother _____ played football for France once.

6 We're taking the train _____ leaves at 10.15.

7 People _____ always think about money are sad, I think.

Which of the sentences do not need a relative pronoun?

B Fill in the gaps using a relative clause with this information:

cut/hair   sell/meat   sell/fruit and vegetables   write/newspaper articles
open/tins   protect you/from the sun

1 A barber is a man _____ .

2 A woman _____
is called a hairdresser.

3 Someone _____
is a greengrocer.

4 A man or a woman _____
is called a journalist.

5 A tin-opener is something _____ .

6 A butcher is a man _____ .

7 A parasol is something

_____ .

C Do you know someone who ...?

Complete the sentences following the model:

e.g. I know someone who can speak 3 languages.
OR   I don't know anyone who can speak 3 languages.

1 _____ has been to Iceland?

2 _____ can play the guitar?

3 _____ doesn't know how to swim?

4 _____ wants to be an actor or actress?

D Make one sentence from the two sentences following the model:

e.g. I found a pen. You were looking for it.
 I found the pen you were looking for.

1 Mr Davies is a dentist. My family goes to him.
2 Euro-net is a marketing company. My sister works for it.
3 Wine and cheese are the local products. This region is famous for them.
4 Simon is a friend of mine. He has just gone to New Zealand.

Cycle 4

UNIT 73 Adjectives with *to* clauses

1 Some common adjectives usually have a *to-infinitive* clause after them. These usually give an idea of the probability of something:

bound   due   likely   unlikely

or of someone's desire or ability to do something:

able   prepared   ready   willing   unable   unwilling

The train is **due to arrive** at 7.50.

Your mum is **bound to be** angry when she sees what we've done.

It's **likely to rain** tomorrow.

The police were **unable to help** us.

Is anybody **prepared to stay** late and help me clean up?

I'm **willing to try** anything once.

2 You can use a *to-infinitive* clause with adjectives to say how someone feels about something:

afraid   disappointed   frightened   glad   happy   pleased   sad   surprised   unhappy

We were really **happy to see** everyone.

'Jack, this is Samantha'. 'I'm **pleased to meet** you.'

3 When you are talking about how one person feels about another person or thing, you use a *that* clause:

The teacher was **disappointed that** the students did so badly.

I'm **afraid that** you can't stay here.

You can also use a *that* clause with:

awful   bad   funny   good   important   interesting   obvious   sad   sorry   true

'I'm **sorry that** I was late'.

We were **sad that** you couldn't come to our wedding.

It's **true that** we didn't have much time to get ready.

4 You can give your opinion about someone or something using:

crazy   difficult   easy   impossible   mad   possible
right   stupid   wrong   important   essential   necessary

We were **mad to buy** this house.

The exercise was **difficult to finish**.

You were **wrong to criticize** them for something they didn't do.

5 You can also use adjectives with *to-infinitive* after *It*:

It is **good** of you **to come** and see me.

It is **difficult** for my grandmother **to read** without glasses.

Cycle 4

A Combine the two clauses:

1 It's unlikely	to go out tonight?
2 The football match is due	to save the patient's life.
3 Will your brother be able	to be late.
4 There's so much traffic, we're bound	to start at 3 p.m.
5 The price of petrol is likely	to do anything to get rich.
6 When will you be ready	to rain in August.
7 Some people are prepared	to go up next year.
8 The doctors were unable	to lend us some money?

B Rewrite these sentences using *It* and a *to + infinitive* clause:

1 Criticizing young people is easy. *It's easy to criticize young people.*

2 Learning how to use a computer isn't easy. It isn't _____

3 Having a clean driving licence is essential. It's _____

4 Being polite to customers is important. It's _____

5 Arriving late is very rude. It's _____

6 Driving long distances when you're tired is stupid and dangerous. It's _____

7 Making everyone happy at the same time is difficult. _____

C Rewrite these sentences using a *to + infinitive* clause:

e.g. Jeremy met his girlfriend's parents. He was happy.

Jeremy was happy to meet his girlfriend's parents.

1 I didn't watch the film on my own. I was frightened. _____

2 My cousin didn't go home on foot. He was afraid. _____

3 I heard the bad news. I was sad. _____

4 We met an old friend in Japan. We were surprised. _____

5 The boys went home early. They were glad. _____

6 Eric did badly in the test. He was disappointed. _____

D Rewrite these sentences using a *that* clause:

1 Everyone was on time. I was pleased. *I was pleased that everyone was on time.*

2 We got home before dark. My parents were happy.

_____

3 The price of food is going up. The restaurant manager is worried.

_____

4 Henry couldn't find the right address. We were surprised.

_____

5 The weather wasn't very good. The tourists were disappointed.

_____

Too/enough

1 You use *enough* to say someone has as much of something as necessary. You use it:

a before plural count nouns:
We have got **enough sandwiches** for everyone.
The library doesn't have **enough books** on this subject.

b before uncount nouns:
Have you had **enough food**?
Fortunately we had **enough time** to visit both cathedrals.
We can't buy more magazines because we haven't got **enough money** with us.

2 You also use *enough* after adjectives and adverbs:

You are **old enough** to know what is right.   Can you hear? Am I speaking **loud enough**?

They missed the bus because
they didn't run **fast enough**.

'Is this water **warm enough** for your bath?'

3 Look at this useful structure:

(adj/adv) + *enough* **(+ noun) (for someone) + to do something**

I've cooked **enough cakes for everyone to have** some.
My French is **good enough for me to understand** people.
You are not **old enough to see** that film.

4 You use *too* to say there is more than necessary, or more than is acceptable:

a *too* **+ adjective/adverb:**
I like that picture, but I think it's **too expensive**.
You can't walk from here to the beach! It's **too far**.
I'm not surprised you feel sick. You ate **too quickly!**

b *too* **+** *many/few* **+ plural countable noun:**
There were **too many people**. We couldn't sit down.
The hotel is closed in winter because we have **too few visitors**.

Be careful: you don't say *too* **+ adj + noun:**
NOT: These are too expensive shoes.
BUT: These shoes are **too** expensive.

c *too* **+** *much/little* **+ uncountable noun:**
We didn't see the museum because we had **too little time**.
This tea is terrible. You put **too much sugar** in it !

'These jeans are **too big** for me.'

A Complete the sentences using:

> too many   too much   not enough   well enough   clearly enough   too many   enough   too little

1 Paul felt sick because he had eaten _____ sweets.

2 I'm not an expert, but I play _____ to be in the school team.

3 Don't spend _____ time doing the shopping. We are in a hurry.

4 The concert was cancelled because _____ people had bought tickets.

5 You should have finished by now. I gave you _____ time!

6 We didn't wait for the bus because there were _____ people in the queue.

7 You must speak _____ for everyone to understand.

8 I think I put _____ milk in this tea. It's still very black.

B Change the sentences following the model:

e.g. He's very busy. He can't go to the theatre tonight.
   He's too busy to go to the theatre tonight.

1 My brother's very young. He can't drive a car. _____

2 You look very tired. You shouldn't go out tonight. _____

3 That dress looks very expensive. I'm not going to buy it. _____

4 The book is very long. We can't finish it now. _____

5 It's very cold outside. They can't play football. _____

6 This is a very difficult question. We can't do it. _____

C Fill in <u>one</u> of the blanks in each sentence with *too* or *enough*:

1 I'm afraid the doctor can't see you today because he's _____ busy _____ .

2 You don't look _____ old _____ to be married.

3 Did I put _____ sugar _____ in your coffee?

4 If you sit in the sun for _____ long _____ you'll get burnt.

5 The car isn't _____ big _____ for us all to go in.

6 'You're never _____ old _____ to rock and roll!' he shouted.

7 A workaholic is someone who works _____ much _____ .

8 We invited _____ many _____ people to the party, and there wasn't _____
   drink _____ for everybody.

9 There weren't _____ chairs _____ either. A lot of us had to stand up all night.

10 It's _____ soon _____ to know the results of the test.

Present tenses with *if, when* etc

1 Look at the verb tenses in these sentences:

We will start **when we are ready**.   I'll ask him **if I see him**.

I'll wait for you in the car tomorrow **while you are doing** the shopping.

We are going to get married **as soon as we have** enough money.

You normally use a present tense to talk about the future in clauses with *if* or with time words like *when, while, before, as soon as, after, until.*

Look at these sentences. The *if* clause or the time clause is indicated in each one:

I will come round tomorrow **if I have time**.   **If I see Jack** I will give him your message.

'**When Red Riding Hood comes**
I'm going to eat her up.'

'**If I don't hurry** it'll be dark **before I get to
Grandma's house.**'

You will break those glasses **if you're not careful**.   I'm not coming **until I'm ready**.

2 There are some very common expressions with *if*. You should practise these expressions:

If I can   If I have time   If you like   If you want (to)

Notice that all these phrases use a present tense to talk about the future:

A Will you do the shopping?   B Yes, if I **have** time.

A Will you be home early tonight?   B Yes, I will if I **can**.

A Shall we go to the cinema?   B Yes, we can if you **like**.

A May I borrow this book?   B Yes of course, if you **want** (to).

3 When you think something might happen and might be important in some way you can say *What if ...?* or *Suppose ...?* with the present tense:

What if it rains?   **What if** it breaks?   **Suppose** you hurt yourself?   **Suppose** you fall ill?

A Match the clauses to make sentences:

1 I'll take an umbrella
2 I'm sure we will enjoy the match
3 Would you like a hot drink
4 You will probably catch the train
5 We will have dinner
6 You will hear the dog bark

if you take a taxi.
as soon as your father gets home.
if it rains.
before you go to bed?
if anyone comes to the door.
if we can get tickets.

B Rewrite these sentences using the word given:

1 You will go to town tomorrow and I will look after the children.

When _you go to town tomorrow I will look after the children._

2 Mary will be late. I will meet her at the station.

If _____ .

3 Bill is going to write to me. I will tell you all his news.

_____ when _____ .

4 You will go to the supermarket. You can buy some bread.

If _____ .

5 I won't go to bed. Peter will get home at midnight.

_____ until _____ .

6 She is going to finish her homework. She can't go out.

_____ until after _____ .

7 The weather will probably be very bad next week. We will be on our holidays.

_____ while _____ .

8 You will get your exam results next week. Then you can write to Mary.

When _____ .

9 You won't get home till after midnight. Your mother will be very worried.

If _____ .

10 I will pay you the money. I will get a job.

_____ as soon as _____ .

Look at the sentences again and underline all the *if* clauses and time clauses.

C Make short dialogues from these tables:

A Come round and see us tomorrow.	
A Could you help me with this?	B Yes, I will if I can.
A Would you mind doing this?	B Sure, if you like.
A Will you give this to Peter?	
A Can I borrow your pen?	B Yes, of course, if you want me to.
A Will you phone us when you get there?	

1 You use *wish* followed by a verb in the past tense to talk about something that you would like to happen or be true:

You can make a wish about something to do with the present:

It's cold. I **wish** it **was** a bit warmer. I'm hungry. I **wish** I **had** something to eat.

or about something to do with the past:

I forgot my overcoat. I **wish** I **had brought** it. I **wish** I **hadn't forgotten** it.

Notice the tenses. You use the past tense to talk about the present, and the past perfect to talk about the past. You also use the past tense of the modals.
You do not use *can,* you use *could*:

I'm tired. I **wish** I **could go** to bed. It's late. I **wish** we **could go** home.

If you want someone to do something but they are not going to do it you can say *I wish they would ...*:

He's very silly. I **wish** he **would be** more careful.

They're very noisy. I **wish** they **wouldn't shout** so much.

Often you just say *I wish they hadn't* or *I wish they wouldn't*:

They are making a dreadful noise. I **wish** they **wouldn't**.

He's gone out again. I **wish** he **hadn't**.

2 You can use an *if* clause (conditional clause) to talk about something which isn't happening:

If I **was** a year older I **could drive** a car.

If I **had** enough money I **would buy** a new bike.

Notice that you use past tense forms. Very often you have the past tense in the *if* clause and *would* or *could* or *might* in the other clause:

I'd (I would) certainly come and see you **if I had** time.

If you lived nearer **you could come** over on the bus.

If you left before breakfast **you might get** there before lunch.

Notice that you can use *were* instead of *was* in *if* clauses:

If I **were** older I could drive a car.

But this is very formal, except in the expression *If I were you ...* (see below).

3 There are some very common expressions with this pattern:

If I were you I'd ... is often used to give advice:

A: I'm not very well. What should I do? B: **If I were you I'd see** a doctor.

I would if I could ... is often used to make an excuse:

A: Will you give me a lift? B: **I would if I could,** but I'm just too busy.

A Rewrite these sentences as wishes:

1 It's raining again. *I wish it wasn't raining.*

2 I don't know the answer. _____

3 Jack won't help us. _____

4 I didn't see Angela this morning. _____

5 We don't live here. _____

6 Mary never telephones. _____

7 Paul didn't write last week. _____

8 I haven't enough time. _____

B Match these parts to make conditional sentences:

1 If the weather was warmer
2 If you asked Peter
3 If I had a better job
4 If we got up early
5 If we could borrow the car
6 If I knew the answer
7 If you had a dictionary
8 If I had a coat

a we could get there before lunch.
b you could look it up.
c I would be much warmer.
d we could go for a drive.
e we could go for a swim.
f I would earn more money.
g I would tell you.
h he might help you.

C Rewrite these sentences as conditionals:

1 I'm ill, so I can't play basketball. *If I wasn't ill I could play basketball.*

2 I haven't enough money, so I can't buy it. _____

3 She's not tired, so she won't go to bed. _____

4 We haven't much time so we can't wait for him. _____

5 He's so big it won't fit him.

If _____

6 'It's so cold we can't go out today.'

If _____

7 They haven't got a map so they can't find the way. _____

8 They don't know the way so they need a map. _____

9 Oh dear! I've got them all wrong. I'll do the exercise again. _____

187

Cycle 4

UNIT 77 Purpose and reason

1 **You use** *... because I want to ...* **or** *... because I wanted to ...* **to explain your purpose in doing something:**

We are travelling overnight **because we want to get** there early tomorrow.

You can also use *to* **or** *in order to* **to mean the same thing:**
They locked the door **to keep** everybody out.   He gave up his job **in order to spend** more time at home.

The wolf ran fast **because he wanted to get** there before Red Riding Hood.

Red Riding Hood stopped **in order to collect** some flowers for her Grandmother.

To make a purpose clause negative you say *so as not to* **or** *... because I didn't want to:*
I spoke quietly **so as not to wake up** the baby.

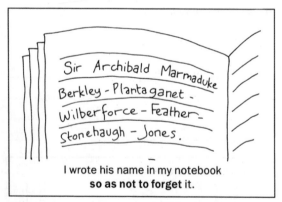

Sir Archibald Marmaduke Berkley - Plantaganet - Wilberforce - Feather - Stonehaugh - Jones.

I wrote his name in my notebook **so as not to forget** it.

'He always does that **because he doesn't want to be left behind**.'

2 **You can also use** *so* **or** *so that* **for a purpose clause. If you do this you usually use a modal verb – a word like** *can, could, will* **or** *would:*

I have drawn a map **so that you can get** here easily.
They put up a very large notice **so that everybody would see** it.

3 **You use** *because* **to explain why someone does something or why it happens:**

We went to bed early **because we were** very tired.
I spoke very slowly **because he didn't understand** English very well.

4 **You use** *so* **to say what the result of an action or situation is:**

We were very tired **so we went** to bed early.   He couldn't understand English very well **so I spoke** very slowly.

Cycle 4

A Here are the words of a well known folk song:

I know an old lady who swallowed a fly

I don't know why she swallowed the fly ... perhaps she'll die.

I know an old lady who swallowed a spider that wriggled and tickled and jiggled inside her.

She swallowed the spider to catch the fly, but I don't know why she swallowed the fly ... perhaps she'll die.

I know an old lady who swallowed a bird. Well how absurd – to swallow a bird.

She swallowed a bird ____ _____ _____ _____ that wriggled and tickled and jiggled inside her. She swallowed the spider to catch the fly, but I don't know why she swallowed the fly ... perhaps she'll die.

I know an old lady who swallowed a cat. Well fancy that – she swallowed a cat.

I know an old lady who swallowed a dog. What a hog to swallow a dog.

I know an old lady who swallowed a goat. She just opened her throat and swallowed a goat.

I know an old lady who swallowed a cow. I don't know how she swallowed the cow.

I know an old lady who swallowed a horse – she died of course.

> **wriggle** When a person or animal **wriggles** or when they **wriggle** part of their body, they twist and turn their body with quick movements e.g. *She wriggled her toes.*
>
> **tickle** When something **tickles** you or **tickles**, it produces an irritating but sometimes pleasant feeling in a part of your body by touching it lightly.
>
> **jiggle** If you **jiggle** about you move up and down or from side to side in a quick and jerky way.
>
> **absurd** Something that is **absurd** is ridiculous because it is totally different from what you would normally expect. e.g. *That hat looks absurd.*
>
> **fancy** You say '**fancy**' when you want to express surprise or disapproval. e.g. *Fancy that!*
>
> **hog 1** A hog is a male pig. **1.2** a greedy, person; an informal use.

Cover the page and see if you can say:

'She swallowed the cow because she wanted to catch the goat. She swallowed the goat because she wanted to catch the dog. She swallowed the dog .... cat............ bird .... spider .... fly – but I don't know why she swallowed the fly. Perhaps she'll die.'

Can you do the same saying *in order to*?

Work with a friend. Ask and answer questions like *Why did she swallow the dog*?

1 You use patterns with *so* or *such* followed by *that* to talk about result:

Look at Unit 65 for patterns with *so* and *such*:

The food was **so delicious that** I helped myself to more. (*so* + adjective + *that*)

It was **such a nice day that** I had to go for a swim. (*such a* + adj + count noun + *that*)

We had **such good weather that** we came back with tans. (*such* + adj + uncount noun + *that*)

She made **such beautiful cakes that** they are all sold out. (*such* + adj + plural noun + *that*)

You use *so* with an adverb:

We arrived **so late** we almost missed the party.

He talked **so much** that she couldn't get a word in edgeways.

Patterns with quantifiers: *so much* (with uncount nouns); *so many* (with count nouns); *so few* (with count nouns); *such a lot of* (with either count or uncount):

We had **so many things** to carry that we had to ask Sophie to help us.

There were **such a lot of people** the e that we couldn't get a seat.

There was **so much food** left we had to throw some away.

2 You often use *enough* with an adjective, an adverb or a noun. It comes after an adjective or adverb:

A: Are those shoes comfortable?   B: Not really. They're not **big enough.**

I can't hear him. He never speaks **loud enough.**

It comes in front of a noun:

A: How is your orange juice?   B: It's very nice, but there's not **enough sugar** in it.

OK. Let's start the meeting.   There are **enough people** here now.

These patterns are followed by the *to - infinitive* to talk about result:

The children are **old enough to go** to school.   We ran **fast enough to catch** him.

I haven't **enough money to buy** a new car.   There's **enough time to have** lunch.

You can use adverbs such as *nearly*, *just* and *easily* with *enough*:

We have **just enough time** to have lunch.   They're **easily old enough** to go to school.

3 Enough can be used on its own as a pronoun:

I've got **enough** to worry about.   **Enough** has been said about this already.

4 You often use *too* with an adjective or adverb to talk about a negative result:

A: Have the children started school yet?   B: Oh no. They're still **too young.**

A: Let's go out for a meal.   B: Oh no. It's **much too expensive.**

They were **too tired** to walk any further. (They were so tired that they could not walk any further.)

A Join these sentences using *so/such ... that*:

1 He was very pleased. He wrote a letter to thank me for my help.
   He was so pleased that he wrote a letter to thank me for my help.

2 They worked very hard. They finished everything in one afternoon.

3 She is very kind. She will help anyone who asks her.

4 It's a nice day. We should go out for a walk in the fresh air.

5 She had a very bad cold. She could not possibly go to work.

6 He had a big car. There was plenty of room for everybody.

7 The flat was very small. Three of us had to share a room.

8 They have a lot of friends. They go out almost every evening.

B Complete these sentences using *enough* or *too*:

1 I won't be able to come tomorrow. I'm afraid I'm ___*too busy*___ . (busy)

2 Katherine can go to school by herself. She's certainly _____ . (old)

3 You shouldn't go out without an overcoat. It's much _____ . (cold)

4 We won't telephone you when we get back. It will be _____ . (late)

5 You can walk there in about ten minutes. It's _____ . (close)

6 You can't drive there in a day. It's _____ . (far)

7 She cycles to the shops every day. She's still _____ . (fit)

8 We can't afford to stay in a hotel. It's _____ . (expensive)

Now rewrite the sentences using *too/enough ... to ...* :

1 *I'm afraid I'll be too busy to come tomorrow.*

2 _____

3 _____

4 _____

5 _____

6 _____

7 _____

8 _____

Contrast and comparison

1 **When you want to contrast two statements you can say *although* or *even though*:**

Although he was late he stopped to buy a sandwich.
He went to work every day **even though** he was very ill.

Sometimes you use the word *still* to emphasise the contrast:
I **still** like Anna, **even though** she is sometimes very annoying.
He was **still** cheerful, **even though** he was very ill.

2 **Another way of making a contrast is to use *in spite of ...* with a noun:**

He is still very fit **in spite of his age**.
She worked very hard **in spite of the difficulties**.

In spite of is often followed by an *-ing* form:
He still failed his exams **in spite of working** really hard.
He won the race **in spite of being** the youngest competitor.

3 **You can compare things by using a comparative adjective with *than*, or by using *as ... as ...* (see Unit 64):**

This pullover is **much nicer than** that one, and it's **a bit cheaper** too.
Their house is **as big as** ours.　　It's **not as easy as** you think.

4 **You use *like* with a few verbs to talk about things which are almost the same in some way:**

Ken **is just like** his father.　New York **is like** London in many ways.
An okapi **looks like** a small giraffe.　Who's that? It **sounds like** Henry.

These verbs are very commonly used with *like*:
be　feel　look　seem　smell　sound　taste

Questions with *like* are very common (see Unit 14):
What's it **like**?　What does it look **like**?　What did it sound **like**?

You use some adverbs of degree with *like*:
exactly　just　rather　a bit　a little bit　nothing

He looks **exactly like** his father.

'They sound **a bit like** the Beatles.'

A Use these phrases to complete the sentences below:

we drove very fast	we were really hungry	I was very angry
they didn't hear us	I haven't finished it yet	he was looking very well
we are very good friends	we don't see her very often	he looked very fierce
it's much more expensive	he still didn't earn very much	the sun was shining

1 Although _____*we were really hungry*_____ there was no time to stop and eat.

2 _____ even though we have only just met.

3 Although he worked very long hours _____ .

4 _____ even though she lives next door.

5 The journey took over four hours even though _____ .

6 _____ even though he had just been ill.

7 Although _____ I tried to speak quietly and calmly.

8 This coat doesn't look as smart as that even though _____ .

9 It was still bitterly cold even though

_____ .

10 He was really quite friendly, although

_____ .

11 I must take this book back to the library even though _____ .

12 _____ even though we knocked very loudly.

B Rewrite these sentences using *in spite of*:

1 We arrived on time although we got lost on the way.

We arrived on time _*in spite of getting lost on the way.*_

2 He still takes a lot of exercise even though he is over seventy.

He still takes a lot of exercise _____ .

3 Although she was injured she still finished the match.

_____ she still finished the match.

4 He looks just like his brother although he's much younger.

He looks just like his brother _____ .

5 She still has a job although she has three children to look after.

She still has a job _____ .

1 Look at the clauses in Unit 72. You use these relative clauses to identify the person or thing you are talking about:

A: I saw a friend of yours today.   B: Who was that?

A: That man **who worked with you in Manchester.**   B: Oh, you mean George.

A: Have you seen my shirt? B: Which shirt?
A: The one **I wore at the party last week.** B: Oh yes. It's here, in the drawer.

2 You also use relative clauses to tell you more about the person or thing you are talking about:

Once upon a time there was a little girl called Red Riding Hood, **who lived in a little house in the forest with her mother and father.**

There was a wicked wolf, **who wanted to catch Red Riding Hood and eat her up.**

I bought the car from Professor Jones, **who lives just across the road.**

They go to the King's School, **which is quite close to home.**

These relative clauses are 'describing clauses'. You always start a describing clause with a relative pronoun. You use *who* to talk about people and *which* to talk about things:

She works with Alex, **who used to go to school with her brother.**

I teach at the University, **which is in the centre of town.**

⚠ WARNING : You do not use *that* in describing clauses.

3 You can use *when* and *where* in describing clauses to talk about times and places:

We haven't seen them since January, **when we were on holiday together.**

They live in Birmingham, **where Rebecca was born.**

4 You can use a describing clause beginning with *which* to say something about a situation:

I've lost my key, **which is very annoying.** He shouted at us, **which was very rude.**

A Complete these sentences using *who, which, when* or *where*:

1 Tomorrow we are going to Leeds, _____*where*_____ William and Jenny live.

2 On Tuesday it's the carnival, _____ everybody gets dressed up in a fancy costume.

3 We'll meet at Wendy's house, _____ is about a couple of miles out of town.

4 This is the store room, _____ we keep most of our equipment.

5 I'll introduce you to Monica, _____ has the office next to mine.

6 It's time for our coffee break, _____ we meet everyone in the canteen.

7 He stays at home and looks after the children, _____ is very hard work.

8 This is Dan, _____ works here on Mondays and Wednesdays.

B Match these parts to make sentences. Some of them you will know, but some are very difficult:

1 We spent a week in Stratford-on Avon,	a where we saw the Parthenon.
2 I am reading about Marconi,	b which is a kind of cheese.
3 They live in Brussels,	c who discovered America.
4 John Logie Baird was a Scotsman,	d when we celebrate carnival.
5 You could come in December,	e where William Shakespeare was born.
6 It's a haggis,	f who discovered radium.
7 Valladolid is the birthplace of Cervantes,	g which is a very popular dish in Scotland.
8 We change planes in Canberra,	h who invented the radio.
9 We stopped off in Athens,	i when we celebrate Christmas.
10 This book is about Christopher Columbus,	j where the European Parliament is.
11 This is gorgonzola,	k who wrote Don Quixote.
12 I've just seen a film about Marie Curie,	l who invented television.
13 It's a microscope,	m which is the capital of Australia.
14 Next week is Mardi Gras,	n which is used to study very small objects.

Work in pairs. One person closes the book. The other person gives the first part of a sentence to see if his/her partner can complete it correctly.

C Rewrite the following as single sentences using *who, which, when* or *where*:

1 My grandfather was born in 1914, *when the First World War started.*
(The First World War started in 1914.)

2 He lived most of his life in Newcastle, _____ .
(He was born in Newcastle.)

3 When he was at university he met my grandmother, _____ .
(She was studying mathematics.)

4 They got married in 1938, _____ .
(They left university in 1938.)

5 My mother was born in Bournemouth, _____
(Bournemouth is in the south of England.)

Review: Cycle 4 – Units 66–80

Unit 66: Verbs not used in continuous tenses

A Complete the following dialogues with the verb in the present simple or the present continuous:

A What (you /cook?)

(1) _____? It (smell)

(2) _____ wonderful.

B I (make) (3) _____ a chocolate cake.

(You like?) (4) _____ chocolate cake?

A Yes, I (love) (5) _____ it. Mmm, it

(taste) (6) _____ good.

A (Be) (7) _____ this your bike?

B No. I (think) (8) _____ it (belong)

(9) _____ to my neighbour's daughter.

I (know) (10) _____ she (have)

(11) _____ one like that.

B Complete these sentences with the correct form of the verb:

1 Mary's upstairs. She (a) *has/is having* a rest.
2 Be quiet. I (b) *think/am thinking* I (c) *am hearing/can hear* someone downstairs.
3 We were out very late last night because we (d) *saw/were seeing* some old friends.
4 Jack (e) *doesn't like/isn't liking* maths because he (f) *doesn't understand/isn't understanding* it very well.
5 Ivan was very rich. He (g) *owned/was owning* a big car and a house in the country.
6 Can you turn the TV down please? I (h) *try/am trying* to do some work. I (i) *think/am thinking* about my homework.
7 A: That (j) *looks/is looking* interesting? What is it?
  B: It's a cigarette lighter. It (k) *belonged/was belonging* to my grandfather.
8 A: Where's Jenny?
  B: She's at the Arts Centre. She (l) *learns/is learning* to paint.
  A: That (m) *sounds/is sounding* interesting.

Review: Cycle 4 – Units 66–80

Unit 67: The passive

C Rewrite these sentences in the passive:

1 We keep the glasses in this cupboard.

   The glasses _are kept in this cupboard._

2 Someone found Jim's wallet lying in the street.

   Jim's wallet _____ .

3 You can obtain this book at your local library.

   This book _____ .

4 Someone told me to park my car outside in the street.

   I _____ .

5 They sold their house for over £200,000.

   Their house _____ .

6 Nobody has heard of John since he went to live in America.

   John _____ .

7 They sell newspapers at most corner shops.

   Newspapers _____ .

8 They do not allow you to borrow more than three books.

   You _____ .

9 Someone gave her a computer for her birthday.

   She _____ .

10 You must wear protective clothing in the factory.

   Protective clothing _____ .

D Choose the right form of the verb:

1 A Birmingham woman (1) *attacked/was attacked* with a knife on her way home from work. Mrs Fung (2) *had just left/had just been left* her shop in South Street when she (3) *stopped/was stopped* by a young man who (4) *tried/was tried* to snatch her handbag. When Mrs Fung (5) *was fought /fought back*, the man (6) *took/was taken* out a knife. Mrs. Fung's face (7) *badly cut/ was badly cut* and she (8) *took/was taken* to hospital.

2 Germany (9) *were won/won* the football World Cup in 1990, when they (10) *beat/were beaten* Argentina. In 1994 the Germans (11) *beat/were beaten* by Bulgaria in the quarter final, and the cup (12) *won/was won* by Brazil.

3 John F. Kennedy (13) *born/was born* in 1973. He (14) *elected/was elected* President of the US in 1960. On 22 November, 1963, he (15) *shot/was shot* dead by Lee Harvey Oswald, during a visit to Dallas, Texas. Two days later Oswald himself (16) *shot/was shot* and killed.

Review: Cycle 4 – Units 66–80

Unit 68: *Reporting the past*

E Look at this dialogue:

A Hi Ken! Where are you going?

B I'm going into town to do some shopping. Why?

A Can you give me a lift? I'm late for work.
  My car has broken down. It won't start.

B I'm sorry, I'm not going into town,
  but I can give you a lift to the railway station.

Now complete this report, putting the verbs in the right tense:

As I (1) (get) _____ into my car my neighbour (2) (shout) _____ out of

his front window and (3) (ask) _____ me where I (4) (go) _____ . When I

(5) (tell) _____ him I (6) (go) _____ to town he (7) (ask) _____

if I (8) (can) _____ give him a lift into work. He (9) (be) _____ afraid he

(10) (be) _____ late for work because his car (11) (break down) _____ and it

(12) (not start) _____ . I explained that I (13) (not/go) _____ into town

but I (14) (can) _____ give him a lift to the railway station.

F Now do this one in the same way:

'Tell me why do you want to
be a computer programmer?'

A Tell me, why do you want to be a computer
  programmer?

B Well I've always been interested in computers.

A When have you used them before?

B Well, we used computers for some of our work at
  school. And in my last job all the records were kept
  on computer.

A Yes, but do you have any experience as a
  programmer?

B No, not yet. But I have read a lot and I have been
  studying programming at night school.

A I see. And do you have any qualifications?

B Not yet. But I'm going to take my certificate exam
  next month.

Annette was asked why she (1) _____ to be a computer programmer. She said that

she (2) _____ always been interested in computers. She said she

(3) _____ them at school and also in her last job, where all the records

(4) _____ computerised. She (5) _____ any experience

as a programmer, but she (6) _____ programming at night school. Although she

(7) _____ no qualifications she (8) _____ to take her

exam the next month.

Review: Cycle 4 – Units 66–80

Units 66, 67, 68

G Choose the form in brackets which best completes the story:

'Do you think you could take my carpets too?'

One day as Mrs. Jackson (1) *was looking/had looked* out of the window she (2) *saw/ was seeing* two men in the garden next door. They (3) *carried/were carrying* some expensive carpets down the path towards a large van. Mrs Jackson (4) *called out/was calling out* and (5) *asked/asking* them what they (6) *are doing/were doing/do/did*. One of the men (7) *explained/was explaining* that the carpets (8) *are taking/were taking/are being taken/were being taken* away to be cleaned.

Mrs. Jackson (9) *was thinking/thought* she (10) *will like/would like/liked* her carpets cleaned too and asked the two men if they (11) *can/could* put them on the van. The men agreed and explained that they (12) *will return/would return* the carpets in three weeks time. A week later the neighbours came back and found that their carpets (13) *have stole/had stolen/have been stolen/had been stolen*. Poor Mrs. Jackson realised that she (14) *has given/had given* the thieves her carpets too.

Unit 69: Short answers

H Write a short sentence in response to each of the questions:

1 Mrs. Jackson saw two men, didn't she? *Yes she did.* _____

2 Were they carrying a carpet? _____

3 Were they thieves? _____

4 Did Mrs. Jackson call the police? _____

5 Did Mrs. Jackson want her carpets cleaned? _____

6 Could they put the carpets on the van? _____

7 Would the neighbours be happy? _____

8 Was Mrs. Jackson silly? _____

Cycle 4

Review: Cycle 4 – Units 66–80

Unit 70: Question tags

Add tags to these questions:

1 You live quite near here, _____ ?
2 I'm not late, _____ ?
3 Columbus discovered America, _____ ?
4 You're not tired, _____ ?
5 You'll come with us, _____ ?
6 We haven't met before, _____ ?
7 There's plenty of time, _____ ?
8 You've been to Britain, _____ ?
9 You went there last year, _____ ?
10 You can't lend me a pound, _____ ?
11 He looks unhappy, _____ ?
12 It isn't going to rain, _____ ?
13 You didn't enjoy it much, _____ ?
14 I'm next, _____ ?
15 You should work harder, _____ ?
16 We have to go soon, _____ ?
17 You won't forget, _____ ?
18 We'll all be late, _____ ?

Unit 71: Too/either/so/neither

Complete the sentences below using *too*, *either*, *so* or *neither*.

1 There were lots of children at the circus, and quite a lot of adults _____ .

2 We didn't enjoy the film much and _____ did our friends.

3 My mother is a wonderful cook, and _____ is my father.

4 I didn't see Jill and I didn't see her sister _____ .

5 She bought a new dress, and some new shoes _____ .

6 I haven't booked a seat for the theatre yet and I haven't bought a ticket _____ .

7 I know Jane will be happy to see you, and _____ will her family.

Unit 72: Defining relative clauses

Make sentences like 1 (b) below:

1 (a) He was carrying an old bag. It looked really heavy.

  (b) The old bag *he was carrying looked really heavy.* _____

2 (a) Some people drive too fast. They are really dangerous.

  (b) People _____ .

3 (a) We went to a concert in London. It wasn't very good.

  (b) The concert _____ .

4 (a) I'd like to buy that red dress. I saw it in your shop yesterday.

  (b) I'd like to buy that red dress _____ .

5 (a) We know some people. They live very near you.

  (b) We know some people _____ .

Review: Cycle 4 – Units 66–80

Unit 74: Too/enough

L **Complete these sentences using *too much, too many* or *enough*:**

1 I'm sorry I can't help. I just don't have _____*enough*_____ time.

2 I can't drink this coffee. There's _____ sugar in it.

3 I hate shopping on Saturday. There are always _____ people in town.

4 David can't drive the car yet. He's not old _____ .

5 If we are going camping we must take _____ food for three days.

6 Everything is very wet. We have had _____ rain over the weekend.

7 There are _____ people. We haven't got _____ chairs for everybody.

8 I don't feel very well. I think I've had _____ to eat.

Units 69 – 74

M **Read this dialogue and underline the correct answers:**

Travel Agent: Good morning. What can I do for you?

Helen: Good morning. We are looking for a holiday in the sun. We'd like to go next week. We're not .
    (1) *very late/too late/late enough* (2) *aren't we/are we/is it?*

Travel Agent: No. I think I can help you. What about the Greek Islands?

Susan: No, we've been to Greece, (3) *have we/haven't we/don't we* Helen?

Helen: Yes, we (4) *go/have gone/went* to Crete last year.

Travel Agent: I see. You want a country (5) *which you haven't visited it/you haven't visited* before. And you
    want somewhere sunny, (6) *is it/are you/do you?* Well Portugal isn't (7) *expensive enough/too*
    expensive, and it's certainly (8) *enough warm/warm enough* at this time of year.

Helen: (9) *Is it/does it* really? I haven't heard much about Portugal.

Travel Agent: (10) *Have you/Haven't you?* Well it's a popular place nowadays, with plenty of good resorts.

Review: Cycle 4 – Units 66–80

Unit 75: Present tense with if, when etc

N Complete these sentences putting the verbs in the right tense:

a If it (1) *is/will be* fine tomorrow we (2) *have/can have* lunch in the garden...

... but if it (3) *will rain/rains* we (4) *eat/will eat* in the house.

b I (5) *get/ will get* home early tonight if I (6) *catch/will catch* the train at seven thirty.

c If you (7) *will want to/ want to* you (8) *can stay/stay/will stay* with us when you (9) *come/will come* to London.

d I (10) *look after/am looking after/will look after* the children while you (11) *go/will go* to work.

e Joe says he (12) *comes round/will come round* tonight if he (13) *has/will have* time.

f The children are tired out. They (14) *fall/will fall* asleep as soon as they (15) *will get/get home*.

Unit 76: Conditional sentences and wishes

O Complete these sentences putting the verbs in the right tenses:

1 What *would you do/ will you do* if you *are/were* the richest person in the world?

2 I don't know where Anne lives. If I *know/ knew* I *would go/ will go* to see her.

3 A Oh dear. I've forgotten my pen.
  B Never mind. You *can/ could* borrow mine if you *haven't/hadn't* got one.

4 A Do you know what time the train goes?
  B No, I'm sorry. If I *am/was/were* you I'll/I'd telephone the station and find out.

5 A I'm hungry.
  B Okay. If you *are/were* hungry we *will/would* go out and get something to eat.

6 I wish Jack *would telephone/telephoned/had telephoned* yesterday.

7 A I wish Marie *is/will be/was* here.
  B Yes, if she *is/will be/was* here she *will know/knows/would know* what to do.

8 If you *see/will see/saw* Henry tomorrow *will you give/did you give/do you give* him a message, please?

Unit 77: Purpose and reason

P Rewrite these sentences using *used ... to ...*:

1 She opened the bottle with a corkscrew.
   She used a corkscrew to open the bottle.

2 I found what the word meant in a dictionary.
_____

3 He mended the chair with a piece of string.
_____

4 She polished her shoes with a wet cloth.
_____

5 I caught the mouse with a trap and a big piece of cheese.
_____

6 Our teacher always marked our books with a red pen.
_____

7 She looked at the leaf under a microscope.
_____

8 He bathed the baby in a bucket.
_____

Review: Cycle 4 – Units 66–80

Unit 78: Result

Q Rewrite these sentences using *so ... that ...* or *such ... that ...*:

1 I couldn't work any more because I was very tired.
   I was so tired that I couldn't work any more.

2 We couldn't go out because it was a very wet day.
   _____

3 My bicycle was very old. It was always breaking down.
   _____

4 Don is a very good friend. He will always help me if I ask him.
   _____

5 My father lives a long way from his office. He has to drive to work every day.
   _____

6 It was dark when we arrived because the journey took a very long time.
   _____

7 He was very angry. He wouldn't speak to me.
   _____

8 I was very frightened. I didn't know what to do.
   _____

Unit 79: Contrast and comparison

R Complete these sentences using *because* or *even though*:

1 She speaks good English _____ she hasn't been learning it very long.

2 I switched on the TV _____ I wanted to listen to the news.

3 We enjoyed the game _____ we didn't win.

4 He never goes out _____ he's always playing computer games.

5 He's very tall _____ he's only fourteen.

6 Katy didn't look very happy _____ it was her birthday.

7 Don was saving up _____ he wanted to buy a camera.

Review: Cycle 4 – Units 66–80

Unit 80: Describing clauses

S Combine these sentences using the words *who*, *which*, *where*, or *when*:

1 We are going on holiday to Brighton. My mother was born in Brighton.
   We are going on holiday to Brighton, where my mother was born.

2 I'll telephone you at six o'clock. I get home at six o'clock.

3 She comes from Sofia. Sofia is the capital of Bulgaria.

4 This is my old friend, Tom. Tom is staying with us this week.

5 I'm reading a book about Ronald Reagan. He used to be President of the USA.

6 This is the garage. We keep all the garden furniture.

BUCKINGHAM PALACE

7 Pele is a famous footballer. He played for Brazil at the age of seventeen.

8 We visited Buckingham Palace. The royal family lives in Buckingham Palace.

Review: Cycle 4 – Units 66–80

Units 75 – 80

T Use the following words to complete the story: *and, although, because, enough, if, so, who, to:*

This story is about the Hodja, (1) _____ is a well-known character in the Middle East. One

day the Hodja went to his neighbour's house (2) _____ he wanted to borrow a cooking pot.

'A lot of my relatives are coming to stay and my wife doesn't have a big (3) _____ pot,' he

explained. '(4) _____ you can lend me a big pot I will bring it back next week,' he promised.

Although the neighbour did not trust the Hodja he agreed to lend him a pot, (5) _____ the

Hodja went off happily. After two weeks the neighbour went to see the Hodja (6) _____ the

pot had not been returned. 'I am sorry,' said the Hodja. 'I have been looking after your pot very carefully

(7) _____ I realised it was pregnant. The baby was born yesterday. Here it is.' He gave his

neighbour the big pot and also a small one. (8) _____ the neighbour was very surprised he

took the pots and went home happily. A week later the Hodja went to his neighbour's house again

(9) _____ borrow another large pot. 'I will lend you the same pot again,' his neighbour said,

'(10) _____ you promise to bring it back next week.' The Hodja promised and off he went

with the pot. Again two weeks went by (11) _____ the neighbour went to the Hodja's house

(12) _____ ask for his pot. 'I am very sorry,' said the Hodja. 'I cannot give you your pot

(13) _____ it has died.' The neighbour was (14) _____ angry that he

shouted at the Hodja. 'Don't think I am foolish (15) _____ to believe a story like that.

Everyone knows that cooking pots don't die.' 'Please don't be angry,' said the Hodja.

'(16) _____ you believed me when I said your pot was pregnant you should certainly believe

me (17) _____ I tell you it has died.'

General review E

General Revision

A Verb tenses (Units 1 – 12; 66, 75, 76)

Put these verbs in the right tense:

1 We (live) _____ in England for nearly five years now. We came here when I

   (be) _____ ten years old.

2 'Can you be quiet please?

   I (try) _____ to listen to the

   radio.'

3 'Janet's not at home.

   She (just go) _____ to school.

   She (go) _____ out ten minutes

   ago.'

4 Jim was very tired when he (get) _____ home. He (travel) _____ for over

   eight hours.

5 It was ten o'clock and I still (not finish) _____ my homework.

6 It (be) _____ my birthday tomorrow.

7 We are going to be late if we (not hurry) _____ .

8 I met your brother the other day while I (wait) _____ for the bus.

9 If I (be) _____ seventeen I (can drive) _____ my father's car.

10 I wish I (can) _____ come to your party.

11 We (go) _____ to London for our holidays this year.

12 I (not play) _____ football since I (break) _____ my leg six weeks ago.

13 I (learn) _____ Greek ten years ago while I (work) _____ in Athens.

14 I (telephone) _____ Bill as soon as I (get) _____ home this evening.

15 It was eleven o'clock and we (just go) _____ to bed when the telephone (ring)

   _____ .

16 A: Aren't you enjoying the film?

    B: No I (not like) _____ these horror films.

17 I (see) _____ that word yesterday, but I (not remember) _____ what it

    means now.

18 I wish we (live) _____ a more interesting place.

General review E

B Questions (Units 14, 15)

Complete these dialogues by making questions to go with the answers:

1 A: _____ ?

   B: It's nearly six o'clock.

2 A: _____ ?

   B: I'll be seventeen next month.

3 A: _____ ?

   B: No, there's no milk in the fridge, but there's a bottle on the table.

4 A: _____ ?

   B: No, I've never met Marie, but I know her brother well.

5 A: _____ ?

   B: Jack? He looks just like his father.

6 A: _____ ?

   B: I'll probably stay at home and do some gardening.

7 A: _____ ?

   B: We've got an old Ford.

8 A: _____ ?

   B: 21, North Street, Misson.

9 A: We're going on holiday next week.

   B: _____ ?

   A: Spain.

10 A: We'll come round and see you.

   B: _____ ?

   A: Probably next week.

C Prepositions (Units 30, 48, 49)

Add a preposition where necessary to complete these sentences:

1 Do you go to school _____ your bicycle or _____ foot?

2 The match starts _____ ten o'clock _____ Thursday.

3 John's not very well. He's not _____ work today.

4 The weather is usually warm _____ summer, but it can be very cold _____ December.

5 Jan went to Manchester _____ bus, but I went _____ my friend's car.

6 We will get _____ the bus at the next stop.

7 Dad always reads the newspaper _____ breakfast.

8 We'll come and see you _____ tomorrow.

9 They sell sandwiches _____ the train.

10 We stay with my parents _____ every Christmas.

General review E

D Position of adverbials (Units 27, 28, 47)

Complete these sentences by putting the words in brackets in the right place:

1 We go to the cinema at the weekend. (often)

_____

2 George can tell you what you want to know. (certainly)

_____

3 I don't play football now (very much), but I play tennis. (a lot)

_____

4 I saw Fred but he isn't here now. (a while ago)

_____

5 It rained last night. (quite a lot)

_____

6 The door was locked when I went out. (definitely)

_____

7 We watch television at the weekend. (hardly ever)

_____

8 It is one of the best films I have seen. (ever)

_____

9 I didn't enjoy the film (very much), but I enjoyed the play. (a lot)

_____

10 I met Helen a week, but I haven't seen her since then. (ago)

_____

11 I read the instructions on the medicine bottle. (carefully)

_____

12 We see Richard when we are in Oxford. (always)

_____

E Some common verbs (Units 39, 56)

Use the right verbs to complete these sentences:

1 I've had a long journey. I'm going to _____ a shower.

2 Do you _____ the cooking in your family?

3 Keep very quiet and try not to _____ any noise.

4 Stand still a moment. I want to _____ a photograph.

5 Are you going to _____ a holiday this year?

6 Jan has her examination tomorrow. I'm sure she will _____ very well.

7 I'm sure you will _____ a lot of friends at your new school.

8 What time do you _____ breakfast in the morning?

9 There's Barbara over there. _____ her a smile.

10 Did you _____ much fishing on holiday?

General review E

Grammar Practice

F Choose the form in brackets which best completes the story:

One day a friend of mine (1) (a) *who he was driving* (b) *who driving* (c) *who was driving* home late at night saw a young woman (2) (a) *stand* (b) *stood* (c) *standing* by the side of the road. (3) (a) *A friend* (b) *The friend* (c) *My friend* stopped (4) (a) *to* (b) *for* (c) *and* give her a lift. (5) (a) *A young woman* (b) *Young woman* (c) *The young woman* got (6) (a) *on* (b) *into* (c) *to* the car and closed (7) (a) *the door* (b) *a door* (c) *door*. She (8) (a) *told to my friend* (b) *told* (c) *told my friend* she lived (9) (a) *at* (b) *in* (c) *on* 26 North Street, (10) (a) *which* (b) *where* (c) *that* was just near my friend's house.

The young woman talked happily as they drove along but after ten minutes she fell silent. My friend (11) (a) *looked* (b) *was looked* (c) *was looking* round to see if she was all right. To his astonishment[1] the young woman (12) (a) *vanish*[2] (b) *has vanished* (c) *had vanished*. At first my friend (13) (a) *did not know* (b) *was not knowing* (c) *has not known* what to do. Finally he decided (14) (a) *going* (b) *to go* (c) *go* to 26, North Street to see if anyone there (15) (a) *was knowing* (b) *knew* (c) *knows* the woman.

He went up to (16) (a) *a* (b) *the* house and knocked on the door. It (17) (a) *opened* (b) *was opened* by a middle-aged woman. My friend explained how he (18) (a) *was meeting* (b) *has met* (c) *had met* the young woman and (19) (a) *giving* (b) *given* (c) *give* her a lift. He (20) (a) *told to* (b) *told the* woman (21) (a) *who had answered* (b) *who she had answered* (c) *answered* the door that the young woman had said she lived (22) (a) *at* (b) *in* 26, North Street.

I (23) (a) *know* (b) *am knowing* the story said the woman at the door. A young woman who lived here fifteen years ago (24) (a) *killed* (b) *was killed* by a car on that road. It happened exactly (25) (a) *since ten years* (b) *ten years ago* (c) *before ten years*. Every year since then the young woman (26) (a) *had seen* (b) *had been seen* on the road and asked for a lift home to 26, North Street.

---

[1] You say *to his astonishment* or *to her astonishment* when someone is very surprised.
[2] *To vanish* means *to disappear* suddenly or in a way that nobody can explain.

Spelling

Verbs

A For the third person singular of most verbs, but not modals, add -s:

Drink – He drinks a lot.
Want – She wants to see you now.
Like – The dog likes water.
Break – Glass breaks easily.

For verbs ending in -sh, -ch, -ss, -x, -z and -o, add -es:

Finish – It finishes at 8.
Watch – He watches everything.
Pass – The train passes here, but it doesn't stop.
Mix – This colour mixes well.
Buzz – The bell buzzes.
Go – She goes every Friday.

For verbs ending in *consonant* + *y*, change the -y to -ies:

Try – He tries very hard.
Worry – He worries too much.
Study – She studies in France.
Cry – It cries a lot.

For verbs ending in *vowel* + *y* just add -s:

Play – She plays with us sometimes.
Say – Who says so?

B For the past simple and past participle of most regular verbs, add -ed:

Finish – We finished early.
Clean – Who cleaned this?

For verbs ending in -e, add -d, not -ed:

Dance – We danced all night.
Move – They moved in last week.

For verbs ending in *consonant* + -y, change the -y to -ied:

Try – They tried to help.
Study – We've studied hard.

For verbs of one syllable ending in a single vowel + single consonant (e.g. -ip, -op, -an), double the final consonant and add -ed:

Drop – He dropped the ball.
Drip – The tap dripped all night.
Plan – They planned it well.
Stop – We stopped at Dover.

For verbs ending in one vowel and the consonants *y, w* or *x*, just add -ed:

Play – We haven't played with the children.
Mix – She mixed the ingredients for the meal.

For verbs of more than one syllable ending in a single vowel and a consonant, double the final consonant when the stress is on the last syllable:

Refer – I referred to it.
Prefer – She preferred my cake.

When the last syllable is not stressed, just add -ed:

Offer – They offered to pay.
Develop – It developed fast.

An exception: In British English verbs ending in -l double the l even if the last syllable is not stressed:

Travel – He's travelled a lot.

Many common verbs are irregular and do not add -ed in the past tense or the past participle. Here is a list of some of them:

Base form	Past simple	Past participle
be	was/were	been
become	became	become
begin	began	begun
break	broke	broken
bring	brought	brought
build	built	built
buy	bought	bought
catch	caught	caught
choose	chose	chosen
come	came	come
cost	cost	cost
cut	cut	cut
drink	drank	drunk
drive	drove	driven
eat	ate	eaten
fall	fell	fallen
feel	felt	felt
find	found	found
fly	flew	flown
forget	forgot	forgotten
get	got	got
go	went	gone
have	had	had
hear	heard	heard
hide	hid	hidden
hold	held	held
keep	kept	kept
know	knew	known
leave	left	left

Spelling

let	let	let
lose	lost	lost
make	made	made
mean	meant	meant
meet	met	met
pay	paid	paid
put	put	put
read	read	read
ride	rode	ridden
rise	rose	risen
run	ran	run
see	saw	seen
sell	sold	sold
send	sent	sent
shut	shut	shut
sing	sang	sung
sit	sat	sat
sleep	slept	slept
speak	spoke	spoken
stand	stood	stood
steal	stole	stolen
swim	swam	swum
take	took	taken
teach	taught	taught
think	thought	thought
understand	understood	understood
wear	wore	worn
write	wrote	written

C For the -ing form or present participle, just add -ing for most verbs:

Do – What are you doing?
Sleep – He's sleeping.
Sing – Who's singing?
Finish – We're finishing soon.
Cry – Someone's crying.
Play –They're playing now.

For verbs ending in e, leave off the e and add -ing:

Dance – He's dancing now.
Hope – We're hoping for the best.

For verbs ending in ee just add -ing. See, agree and disagree become seeing, agreeing and disagreeing.

For verbs of one syllable ending in a single vowel and a consonant, double the final consonant and add -ing:

Begin – It's beginning now.
Get – He's getting the car.

For longer verbs with the stress on the final syllable, double the consonant and add -ing:

Refer – I'm not referring to you.

Nouns and adjectives and adverbs

A Most count nouns form the plural by adding -s, which is pronounced either /s/ or /z/:

A cat – two cats
One table – two tables
A tree – many trees
A day – several days

Nouns ending in -se, -ze, -ce or -ge add an -s, but are pronounced /iz/ and so sound one syllable longer than in the singular:

A rose – A bunch of roses.
The prize – We all won prizes.
A service – The services.
A cage – Animals hate cages.

Nouns ending in -sh, -ch, -ss, -x or -s, add -es and are pronounced /iz/ as well:

Bush – They cut the bushes.
Watch – He bought us all watches.
Pass – The mountain passes are blocked with snow.
Box – Where are those boxes?
Bus – Take one of the buses.

With nouns ending in a consonant + y, change the y to ies:

Lady – Good evening, ladies.
City – The cities of Europe.

Nouns ending in -f or -fe change to -ves:

Knife – Careful with those knives!
Shelf – Paco is putting up shelves.
Wife – The officers and their wives had a special party.

Many nouns ending in -o add -s:

A photo – Here are your photos, sir.
My radio – Those radios look expensive.

But these nouns have the plural form -oes:

A tomato - Sun-ripened tomatoes.
An echo - The sound of echoes.
Potato - A kilo of potatoes.
Hero - He's one of my heroes.

Spelling

B To form comparative and superlative forms of most adjectives, you add -er and -est:

soon – sooner – soonest

cheap – cheaper – cheapest

With words ending in -e, you just add -r and -st:

late – later – latest

wide – wider – widest

With adjectives ending in -y, you change -y to -ier and -iest:

dry – drier – driest

dirty – dirtier – dirtiest

happy – happier – happiest

silly – sillier – silliest

Warning; with shy, you keep the y: shyer/shyest.

With adjectives ending in one vowel and one consonant, you double the final consonant, except with w:

fat – fatter – fattest

big – bigger – biggest

BUT: slow – slower – slowest

C To make adverbs, you generally add -ly to the adjective:

slow – slowly

late – lately

cheap – cheaply

Adjectives ending in -l, change to -lly:

real – really

hopeful – hopefully

With adjectives ending in -y, the -y changes to ily:

happy – happily

easy – easily

Adjectives ending in -le change to -ly:

simple – simply

idle – idly

With adjectives ending in -ic, you add ally, not ly, but the ending is pronounced like ly:

artistic – artistically

automatic – automatically

specific – specifically

D Capital letters:

You must use a capital letter for:

1 the first letter of the first word in every sentence.

2 names of people and places:

This is Arlene. She works in the Education Department.

Have you met Rajan? He's from Malaysia, I think.

3 the days of the week and the months of the year:

See you on Monday or Tuesday. I love September.

4 adjectives and nouns of nationality, and languages:

He's not French or Belgian. He's Swiss.

Can you speak Russian? I met an American last night.

Most people seem to drive Japanese cars nowadays.

5 titles used in front of someone's name:

Do you know Professor Blum? This was Queen Victoria's home.

6 the pronoun *I*:

I know I told you that I was busy.

E Common spelling problems

Here is a list of words that many students find difficult to spell:

accommodation	government	responsible
across	holiday	science
address	language	secretary
argument	library	separate
beautiful	medicine	succeed
beginning	necessary	surprise
blue	occasion	though
businessman	occurred	through
calendar	parliament	tomorrow
embarrassing	professor	vegetable
February	recommend	Wednesday
foreign	referred	

Pronunciation

1 Vowels

1	/ɑ:/	far; start; large[1]; father.
2	/æ/	have; fat; bad.
3	/e/	egg; bed; head.
4	/ɪ/	sit; give; sing.
5	/iː/	me; eat; agreed; piece.
6	/ɒ/	hot; lost; long.
7	/ɔ:/	saw; more; four.[1]
8	/ʊ/	could; good; would.
9	/ʌ/	but; cut; blood.
10	/u:/	you; use; fool; do.
11	/ɜ:/	learn; third; word.[1]
12	/ə/	mother; about; forget.[1]
13	/i/	city; very; jockey.

A Find these words in the list above and write them down

1 /hæv/ _have_   6 /lɒst/ _____   11 /get/ _____   16 /əbaʊt/ _____

2 /fɑ:/ _____   7 /fəget/ _____   12 /gʊd/ _____   17 /gɪv/ _____

3 /lɜ:n/ _____   8 /bʌt/ _____   13 /blʌd/ _____   18 /pi:s/ _____

4 /fu:l/ _____   9 /sɔ:/ _____   14 /du:/ _____   19 /stɑ:t/ _____

5 /i:t/ _____   10 /sɪt/ _____   15 /wɜ:d/ _____   20 /əgri:d/ _____

2 Consonants

14	/b/	bed; big; brother.
15	/d/	did; dog; bed.
16	/f/	five; if; coffee.
17	/g/	good; leg; pig.
18	/h/	hat; have; who.
19	/j/	you; yellow; young.
20	/k/	can; kicking; lucky.
21	/l/	leg; yellow; old.
22	/m/	me; money; summer.
23	/n/	no; money; can.
24	/p/	put; happy; up.
25	/r/	run; hurry.
26	/s/	see; hits; mass.
27	/t/	time; put; winter.
28	/v/	van; have; lovely.
29	/w/	with; white; woman.
30	/z/	zoo; nose; runs; easy.
31	/ʃ/	ship; sugar; wish.
32	/ʒ/	pleasure; measure.
33	/ŋ/	sing; running; singer.
34	/tʃ/	cheap; watch; reaching.
35	/θ/	thin; thick; bath.
36	/ð/	then; weather.
37	/dʒ/	joy; judge; general.

B Find these words in the list above and write them down:

1 /weðə/ _weather_   7 /dɒg/ _____   13 /leg/ _____   19 /sɪŋə/ _____

2 /jʌŋ/ _____   8 /mʌni/ _____   14 /hʌri/ _____   20 /si:/ _____

3 /lʌvli/ _____   9 /wɪntə/ _____   15 /brʌðə/ _____   21 /kɒfi/ _____

4 /hæt/ _____   10 /kɪkɪŋ/ _____   16 /sʌmə/ _____   22 /hæpi/ _____

5 /dʒʌdʒ/ _____   11 /θɪk/ _____   17 /rʌnɪŋ/ _____   23 /ri:tʃɪŋ/ _____

6 /pleʒə/ _____   12 /wɒtʃ/ _____   18 /rʌnz/ _____   24 /wʊmən/ _____

C Can you write out these words and put them in the right order?

1 /sevən/ _seven_   3 /sɪks/ _____   5 /fɔ:/ _____   7 /θri:/ _____

2 /wʌn/ _____   4 /ten/ _____   6 /tu:/ _____

Which three are missing? _____ and _____

---

[1]In standard British English the /r/ is not heard in these words. In most American accents and some British dialects you would hear the /r/: /fɑ:r/ /stɑ:rt/ /lɑ:rdz/

Pronunciation

3 Diphthongs

38	/aɪ/	five; nine; alive; why
39	/aɪə/	fire; higher
40	/aʊ/	out; down; sound
41	/aʊə/	flower; sour
42	/eɪ/	say; eight; paint; again
43	/eə/	there; hair; where; bear
44	/ɪə/	hear; nearly
45	/oʊ/	going; so; slowly
46	/ɔɪ/	boy; toilet; coin
47	/ʊə/	poor; sure

D Find these words in the list above and write them down:

1 /ðeə/ _there_

2 /peɪnt/ _____

3 /əlaɪv/ _____

4 /nɪəlɪ/ _____

5 /flaʊə/ _____

6 /goʊɪŋ/ _____

7 /saʊnd/ _____

8 /kɔɪn/ _____

9 /haɪə/ _____

10 /ʃʊə/ _____

11 /əgeɪn/ _____

E Match the words in list A with the words in list B, the words in list C with the words in list D and the words in list E with the words in list F:

A	B	C	D	E	F
/lʌndən/	/ɒstreɪljə/	/red/	/kɒfi/	/bred/	/tʃɪps/
/pærɪs/	/i:dʒɪpt/	/gri:n/	/gra:s/	/sɒlt/	/bʌtə/
/mədrɪd/	/ɪŋglənd/	/braʊn/	/mɪlk/	/ʃu:z/	/ɪŋk/
/lɪzbən/	/fra:ns/	/waɪt/	/ðə skaɪ/	/pen/	/pepə/
/toʊkjoʊ/	/gri:s/	/blu:/	/ɪŋk/	/fɪʃ/	/sɒks/
/mɒskoʊ/	/ɪndəni:zjə/	/blæk/	/ðə sʌn/		
/wɒʃɪŋtən/	/ɪtəli/	/jeloʊ/	/ə təma:toʊ/		
/æθənz/	/dʒəpæn/				
/roʊm/	/dʒɔ:dən/				
/æma:n/	/pɔ:tjəgəl/				
/dəmæskəs/	/rʌʃə/				
/kænbrə/	/speɪn/				
/kaɪroʊ/	/sɪrɪə/				
/dʒəka:tə/	/ðə ju:naɪtɪd steɪts/				

4 The schwa

The commonest vowel in English is /ə/, which is often called *schwa*.

F Look at these words. You have read them all before. Can you write them out?

1 /bəna:nə/ _banana_

2 /sɪstə/ _____

3 /lesənz/ _____

4 /elɪfənt/ _____

5 /lʌndən/ _____

6 /pleʒə/ _____

7 /æpəl/ _____

8 /fa:ðə/ _____

9 /taɪgə/ _____

10 /ɒstreɪljə/ _____

11 /sʌmə/ _____

12 /meʒə/ _____

13 /brʌðə/ _____

14 /mʌðə/ _____

15 /lɪzbən/ _____

16 /dʒəpæn/ _____

17 /weðə/ _____

18 /mɪstə/ _____

Pronunciation

G Read these sentences. If a sentence is true about you mark it with a tick. If it is not true mark it with a cross:

1 /aɪm ə tiːtʃə/
2 /aɪm ə bɔɪ/
3 /aɪ əm mærɪd/
4 /aɪ hæv ə sɪstə/
5 /aɪ lɪv ɪn ə haʊs/

6 /aɪm ə stjuːdənt/
7 /aɪm ə gɜːl/
8 /aɪ əm nɒt mærɪd/
9 /aɪ hæv ə brʌðə ənd sɪstə/
10 /aɪ laɪk ɪŋglɪʃ lesənz/

11 /aɪ lɪv ɪn lʌndən/
12 /maɪ neɪm ɪz piːtə/
13 /aɪ hæv ə brʌðə/
14 /aɪ lɪv ɪn ə flæt/
15 /aɪ doʊnt laɪk ɪŋglɪʃ lesənz/

H Arrange these words in six groups with three words in each group. Copy down one word from each group in phonetic symbols. Give them to a friend and see if he or she can read them:

/kaʊ/ /desk/ /treɪn/ /æpəl/ /taɪgə/ /ʃɜːt/ /tʃeə/ /elɪfənt/ /hɔːs/
/bənɑːnə/ /dʒækɪt/ /teɪbl/ /bʌs/ /ɒrɪndʒ/ /kɑː/ /blaʊz/ /laɪən/ /ʃiːp/

_____ _____ _____ _____ _____ _____

_____ _____ _____ _____ _____ _____

5 The definite article

The definite article, *the,* has only one form in writing:
Give me *the* money.   This is *the* end.

But there are two ways of pronouncing it:
Give me *the* money. /ðə/
This is *the* end. /ði/

Before a consonant *the* is /ðə/:
/ðə mʌni/ /ðə bənɑːnə/ /ðə dɒg/ /ðə kæt/ /ðə laɪən/ /ðə taɪgə/

Before a vowel *the* is /ði/:
/ði end/ /ði æpəl/ /ði ɑːnsə/ /ði iːvnɪŋ/ /ði aɪdɪə/ /ði ɒfɪs/ /ði oʊld mæn/

I Divide these words into two groups, those with /ðə/ and those with /ði/:

/ðə/	/ði/
the name	*the ink*
_____	_____
_____	_____
_____	_____

elɪfənt   kɑː   deɪ

ɒrɪndʒ   neɪm   ədres

kɔɪn

aɪ   mæn   ɪŋk

Can you write them out?

Pronunciation

6 The indefinite article

The indefinite article has two forms: *a* /ə/ and *an* /ən/. /ə/ is used before consonants and /ən/ before vowels.

J Divide these words into two groups, those with *a* /ə/ and those with *an* /ən/.

/ə/	/ən/
a glass	an apple
_____	_____
_____	_____
_____	_____
_____	_____

æpəl   baɪk   bɔɪ   endʒɪn

glɑːs   æktə   haʊs

ɒfɪs   eg

Can you write them out?

7 Stress

In English words with more than one syllable, one syllable is accented. The position of the accent may be:

On the first syllable:

famous /feɪməs/   person /pɜːsən/   secretary /sekrətəri/   yesterday /jestədeɪ/   difficult /dɪfɪkəlt/
definitely /defɪnətli/

On the last syllable:

behind /bɪhaɪnd/   before /bɪfɔː/   understand /ʌndəstænd/   cigarette /sɪgəret/

On the syllable before the last :

important /ɪmpɔːtənt/   excitement /eksaɪtmənt/   decision /dɪsɪʒən/   determined /dɪtɜːmɪnd/

Words ending in -*tion* /ʃən/ have the accent on the syllable before last:

nation /neɪʃən/   examination /egzæmɪneɪʃən/   information /ɪnfəmeɪʃən/   repetition /repɪtɪʃən/

K Write out these words:

1 /ɪnʌf/ _enough_
2 /eksplənəɪʃʌn/ _____
3 /dʒenrəl/ _____
4 /evrɪθɪŋ/ _____
5 /endʒɔɪmənt/ _____
6 /juːnɪvɜːsəti/ _____
7 /ɪntenʃən/ _____
8 /tʃɪldrən/ _____
9 /keəfəl/ _____
10 /dɪsembə/ _____
11 /wensdeɪ/ _____
12 /gʌvənmənt/ _____

L Mark the accented syllable in these words and write them out:

1 /bɒroʊ/ _borrow_
2 /ɪmpɔːtəns/ _____
3 /mægəziːn/ _____
4 /pəzɪʃən/ _____
5 /evrɪbɒdi/ _____
6 /nesəsəri/ _____
7 /fəgɒtən/ _____
8 /æksənt/ _____
9 /əmerɪkən/ _____
10 /prɒbəbli/ _____
11 /septembə/ _____
12 /sɪləbəl/ _____

Pronunciation

8 Putting words together

When we put two words together the sounds of the words sometimes change.

/n/ → /m/	/braʊm bred/	(brown bread)
/nd/ → /m/	/braʊm bred əm bʌtə/	(brown bread and butter)
/n/ → /ŋ/	/teŋ griːm bɒtəlz/	(ten green bottles)
/d/ → /b/	/gʊb bɔɪ/	(good boy)
/d + j/ → /dʒ/	/wʊdʒuː/ /kʊdʒuː/ /dɪdʒuː/	(would you, could you, did you)
/t + j/ → /tʃ/	/wəʊntʃə/ /dəʊntʃə/	(won't you, don't you)
/t + m/ → /pm/	/lep mɪ/ /pʊp mɪ daʊn/ /gep mə bʊk/	(let me, put me down, get my book)

M Try to read these sentences quickly:

1 /ðə wə teŋgriːm bɒtəlz hæŋɪŋ ɒn ðə wɔːl/ (There were ten green bottles hanging on the wall.)
2 /wʊdʒu: laɪk səm braʊm bred əm bʌtə?/ (Would you like some brown bread and butter?)
3 /ðɪʃ ʃɒp selz gʊb braʊm bægz/ (This shop sells good brown bags.)
4 /kɑːntʃə lem mɪ ə paʊnd?/ (Can't you lend me a pound?)
5 /kæn jə gep mɪ ə kʌpə tiː?/ (Can you get me a cup of tea?)

9 Weak forms

Some very common words in English have weak forms which are normally used in connected speech.
Sometimes these weak forms can be shown in writing:

I am tired → I'm tired   She is not here → She's not here → She isn't here
She did not know → She didn't know   They have gone → They've gone
We will come tomorrow → We'll come tomorrow   He would help → He'd help

Most of these weak forms use the schwa /ə/. Words commonly used with the weak form are:

Auxiliary and modal verbs:

I was there.	/aɪ wəz ðeə/
They were friends.	/ðeɪ wə frenz/
I could come.	/aɪ kəd kʌm/
She would know.	/ʃiː wəd nəʊ/
You can go.	/juː kən gəʊ/
What have you done?	/wɒt əv juː dʌn/

Pronouns:

I was there.	/aɪ wəz ðeə/
You can go.	/juː kən gəʊ/
Tell them a story.	/tel ðəm ə stɔːri/

Prepositions:

A glass of water.	/ə glɑːs ə wɔːtə/
I'm from England.	/aɪm frəm ɪŋglənd/
Is that for me?	/ɪz ðæt fə miː/
I'm going to bed.	/aɪm gəʊɪŋ tə bed/

Pronunciation

N Match the sentences in list A and list B. Read out list B:

<table>
<tr><td colspan="2">A</td><td colspan="2">B</td></tr>
<tr><td>1</td><td>Who was that?</td><td>a</td><td>/wʊdʒə laɪk ə glɑ:s ə mɪlk?/</td></tr>
<tr><td>2</td><td>Where were you going?</td><td>b</td><td>/kʊd aɪ hæv ə kʌp ə ti: pli:z?/</td></tr>
<tr><td>3</td><td>What do you want?</td><td>c</td><td>/wi: wə weɪtɪŋ fər ə bʌs/</td></tr>
<tr><td>4</td><td>Could I have a cup of tea please?</td><td>d</td><td>/jə kən goʊ ɪf jə laɪk/</td></tr>
<tr><td>5</td><td>Do you know who it is?</td><td>e</td><td>/wɒdʒə wɒnt?/</td></tr>
<tr><td>6</td><td>Would you like a glass of milk?</td><td>f</td><td>/weə wə jə goʊɪŋ?/</td></tr>
<tr><td>7</td><td>We were waiting for a bus.</td><td>g</td><td>/dʒə noʊ hu: ɪt ɪz?/</td></tr>
<tr><td>8</td><td>You can go if you like.</td><td>h</td><td>/hu: wəz ðæt?/</td></tr>
</table>

10 Common phrases

Some phrases in English are so common that the words are run together and pronounced very quickly:

Would you mind → /wʊdʒəmaɪnd/.   Do you mind → /dʒəmaɪnd/.   Do you think → /dʒəθɪŋk/.
Don't you think → /dʌntʃəθɪŋk/.   I don't know → /aɪdənoʊ/.   Did you know → /dɪdʒənoʊ/.
Where's the ... → /weəzə .../.   What's the matter → /wɒzəmætə/.
What's the matter with you → /wɒzəmætəwɪju:/.   Who's that → /hu:zæt/.
I want to → /æwɒnə/.   I'm going to → /æmgənə/.

O Can you read these sentences? Can you write them out in full?

1 /weə dʒə lɪv?/
2 /wɒtʃə gənə du: təmɒrə/
3 /tel əm tə kʌm ət fɔ:r ə klɒk/
4 /aɪ wɒnə goʊ hoʊm/
5 /aɪ dɪdn noʊ wɒdə du:/
6 /wɒ dʒə wɒnə du:/
7 /aɪ dənoʊ wɒtʃə mi:n/
8 /hu: zæt oʊvə ðeə/
9 /aɪ hæftə goʊ hoʊm naʊ/
10 /jə kən du: wɒtʃə wɒnt/
11 /aɪv gɒtə lɒtə mʌni/
12 /aɪm gənə getə kʌpə ti:/
13 /hu: dʒə wɒnə si:/
14 /aɪl tel jə wɒt aɪ wɒnt/
15 /haʊ dʒə noʊ/

1 *Where do you live?* _____
2 _____
3 _____
4 _____
5 _____
6 _____
7 _____
8 _____
9 _____
10 _____
11 _____
12 _____
13 _____
14 _____
15 _____

Numbers

A Cardinal numbers: one, two, three, four etc:

1 There are different names for the number *0*.
When you count, and in mathematics, you say
nought:

*The substance weighs nought point five grammes
(0.5 grammes)*

In most sports, you say *nil*:
We lost five – nil (5-0)

In tennis, you say *love*:
Becker leads forty – love (40-0)

When you talk about the temperature, you say
zero:
*In the winter it can get as cold as twenty-five
degrees below zero.*

When you are talking about phone numbers, you
say each number separately, and 0 is *oh*:
*Oh two seven two five five oh nine
0 2 7 2 5 5 0 9*

You also say *oh* for dates and for numbers less
than one:
*Nineteen oh one (1901)
Nought point oh oh five (0.005)*

2 You say *and* between the hundreds and the rest
of the number:

*two hundred and fifty (250)
one hundred and twenty-one (121)
three thousand nine hundred and ten (3910)*

3 Numbers like *hundred, thousand* and *million* do
not have a plural -s when they are exact
numbers:

*Three million two hundred thousand four hundred
and one (3200401)
There were millions of people at the concert.
They say this tree is a hundred years old.
I've told you hundreds of times, you mustn't smoke
in here!*

4 You can often make numbers into compound
adjectives, using the structure: number +
singular noun. You normally link the two parts
with a hyphen '-':

*The team played with ten men: It was a ten-man
team.
The watch cost forty pounds: It's a forty-pound
watch.*

B Ordinal numbers: first, second, third etc:

1 You use ordinal numbers to say where someone
or something is in a sequence or group:

*We lived on the fifth floor.
He was second in the race.
This is the tenth time I've seen the film.*

2 You can use an ordinal and a cardinal number
together, with the ordinal first:

*The first five rows are the most expensive.
The first three people who come in to the shop will
win £100, the second five will win £50.*

3 You use ordinals in dates. When you write dates,
you can use a short form 1st, 2nd, 3rd, 4th etc:

*Today is the first of May (May 1st).
The play opens on the twenty-second of March
(March 22nd).*

C To talk about how often someone does something, you use *once, twice*. With numbers above two, you say *three times, four times* etc:

*I've read that book twice.
The clock struck four times.
You must take this medicine three times a day.*

Numbers Practice

A Look at these sporting results and work out the places of the runners using these ordinals:

first second third fourth fifth sixth

1 Team A finished in 49 seconds.
2 Team B finished in 51 seconds.
3 Team C finished last.
4 Team D finished in 48 seconds.
5 Team E finished in 55 seconds.
6 Team F finished in 50.5 seconds.

B Read these sentences and decide if the 0 in each sentence is:

oh zero nought nil love

1 The area code for Bath is 01225.
2 Germany won the match 2-0.
3 My great-grandfather was born in 1909, I think.
4 The score here at Wimbledon is 40-0 to Lendl.
5 In rugby you sometimes have scores of 70-0!
6 We want to reduce inflation to 0.5% this year.
7 0.004 milligrammes of this substance can poison a man.
8 It was very cold. The temperature was below 0.

C Complete these sentences using compound adjectives:

e.g. The book has 120 pages.

It's a one hundred and twenty page book.

1 The pass lasts for three days.

It's a _____ pass.

2 The speed limit here is 80 miles per hour.

There's an _____ speed limit here.

3 The baby weighed five pounds when she was born.

She was a _____ baby.

4 The journey to Cornwall takes 3 hours by train.

It's a _____ train journey to Cornwall.

5 My new shirt cost £22.

This is a _____ shirt.

6 The meal we ate had three courses.

We had a _____ meal.

D Look at this plan of Bob's activities, then complete the sentences using:
once twice three times etc

	Mon	Tues	Wed	Thurs	Fri	Sat	Sun
shopping		✓	✓		✓	✓	
swimming	✓			✓			
gardening					✓	✓	✓
watch TV		✓	✓	✓	✓		✓
eat in restaurant						✓	

1 Last week Bob went shopping _____ .

2 He went to the swimming pool_____ .

3 Bob watched TV _____ last week.

4 He only went out for a meal _____ .

Letters

A There are 26 letters in the English alphabet. Can you arrange them in the right sequence?

Q W E R T Y U I O P A S D F G H J K L Z X C V B N M

1		8		15		22	
2		9		16		23	
3		10		17		24	
4		11		18		25	
5		12		19		26	
6		13		20			
7		14		21			

B Some of the letters are not pronounced like in other languages. Here are the phonetic symbols for the sounds of English:

Vowels

/iː/	tree		/ʊ/	good
/ɪ/	big		/uː/	moon
/e/	get		/ʌ/	cut
/æ/	hat		/ɜː/	bird
/ɑː/	car		/ə/	father
/ɔː/	door		/ɒ/	pot
			/i/	very

Diphthongs

/eɪ/	day
/oʊ/	no
/aɪ/	my
/aʊ/	now
/ɔɪ/	boy
/ɪə/	near
/eə/	hair
/ʊə/	sure
/aɪə/	fire
/aʊə/	flower

Consonants

/p/	pen		/f/	fall		/h/	hello
/b/	book		/v/	very		/m/	mum
/t/	tea		/θ/	thin		/n/	not
/d/	did		/ð/	then		/ŋ/	sing
/k/	can		/s/	so		/l/	leg
/g/	go		/z/	zoo		/r/	red
/tʃ/	cheap		/ʃ/	she		/j/	yes
/dʒ/	job		/ʒ/	vision		/w/	wet

C Which letters of the alphabet are these?

1 /zed/	7 /biː/	13 /aɪ/	20 /dʒeɪ/
2 /eɪtʃ/	8 /eɪ/	14 /es/	21 /en/
3 /dʒiː/	9 /keɪ/	15 /ef/	22 /diː/
4 /iː/	10 /eks/	16 /em/	23 /piː/
5 /dʌbəljuː/	11 /el/	17 /juː/	24 /ɑː/
6 /waɪ/	12 /kjuː/	18 /siː/	25 /viː/
		19 /tiː/	26 /oʊ/

1 ____	7 ____	13 ____	20 ____
2 ____	8 ____	14 ____	21 ____
3 ____	9 ____	15 ____	22 ____
4 ____	10 ____	16 ____	23 ____
5 ____	11 ____	17 ____	24 ____
6 ____	12 ____	18 ____	25 ____
		19 ____	26 ____

D How do you pronounce these common abbreviations?

1 UK	6 CD	11 EC
2 GB	7 DJ	12 USA
3 a.m.	8 BBC	13 VIP
4 p.m.	9 TV	14 UFO
5 PTO	10 NATO	15 WWF

1 _____	6 _____	11 _____
2 _____	7 _____	12 _____
3 _____	8 _____	13 _____
4 _____	9 _____	14 _____
5 _____	10 _____	15 _____

Answer Key

Unit 1 Practice

B
1	tick	5	tick
2	tick	6	tick
3	cross	7	tick
4	tick	8	cross

C
1 The big book isn't on the table. It's on the chair.
2 The shoes aren't on the chair. They're under the chair.
3 The exercise book isn't on the chair. It's on the table.
4 The ruler and pen aren't on the chair. They're on the table.
5 The pencil isn't next to the ruler. It's next to the pen.
6 The ball and the book aren't on the floor. They're on the chair.

D
1 My name isn't Kim, it's . . .
2 I'm not three years old. I'm . . .
3 I'm not from Scotland, I'm from . . .
4 I'm not a pop singer, I'm a . . .
5 I'm not English, I'm . . .
6 His/Her name isn't Kim, it's . . .
7 He's/She's not three years old, he's/she's . . .
8 He's/She's not from Scotland, he's/she's from . . .
9 He's/She's not a pop singer, he's/she's a . . .
10 He's/She's not English, he's/she's . . .

Unit 2 Practice

A
1	PA	6	FP
2	FP	7	PA
3	PA	8	PA or FP
4	FP	9	PA
5	PA		

B
1 I'm wearing jeans / I'm not wearing jeans.
2 I'm studying English / I'm not studying English.
3 I'm sitting at home / I'm not sitting at home.
4 I'm watching TV/ I'm not watching TV.
5 I'm smoking a cigarette / I'm not smoking a cigarette.
6 I'm talking with friends / I'm not talking with friends.
7 I'm relaxing / I'm not relaxing.
8 I'm listening to music / I'm not listening to music.

C
1 The boy is eating sweets.
2 The businessman is walking across the road.
3 It's a fine day. The sun is shining.
4 A jogger is listening to music on a walkman.
5 The man at the bus stop is reading a newspaper.
6 The woman in the park is pushing a pram.
7 No-one in the picture is wearing a hat.
8 Some customers are buying fruit.

D
1 To Malta probably.
2 I'm watching a video.
3 Because it's useful.
4 We're going camping.

Unit 3 Practice

A
1	have	6	do
2	lives go	7	does
3	like	8	live
4	has/does	9	likes
5	goes		

B
1	reads	5	comes
2	listens	6	cost
3	travels	7	speaks
4	live	8	knows

Unit 4 Practice

C
1 Do you watch television every day?
2 Do you buy a newspaper every day?
3 Do you go abroad on holiday every year?
4 Do you work in an office?
5 Do you live alone?
6 Do you like rock music?
7 Do you play the piano?
8 Do you live in a big city?

D
1 I haven't any friends in England.
2 Have they a big house?
3 He hasn't much money.
4 They haven't any pets.
5 Has she any nice new clothes?
6 I haven't got any friends in England.
7 Have they got a big house?
8 He hasn't got much money.
9 They haven't got any pets.
10 Has she got any nice new clothes?

Unit 5 Practice

A 1c, 2f, 3a, 4d, 5h, 6b, 7e, 8g

C
a He's eaten too much.
b She's broken her arm.
c They've lost their way.
d She's won a prize.
e He's caught a fish.
f He's fallen down.
g He's had an accident.
h He's lost all his money.

Unit 6 Practice

A
1 When I have finished Oliver Twist I will read Don Quixote.
2 You can do the shopping after you have made the beds.
3 Don't go out before you have done your homework.
4 I'm going to stay in class until I have finished my essay.

B
1 Has your sister passed her exam? I don't know. She hasn't got the results.
2 Has your brother gone to America? No, He hasn't gone yet.
3 Has Peter started school? No, He hasn't started yet.
4 Have you read the newspaper? No, I haven't read it yet.

C
a He's been waiting for a bus.
b They've been skiing.
c She's been playing tennis.
d He's been swimming.
e She's been reading.
f He's been eating.

Unit 7

4 Exercise (as table below)

	Present	Past (positive)	Past (negative)	Question
I	am busy	was busy	wasn't busy	Was I busy?
He	is busy	was busy	wasn't busy	Was he there?
She	is busy	was angry	wasn't busy	Was she there?
It	is cold	was angry	wasn't busy	Was it there?
We	are cold	were angry	weren't busy	Were we late?
You	are sad	were angry	weren't busy	Were you late?
They	are sad	were angry	weren't at home	Were they late?

Unit 7 Practice

A
1 I was in town.
2 No, I was with a friend.
3 It was really hot.
4 No, I was fine, but my brother was ill.
5 I was in bed, but I wasn't asleep.

Answer Key

C 1 was 2 was 3 were 4 were 5 was

D 1 False. Tony Blair is the Prime Minister of Britain.
2 False. Charlie Chaplin was a famous silent movie star.
3 False. Cities are larger now than in 1900.
4 False. The world record for the 100 metres sprint is less than 10 seconds.
5 True.
6 False. English is the most useful international language.

E 1 were, was   4 was, was
2 was, was   5 Was
3 was   6 weren't

Unit 8

3 begin began; break broke; buy bought
come came; do did; drink drank;
drive drove; eat ate; find found;
get got; give gave; go went;
have had; make made; pay paid;
say said; see saw; take took;
tell told; write wrote;

Unit 8 Practice

A 1 saw   5 wrote
2 bought   6 gave
3 went   7 broke
4 ate   8 did

B The police are looking for a man who stole £25 and a jacket from a crowded fashion shop in Brighton last week. The man, who was between 20 and 25, with short brown hair, took the jacket from a staff changing room. 'I'm not worried about the money, really,' said the victim, Sally Walker, 25, who works in the shop. 'But the jacket cost me £150. I got it when I was on holiday in Turkey.' The police do not think the man is dangerous, but warned the public to be careful.

C 1 When did she buy the jacket?
2 Where did she go on holiday?
3 What did he steal?
4 Where did he steal them from?
5 How much did the jacket cost?

D She bought a paper and a magazine for her mother. She had a meeting with the bank manager. She called Export International. She didn't have time to write a letter to Gerry but she wrote a letter to the Directors of XYZ to confirm a meeting. She talked with Jan and John about new products for the company. She didn't have time to send a fax to ISB in Munich. She didn't have time to meet David for lunch. She took a taxi home, packed a suitcase and took a train to London.

Unit 9 Practice

A 1 met, was shopping
2 were walking, began
3 hurt, was working
4 was staying, went
5 was doing, forgot
6 were living, was
7 was working, saw
8 went, were staying

B 1 hurt, went
2 heard, began
3 were listening, came
4 heard, began
5 was talking, went
6 was having, rang
7 had, got
8 were playing, arrived

Unit 10 Practice

A 1b, 2a, 3h, 4c, 5d, 6e, 7f, 8g

B 1e, 2g, 3a, 4h, 5i, 6b, 7j, 8c, 9d, 10f

C 1 went, had finished
2 had gone, was
3 had lived, was
4 had eaten, ordered
5 felt, had caught
6 took, had read

Unit 11

* There is no 30th February!

Unit 11 Practice

Dear Monica,

Many thanks for your letter. I am pleased you are enjoying your holiday. When (do you come) home? It will be great to see you. (We are going) to Greece this year - next Friday in fact. I am trying to get everything ready in time, but it is very difficult with three small children. Our plane (leaves) at six o'clock on Friday morning, so we (are taking) a taxi to the airport at four o'clock in the morning - I hope the children (behave) themselves and (get) ready quickly without too much trouble. Peter (has) three weeks holiday this year so when we (get) back from Greece we (are staying) with his mother in Brighton for a week. She has a big flat right next to the sea. The children love it. Lydia (is starting) school this September. I hope she (likes) it. Jimmy hates going to school. He shouts and screams every morning. Perhaps he will be better when Lydia (starts). Thank you for your news. I am very pleased to hear that Isobel has done so well at University. What (is she doing) next year? Has she decided yet? What about the twins? When (do they leave) school? Give

my love to Norman. I am sorry about his accident. I hope he (gets) better soon. Much love, Teresa.

B 1 My next birthday is on a Friday.
2 This lesson finishes at . . . o'clock.
3 I am . . . tomorrow morning.
4 I have . . . English lessons next week.
5 It is . . . the day after tomorrow.
6 It is the . . . next Thursday.
7 I am having . . . for supper tonight.
8 I am . . . after my lesson.
9 It is . . . .
10 I am . . . years old next birthday.

Unit 12 Practice

A 1c, 2e, 3a, 4f, 5b, 6d,

B 1 will you lend
2 are going to have
3 are going to see
4 will not get back/won't get back
5 are you going to do
6 will share
7 are going to borrow
8 Will there be
9 are not going to come
10 are going to take
11 are going to stay with
12 will be
13 will have/are going to have

C a I will open
b I will write
c I'm going to fall
d We are going to get
e I will cook/I'm going to cook
f I'm going to get into trouble

Unit 13 Practice

A 1 There are . . . people in my class.
2 There are . . . people in the room.
3 There are . . . pictures on the walls.
4 There is a . . . on my desk.
5 There are . . . people in my family.
6 There were two big beds and a little bed in the room.

B 1 There's an English class every day.
2 There will be a meeting at three o'clock.
3 There was an accident this morning.
4 There were a lot of people at the concert.
5 There were three books on the desk.
6 There will be lots of children at the party.
7 There is nothing to eat or drink.
8 There were three people waiting in the shop.

C A Is there anything good on TV tonight?
B No, I don't think there'll be anything very interesting.
A Do you think there's a good film on at the cinema?

Answer Key

B I don't know. There wasn't anything last week.
A Shall we go round and see Joe and Pamela?
B Let's telephone first. Last time we went there was nobody at home.

Unit 14 Practice

A
1 What are they going to do?
2 What work does he do?
3 What does it mean?
4 What time will they arrive?
5 What colour does she want?

B 1d, 2a, 3e, 4b, 5c

C 1 sort 2 time 3 size 4 day 5 colour
6 language 7 kind 8 work

D 1e, 2d, 3a, 4b, 5f, 6c

Unit 15 Practice

A A: Let's go and see Peter and Mary some time.
B: When?
A: Well, we could go this weekend.

A: They live in that big house on the corner.
B: Who?
A: You know - those friends of Michael's.

A: We could probably get there quite quickly.
B: How?
A: Well, we could take a taxi.

A: I'm afraid I've lost it.
B: What?
A: My library book. I don't know where it is.

A: I think they're away on holiday.
B: Where?
A: Italy I think.

B
1 I wonder what she's like.
2 I wonder what she meant.
3 I wonder who this belongs to.
4 I wonder why they're so late.
5 I wonder what he wants.
6 I wonder how old he is.
7 I wonder where they have gone.
8 I wonder what they will say.

C Possible answers include:
1 When did she arrive?
2 Where is she now?
3 How much is it?
4 Where did he go?
5 When does she leave?
6 How do I get there?
7 Where can I find him?
8 Where did he go?
9 Where shall I put this?
10 Where do you live?
11 Where are you going?

D
1 How long will it take?
2 How much will it cost?
3 What does it mean?
4 Where do they come from?
5 When will they arrive?
6 Where has he gone?

Unit 16

4 child, children; fish, fish; sheep, sheep; foot, feet; man, men; tooth, teeth; mouse, mice; person, people; woman, women

Unit 16 Practice

A baby, babies; box, boxes; child, children; shoe, shoes; shop, shops; day, days; church, churches; foot, feet; radio, radios; sandwich, sandwiches; city, cities; story, stories

B
a two buses
b three photos
c four sheep
d five boxes
e six babies
f seven fish
g eight mice
h nine watches
I ten teeth

C Buses are cheaper than taxis.
The bus is going to the station now.
Women work as well as men.
That woman is my neighbour.
Watches were invented a long time ago.
My watch is a Rolex.
Most students work very hard all year.
A student in my class comes from near Buenos Aires.
Books are made of paper.
There is a book about geography on my desk.

D
1 days, week
2 weeks, year
3 hours, day
4 minutes, hour
5 months, year

Unit 17 Practice

A
1 the past
2 the sky
3 the dark
4 the future
5 the moon
6 the sun
7 the world
8 the air

B
1 a drink
2 a sleep
3 a walk
4 a fight
5 a shower
6 a wash

C scissors, binoculars, glasses, tweezers, pyjamas, tights

D
1 a pair of scissors
2 a pair of glasses
3 a pair of tights
4 a pair of tweezers
5 a pair of pyjamas
6 A pair of binoculars

E
1 team
2 staff
3 staff
4 team
5 audience
6 audience

Unit 18 Practice

A
1 snow, wood, metal, glass, gold, ice
2 milk, petrol, coffee, tea
3 dinner, lunch, breakfast, tea
4 food, butter, bread, toast
5 aerobics, maths, physics

B
1 petrol
2 breakfast
3 Gold
4 aerobics
5 tea
6 snow

C
1 a paper
2 paper
3 cheese
4 a cheese
5 a business
6 hair
7 a grey hair
8 Sugar
9 two sugars
10 glass
11 glasses
12 Business

Unit 19

1 a week, a book, a person, a tomato, a cup, a dog, a house

2 a box, a job, a banana, a holiday, a teacher, a hat

3 an elephant, an apple, an aunt, an opinion, an idiot

Unit 19 Practice

A
1 half an hour
2 an hour
3 a kilo
4 a hundred people
5 a few times
6 a lot to do
7 a month

B
1 a student
2 a nurse
3 tourists
4 students
5 a musician
6 nurses
7 a tourist
8 singers

C
1 There's a small table in the kitchen.
2 There are a lot of pictures in the living room.
3 There are some flowers in the living room.
4 There's a lamp in the corner of the living room.
5 There's a TV in the living room.
6 There are some plants in both rooms.
7 There's a guitar in the living room.
8 There are some people in the living room.

Answer Key

Unit 20 Practice

A 1 a, the 2 The, a 3 the, a 4 a, The 5 a, the 6 the, an 7 the, a 8 a, the 9 a, the

B 1 an, 2 a, 3 a, 4 a, 5 the, 6 the, 7 the, 8 the, 9 a, 10 a, 11 a, 12 a, 13 The, 14 the, 15 the, 16 the

Unit 21 Practice

A
1 the guitar   5 the Clintons
2 the Odeon   6 the Ritz
3 the south west   7 the Andes
4 the Nile

C
1 Excuse me, can you tell me the time please?
2 What's the name of the nearest cinema?
3 We went to the cinema last night. Unfortunately we were late so we missed the start of the film.
4 The name of the river that flows through the middle of London is the Thames.
5 The weather in the north of England will get worse on Thursday and Friday. At the weekend the temperature will be 3 degrees and there will be snow during the night.
6 We live near the sea in the south of England. Every day in the afternoon we walk the dogs in the woods for a couple of hours. The scenery is so beautiful.
7 I read in the encyclopaedia you gave me that Mount Everest in the Himalayas is the highest mountain in the world. The longest river in the world is the Nile in Africa.
8 I was thinking of the girls we met in the street when we went to a party in the house next to the restaurant where Michael works. One came from the Republic of Ireland. We invited them to the party but they couldn't go because they were flying to the United States the next day.

Unit 22

1 I, my; he, his; it, its; you, your; you, your; she, her; we, our; they, their

Unit 22 Practice

A
1 my   5 our
2 her his   6 your
3 her   7 its its
4 their   8 its

B
1 his trousers.   4 her number.
2 its handle.   5 your animal.
3 their keys.   6 our ball.

C
1 What's your best friend's name?
2 What's your mother's favourite colour?
3 What's your neighbour's address?
4 What's your teacher's first name?
5 What's your country's main export?
6 What's your region's speciality food?

D
1 My best friend's name is . . .
2 My mother's favourite colour is . . .
3 My neighbour's address is . . .
4 His/Her first name is . . .
5 My country's main export is . . .
6 My region's speciality food is . . .

Unit 23 Practice

A 1b, 2f, 3e, 4a, 5g, 6d, 7h, 8c

B
1 these   6 those
2 this   7 that
3 that, this   8 This
4 that   9 those
5 these

C
1 This song is my mother's favourite.
2 That joke was terrible.
3 This cake is delicious.
4 These shoes are comfortable.
5 That colour is fashionable.
6 Those trousers are my best ones.
7 These books are very popular.
8 That party was great.
9 Those paintings are beautiful.

Unit 24

1 I, me; you, you; he, him; she, her; it, it; we, us; they, them

Unit 24 Practice

A
1 I, we, it   3 I, I, he
2 you, we, you   4 I, I, She, I

B 1 me 2 us 3 him 4 me

C
1 We met them last week.
2 It's in Africa, I think.
3 He's in hospital now.
4 I've seen it three times.
5 It's boring.
6 Paul gave them to me.
7 They eat a lot of pasta.

D
1 She (e)
2 it (c)
3 her, she, me (d)
4 We, We, us (a)
5 them (f)
6 You, me, you, her (b)
7 They, her (g)

Unit 25 Practice

A
1 I love cakes, especially the ones my mother makes!
2 Our car is the black one at the end of the road.
3 I'm not sure if I need a big bottle or a small one.
4 He lost his umbrella, so he wants to buy a new one.
5 The hotel is a modern one on the coast.
6 The books I bought are the ones on the table.
7 I always have two pens with me, a blue one and a red one.
8 Is this museum the one you were talking about?

B
1 'Thanks, I'd love one.'
2 'The brown ones on the desk.'
3 'Your new cotton one.'
4 'The ones of Spain? Yes.'
5 'Sure. Which one?'

C
1 That's all right.
2 That's a lot.
3 That's great.
4 That's why you're tired.

D
1 this, that   3 that, that, This
2 That   4 those

Unit 26 Practice

A
1 his is very old
2 hers is German
3 mine is over there
4 mine is smaller / ours is smaller
5 theirs is black and white
6 ours are second class

B
1 Susan is a friend of ours.
2 The small man is a neighbour of ours.
3 Is singing a hobby of yours?
4 Hamid is a student of mine.
5 Pink is a favourite colour of hers.
6 I am a fan of theirs.
7 Roast beef is a favourite meal of mine.

C
a 'Whose car is that?'
   'It's his.'

b 'Whose is this?'
   'It's his.'

c 'Excuse me, is this yours?'

d 'I haven't got a pen on me.'
   'Here, you can borrow mine.'

Unit 27 Practice

D 1 (F) 2 (T) 3 (F) 4 (T) 5 (F) 6 (T)

Answer Key

Unit 28 Practice

B 1 X I have nearly finished this exercise.
2 correct
3 X I like your new dress a lot.
4 correct
5 X This is a very good book. I enjoyed it very much.
6 X He is very lazy. He doesn't help his parents very much.
7 correct
8 correct
9 X I always enjoy the weekend very much.
10 correct
11 correct

Unit 29 Practice

A 1e, 2a, 3f, 4c, 5b, 6d

B 1 for
2 since
3 from, until
4 From, until
5 until
6 since
7 from, until
8 since
9 since
10 for, for

Unit 30 Practice

A 1 nine o'clock is the odd one out. It takes *at*. The others take *in*.
2 the weekend is the odd one out. It takes *at*. The others take *on*.
3 my sister's birthday is the odd one out. It takes *on*. The others take *at*.
4 winter is the odd one out. It takes *in*. The others take *on*.
5 five o'clock is the odd one out. It takes *at*. The others take *in*.

B 1 in 2 in 3 on 4 at 5 in 6 in 7 at

D 1 in the next century
2 on my birthday
3 on the first of April
4 at dinner
5 in August
6 in the morning
7 at the moment

Review: Cycle 1 – Units 1-30

A 1 is
2 is, am
3 are
4 is
5 does, do
6 have
7 Do, have
8 are

B 1 Do you want to go to the cinema?
2 Does your father work in an office?
3 Does your friend speak English?
4 Do you know that man?
5 Does your mother have a job?
6 Do you want to travel abroad?

C 1 What are you wearing today?
2 Where are you going tonight?
3 What are you doing now?
4 Where are you sitting at the moment?
5 Are you listening to music now?
6 Are you going on holiday with your family this year?
7 Are you wearing a watch?
8 Are you having lunch now?

D 1 Have you ever visited Bath?
2 Have you ever broken your arm or leg?
3 Have you ever cooked for more than 5 people?
4 Have you ever seen a crocodile?
5 Have you ever taken a photograph?
6 Have you ever met a famous person?

E had breakfast had a shower read a newspaper done my homework eaten lunch finished work watched TV spoken English done the washing-up talked to a friend

F 1 I've been cutting onions.
2 I've been revising for my exams.
3 I've been waiting for two hours.
4 I've been playing football.

G 1 were 2 were 3 was 4 was 5 was 6 was 7 was 8 was 9 were 10 were

H 1b, 2c, 3b, 4c, 5a, 6a, 7a, 8b, 9a, 10b, 11a, 12c, 13b, 14b

I 1 found out
2 surprised
3 was shopping
4 was walking
5 knew
6 came
7 was
8 was wearing
9 saw
10 needed
11 was
12 was playing

J 1 Did you go
2 did you buy
3 did you pay
4 were you doing
5 Did you understand, spoke/was speaking

K 1 is
2 I'm getting up/ I get up
3 I'm flying
4 we are having
5 are going
6 leaves
7 begins

L 1 I'll go
2 are having
3 will
4 is going to
5 goes
6 are going to meet

M 1 is going to
2 are going to
3 are going to
4 will
5 will

N 1 What, There, Where, there
2 Where, There, Where
3 how, Where, what, Why, What, There

O 1 brothers, sisters
2 Men, women
3 Are they
4 hair
5 are
6 buses
7 carrots

P 1 a, the
2 a
3 the, the
4 a
5 the, the, the
6 an, a / the
7 the, a, some
8 the, a

Q 1 This, me, mine, my
2 me, this, your
3 you, That, you
4 one
5 you, yours
6 one
7 me, Me
8 Whose, Mine
9 This, one
10 one, me

R 1 last week
2 a lot
3 a lot
4 until
5 since
6 probably
7 probably
8 hardly ever

S 1 in
2 at
3 on
4 in
5 at
6 at
7 in
8 No preposition needed.
9 in
10 No preposition needed.

Unit 31 Practice

A 1 (F) 2 (P) 3 (P) 4 (P) 5 (F) 6 (P) 7 (F) 8 (F)

B 1 The shops may/might be closed now.
2 They may/might be on holiday.
3 The weather may/might be good tomorrow.
4 I may/might get married before I am 30.
5 They may/might go to the disco tonight.
6 It's nice here. I may/might stay an extra week.
7 We may/might go to see the new play at the theatre.
8 They've trained a lot. They may/ might win the match.

Unit 32 Practice

A 1 Can you drive?
2 Can you play the piano?
3 Where could we find someone who can repair clocks?
4 Can any of your friends use a word processor?

C 1 will be able to
2 were able to
3 could, can't
4 couldn't
5 won't be able to/can't
6 can/could

D 1 I enjoy being able to wear casual clothes.
2 I enjoy being able to watch TV when I want.
3 I enjoy being able to see my friends.
4 I enjoy being able to travel abroad.
5 I enjoy being able to stay up late.

Answer Key

Unit 33 Practice

A 1 Could I have another cup of coffee, please?
2 Could I have a cigarette, please?
3 Could you tell me when the train leaves, please?
4 Could we have a table near the window, please?
5 Could I have a ticket to London, please ?
6 Could I go home early today, please?

B 1 Would you like to watch TV now?
2 Would you like soup with your meal?
3 Would you like to go home now or later?
4 Would you like sugar in your tea?
5 Would you like me to type these letters?
6 Would you like us to help you plan the meeting?
7 Would you like a single or a double room?
8 Would you like me to start work early tomorrow?

C 1 Would you mind closing the door?
2 Would you mind turning the music down?
3 Would you mind not smoking?
4 Would you mind not speaking French?
5 Would you mind waiting a minute?
6 Would you mind leaving a message?

Unit 34 Practice

A 1h, 2f, 3d, 4a, 5c, 6g, 7e, 8b

Unit 35 Practice

B 1 mustn't park.
2 mustn't use cameras / take photographs.
3 must be quiet.
4 mustn't smoke.
5 mustn't take dogs here.
6 must carry children.
7 must stop here.
8 must keep off the grass.

D 1 has to
2 has to
3 have to
4 have to
5 have to
6 have to

Unit 36 Practice

A 1 you ought to open the window.
2 you should put the heating on.
3 you should have something to eat.
4 you should go to bed now.
5 you ought to see a doctor.
6 you should see a dentist.
7 you should ask for help.

B 1 In a hospital you should be calm. You shouldn't make a lot of noise.
2 You shouldn't arrive late at work. You should work hard.
3 On the motorway you should drive carefully. You shouldn't drive close to the car in front.
4 You shouldn't play music in the library. You should work in silence.

Unit 37 Practice

A 1 It's a pity
2 It's a good thing/It's lucky
3 It's a good thing/It's lucky
4 it's a pity
5 It's a good thing/It's lucky
6 It's a pity
7 It's a pity

B A: Hello, Who is it?
B: Hello, it's me, Angela.
A: Oh, hi! What's it like in England?
B: Oh, it's great being in London.
A: What about the weather?
B: Well, it's a bit cold, but it's not too bad.
A: It's nice to talk to you.
B: Well, it's ages since I saw you.

A: Did you have a good journey?
B: Not really. I didn't like it very much on the plane.
A: Why not? Was it very uncomfortable?
B: No, it was comfortable, but it was a very long journey.
A: What time is it over there?
B: Eight o'clock. Why?
A: Well, it's four in the morning here in Singapore.
B: Oh, I'm sorry. I didn't know it was so late.
A: Don't worry. It's really nice to hear from you.

Unit 38 Practice

A 1 He cooked them a nice meal.
2 She lent her some money.
3 Hand him that plate.
4 Who'll read them a story?
5 I've made him some coffee.
6 Jack's gone to get her some water.
7 He offered her the job.

B 1 I have booked seats for the children.
2 Can you make a cup of tea for everyone?
3 I've written a letter to my sister.
4 Who's going to cook supper for the family?
5 We can show our photographs to all the visitors.
6 Could you cut some bread for your brothers and sisters?
7 I sold my old skis to your friend.

C 1 for her little brother, Simon.
2 a doll.
3 for her grandfather.
4 to her aunt and uncle.
5 her grandmother.
6 to Richard.

7 for her mother.
8 her father.

Unit 39 Practice

A 1 do 2 do 3 make 4 make 5 make
6 do, do 7 make 8 make 9 make
10 make

B 1 make 2 does 3 make 4 make
5 do

C 1 do, do, make, do
2 make, do, make, do, make

Unit 40 Practice

A 1 advice   5 equipment
2 news   6 information
3 homework   7 money
4 furniture   8 traffic

B 1 Let me give you a piece of advice.
2 There were a few bits of old furniture in the room.
3 I have a couple of bits of homework to do.
4 The fire destroyed a piece of expensive machinery.
5 I wonder if you could help me with a bit of information.
6 I have a piece of good news for you and a bit of bad news.
7 A computer is a very expensive piece of equipment.
8 They had more than a dozen pieces of luggage.

C 1 trouble.   5 music
2 weather   6 happiness
3 work   7 travel
4 fun

Unit 41 Practice

B 1 Two of   8 None of
2 Neither of   9 Both of
3 Both of   10 Neither of
4 One of   11 Most of
5 None of   12 All of
6 Most of   13 Two of
7 Two of   14 One of

Unit 42 Practice

A 1 bread   10 rice/bread
2 cars   11 friends
3 luggage   12 subjects
4 buildings   13 shops
5 animals   14 furniture
6 advice   15 ideas
7 countries   16 traffic
8 weather   17 help
9 houses

228

Answer Key

Answer Key

B 1 I like both of them.
2 There is room for all of them.
3 All of them wanted to come.
4 Both of us stayed at home.
5 They wanted to see both of us.
6 All of them live in a yellow submarine.
7 Both of us come from Liverpool.
8 There is room for both of us.

Unit 43 Practice

A 1 not many/few
2 some/a few
3 not many/few
4 some/a few
5 some/a few
6 some/a few
7 not many/few
8 some/a few

B 1 some
2 any
3 some, some
4 any
5 any
6 any, some
7 some, any
8 any
9 any
10 any
11 any
12 some, any
13 any
14 Some

Unit 44 Practice

A 1 a leather belt (2a)
2 a paper handkerchief (2a)
3 a wooden table (2a)
4 a plastic bag (2a)
5 a kitchen chair (2b)
6 garden furniture (2b)
7 aeroplane seats (2b)
8 a Thursday meeting (2c)
9 a birthday party (2c)
10 a two o'clock appointment (2c)
11 a fifty pound traveller's cheque (2d)
12 a ten pound note (2d)
13 a one hundred kilo bag (2d)
14 a three kilo baby (2d)
15 a cookery book (2f)
16 a fashion magazine (2f)
17 the sports page (2f)
18 a newspaper seller (3)
19 a language teacher (3)
20 a card player (3)

Unit 45 Practice

A 1A, 2B, 3A, 4A, 5B, 6B, 7A, 8A, 9B, 10B, 11A, 12A, 13B, 14A

B 1 here, abroad
2 here, there
3 here, away
4 downstairs, upstairs
5 outdoors, indoors

C 1 under, on
2 under, beside
3 next to, behind

Unit 46 Practice

A 1 during the storm
2 by now
3 during the holidays
4 by the end of the week
5 by six
6 during the lesson
7 by 2020
8 during the demonstration
9 during the morning
10 by bed-time

B 1 at around
2 during
3 By
4 at about
5 after
6 before

C 1 after
2 from, until
3 before
4 before
5 from, until
6 before
7 after
8 before

Unit 47 Practice

A 1 -ly: politely, softly, comfortably, helpfully, fluently, nicely, suddenly, sadly, reasonably
2 -ily: happily, angrily
3 -ically frantically, dramatically
4 -lly: dully

B 1 fluently
2 reasonably
3 softly
4 angrily
5 politely
6 suddenly
7 sadly
8 comfortably

D 1 serious
2 slowly
3 good
4 heavily
5 loud
6 beautiful

Unit 48 Practice

A 1 at the top of the page
2 in Paris last year
3 at Exeter and Portsmouth
4 in a box in my room
5 in the corridor
6 at work
7 in the garden
8 in bed

B 1 in
2 at
3 in
4 at
5 in
6 in
7 at
8 at
9 at
10 at
11 at
12 at

D 1 at, in 2 at 3 in 4 at 5 at 6 at 7 in 8 at

Unit 49 Practice

A 1 Everyone on the plane felt very nervous.
2 I first travelled by plane when I was 14.

3 It's cheaper by coach than by train.
4 The nurse in the ambulance gave me an injection.
5 We watched a video on the coach on the way to the airport.
6 If more people went by bicycle there'd be less pollution.
7 I'll take the shopping on my bicycle if it's not too heavy.
8 We can take 5 people in our car if necessary.
9 When I go by car I take a map.

B 1 off 2 out of 3 off 4 into 5 onto 6 out of 7 into/in

C 1 Tom is going to Mexico by plane tomorrow.
2 Ian went home on foot after the party.
3 We went to Bristol by train.
4 How much does it cost to go to Paris by coach?
5 I went to school by bicycle every day.
6 Last year we went to Scotland by car.
7 Sarah always feels seasick when she goes by ship.
8 They went into the city by taxi.

Review: Cycle 2 – Units 31-49

A 1 Can 2 would 3 Would 4 might 5 will/can/could 6 Can/may 7 will

B 1 It was silly of me
2 It's nice to meet you.
3 It looks like
4 It was kind of you
5 It's a pity
6 It's very expensive
7 It gets very cold

C 1 She invited all her friends round and cooked them a nice meal.
2 I posted the letter to the bank this morning.
3 Can you get a newspaper for your father when you go to do the shopping?
4 Karen showed me her new dress.
5 Her aunt is going to make clothes for the baby when it is born.
6 Will you keep me some food if I'm too late for supper?
7 I usually read the children a story before they go to sleep.
8 James handed the papers to his teacher when he had finished writing.
9 Mr. Wilson teaches us English every Tuesday.
10 I've lent my bicycle to my brother so he can cycle to school.

D 1 do 2 make 3 make 4 do 5 make 6 do 7 do 8 make 9 make 10 do

E 1 luggage
2 ideas
3 advice
4 traffic
5 weather
6 games
7 fun
8 problems
9 furniture
10 music

Answer Key

F
1 lots of
2 both of them
3 All
4 them both
5 all my
6 plenty of, half of it
7 Most
8 Neither of
9 Some of
10 A few of

G
1 a few 2 a few 3 few
4 a few 5 few

H
1 some
2 some, any
3 any
4 some, any
5 Any
6 some
7 some, any
8 any
9 some, any
10 some

I
1 a book about cookery
2 an appointment at two o'clock
3 someone who teaches languages
4 a chair in the kitchen
5 a meeting on Thursday
6 someone who sells newspapers
7 a belt made of leather
8 seats found in an aeroplane
9 a magazine about fashion
10 a note worth ten pounds

J
1 between
2 behind
3 in front of
4 behind
5 behind
6 lamp
7 dog
8 on
9 book
10 chair

K
1 from eleven to twelve thirty
2 from nine o'clock until/to half past ten
3 during the break at about ten forty-five
4 after lunch by two o'clock
5 during
6 about
7 about seven

L
1 A until
  B by
2 A until
  B by

M
1 carefully
2 badly
3 happily
4 sadly
5 fast, slowly
6 hard, badly
7 well
8 sleepily

N
1 at 2 in 3 in 4 at 5 at 6 in 7 in
8 in 9 at

O
1 on, on, by 2 on/off 3 by, on 4 into
5 on 6 on 7 by, by, in 8 off, on 9 on

General review A: Cycles 1 and 2

A
1 How old are you?
2 Where do you live?
3 How long have you lived there?
4 Do you like it in Bromley?
5 Do you work in Bromley?
6 Do you drive to work?

B
1 waited/was waiting
2 have lived/have been living
3 is raining
4 had never been
5 am doing
6 had been working
7 waved
8 were preparing
9 have been working
10 leaves/is leaving

C
1 at, no preposition needed
2 in, on
3 by, on
4 at, at
5 in/at, in
6 at, at/for, in/during
7 in, on
8 in
9 in, in
10 at/around
11 no preposition needed, on
12 at
13 off, at
14 into
15 in, no preposition needed

D
1 I have been to Portugal twice but I have never been to Spain.
2 I enjoyed his first book a lot, but I didn't like his second very much.
3 He was driving quite slowly and that certainly saved his life.
4 You have to work hard if you want to do well.
5 We sometimes play football but we never play hockey.

E
1 Could
2 potatoes
3 rice
4 Would
5 Can
6 some
7 any
8 a few
9 are you going
10 Have you been
11 went
12 will you be
13 on
14 good weather
15 It

Unit 50 Practice

A
1 ought to be/should be an exciting trip.
2 ought to be/should be very comfortable.
3 ought to be/should be a nice day.
4 ought to be/should be a good game.
5 ought to be/should be nice and quiet.
6 ought to be/should be really funny.

B
1 can't be
2 must be
3 must be
4 can't be
5 must be
6 can't be
7 can't be
8 must be
9 can't be
10 must be
11 must be
12 can't be
13 must be

Unit 51 Practice

A
a Could I take this chair, please?
b Can/Could I borrow your pen?
c Could I have a lift home, please?
d Can I play with you?
e Could I ask a question, please?
f Can/Could I go home early tonight?
g Could I have another biscuit, please?
h Can/Could I have a kilo of bananas?

B You don't need to / you don't have to:
1 cook you own meals.
2 make your bed.
3 wash the dishes.
4 tidy your room.
5 clean the windows.
6 clean the furniture.
7 lay the table.
8 clean the bath.

Unit 52 Practice

A
1 Do you feel like seeing that new film?
2 Don't you feel like driving to the mountains this weekend?
3 They felt like getting a video.
4 It was a hot day and everybody felt like going to the beach.
5 I really don't feel like going home now. It's early.
6 Is there anything you particularly feel like doing?

B
1 fishing
2 classical music
3 disco dancing
4 rock music
5 housework
6 travelling abroad
7 playing ball

C
1 Do come in and relax for a moment. How about coming in and relaxing for a moment.
2 Do let me buy you that picture. How about letting me buy you that picture.
3 Do spend the weekend with us. How about spending the weekend with us.
4 Do please write to me with your news. How about writing to me with your news.
5 Do please tell me when you're bored. How about telling me when you're bored.

Unit 53 Practice

A
1 He decided to have the red shirt.
2 I learnt to swim when I was 9.
3 We plan to visit Moscow this year.
4 He promised never to be late again.
5 She expects to be home at ten.
6 He decided not to swim after all.

B
1 advised
2 asked
3 told
4 want
5 asked
6 remind

Answer Key

C
1. understand what
2. forgotten what
3. know how
4. remember where
5. remember what
6. decide what
7. decided when
8. know what
9. forget how
10. explained where
11. explained how
12. understand how

Unit 54 Practice

C
1. Let's go for a drink.
2. Let's go inside.
3. Let's go and see it.
4. Let's do another exercise
5. Let's have a rest.
6. Let's ask someone for help.

D
1. made me depressed
2. made my brother feel better
3. made my father ill
4. made me happy
5. made the cars stop
6. made us go inside

E
1. understand a new word
2. find your way
3. go to sleep
4. find what you want

Unit 55 Practice

A 1 (F) 2 (U) 3 (F) 4 (U) 5 (F) 6 (F)

B Correct Sequence is: 1, 8, 6, 9, 5, 10, 7, 2, 4, 3
1. I saw him get on to his bicycle.
8. I watched him ride down the street.
6. My friend noticed it turn into the street.
9. We heard it driving very fast.
5. We watched it try to overtake the cyclist.
10. We saw it knock the man off his bike.
7. My friend noticed them standing near the traffic lights.
2. We heard it crash into the traffic lights.
4. Everybody heard them scream.
3. We heard it coming to the scene of the accident.

Unit 56

2.

talking and telling:	information, warning, example, speech, report, interview, answer, news
other noises:	cry, laugh, whistle, shout, scream
actions:	kiss, kick, punch, hug, caress, push

Unit 56 Practice

A
1. We had a serious discussion.
2. They were having a quiet chat in the reception room.
3. They have dinner very late in Spain.
4. I had a quick wash, then went to school.
5. Paula had a hamburger for lunch.
6. Most people prefer to have a holiday in the summer
7. I need to have a talk with you about Simon.
8. Mark enjoys having a long bath after playing sport.

B
1. take
2. gives
3. gave
4. give
5. took
6. take
7. gave
8. gave

C
1. They decided to go swimming in the river.
2. If you feel hot why don't you go swimming?
3. When was the last time you went walking across the moor?
4. I think I'll go jogging.
5. The lake is a great place to go fishing.

Unit 57

3 broke into, look after, bumped into (means: meet), looking into (means: investigate)

4 caught up with, date back to, get round to

Unit 57 Practice

A
1. stayed up
2. put up with
3. took up
4. takes after
5. start out
6. Hurry up
7. find out
8. carried out
9. take off
10. broke down

B
Verb + particle
She stayed up
If we start out
Hurry up!
The car broke down

Verb + particle + obj
He took up skiing
Sarah takes after our father
find out what time the train leaves

Three part Verbs
How can you put up with him?

C
1. grew up
2. playing around
3. stayed up
4. got by
5. Hold on
6. Watch out!

D
1. The police followed the robbers, but they got away.
2. I'm trying to find out whose car this is.
3. Most of the students said they wanted to keep on studying.
4. I bumped into an old friend on the ferry. What a surprise!

Unit 58 Practice

A
1. The robbers told the people in the bank to hand over all their money.
2. How old were you when you took up skiing?
3. He pointed out a couple of mistakes.
4. The students handed in their papers at the end of the exam.
5. The shop assistant folded up the clothes and put them in the bag.

B
1. I was very surprised when they invited him out to lunch.
2. The student quickly rubbed them out and wrote it out again.
3. Please help me put them away.
4. I'm going to ring them up and ask her round to dinner.
5. George brought them up and kept his job at the same time.
6. My doctor advised me to give it up.

C
1. take up
2. call back
3. point out
4. fold up
5. clean up
6. knock over
7. tell apart
8. write out

Unit 59 Practice

A
1. Listen to
2. talk about/speak about
3. belongs to
4. complained to/spoke to
5. complain about
6. write to
7. tell about
8. write about
9. dreamt about
10. think about
11. listen to
12. belong to

B
1. laughed at
2. looked at
3. waiting for
4. looked for
5. asked for

C
1. count on/rely on
2. count on/rely on/ depend on
3. depends on
4. depends on

Unit 60

2 I, myself; you, yourself; he, himself; she, herself; it, itself; we, ourselves; you, yourselves; they, themselves;

Answer Key

Unit 60 Practice

A
1. me, myself
2. himself, him
3. themselves, them
4. us, ourselves
5. her, herself
6. itself, it
7. you, yourselves
8. yourself, you

B
1. Sure, help yourself.
2. I taught myself, actually.
3. Enjoy yourselves.
4. I was talking to myself.
5. Let me introduce myself.
6. No, I made it myself.
7. He burnt himself.
8. I think they did it themselves.

C
1. by myself
2. by himself
3. by ourselves
4. for himself
5. for ourselves
6. by herself
7. for yourself
8. to yourself/for yourself

Unit 61 Practice

B
1. annoyed / worried / surprised
2. excited / surprised
3. delighted / excited / surprised
4. bored
5. frightened / worried

C
1. bored, boring
2. interesting, interested
3. terrifying, terrified
4. worrying, worried
5. annoying, annoyed
6. shocked, shocking
7. exciting, excited
8. surprising, surprised
9. disappointing, disappointed
10. amusing, amused

Unit 62 Practice

A
1. something, everybody
2. everybody, something, nothing
3. everybody, something, nobody, everything
4. somebody, something, nobody, anything
5. nothing, nobody, anything
6. everywhere, somewhere

B
1. anyone else
2. somewhere else
3. someone else
4. nobody else
5. something else
6. nothing else
7. something else
8. anywhere else
9. somebody else's
10. Nobody else's
11. somewhere else
12. Nothing else

Unit 63 Practice

A

Group A	Group B
cheap	certain
cold	careful
dark	expensive
full	famous
great	important
green	interested
hard	interesting
high	often
kind	useful
small	

Group A
cheaper, cheapest
colder, coldest
darker, darkest
fuller, fullest
greater, greatest
greener, greenest
harder, hardest
higher, highest
kinder, kindest
smaller, smallest

Group B
more certain, most certain
more careful, most careful
more expensive, most expensive
more famous, most famous
more important, most important
more interested, most interested
more interesting, most interesting
more often, most often
more useful, most useful

B
nicer, nicest   busier, busiest
cleverer, cleverest   later, latest
happier, happiest   better, best
quieter, quietest   worse, worst
bigger, biggest   hotter, hottest

C
1. more expensive
2. more useful
3. younger
4. heavier
5. easier
6. worse, younger
7. worse/colder
8. more important
9. younger
10. worse
11. more expensive

Unit 64 Practice

A
1. Helen, Tom
2. Helen and Bill, Anne
3. Bill
4. Anne, Tom, Helen
5. Anne, Bill
6. Tom, Bill
7. Helen, Tom
8. Helen, Bill, Tom
9. Tom, Helen
10. Bill, Anne

B
1. It's the biggest dog I have ever seen.
2. She's the nicest person I have ever met.
3. It was the funniest story they had ever heard.
4. It was the best book she had ever read.

D
1. The commonest word in English is 'the'.
2. The highest mountain in the world is Mount Everest.
3. The longest river in the world is the Amazon.
4. The biggest city in my country is . . .

Unit 65 Practice

A
1. Why were you in the shop for such a long time?
2. I really like Sue. She's such a nice person.
3. I can never hear him. He speaks in such a quiet voice.
4. We saw you driving your BMW yesterday. It looks such a powerful car.
5. Have you heard the new REM album? It's such a good record.

B
1. that I helped myself to more
2. that we all came back with tans
3. that I couldn't stop to talk
4. that I didn't recognise it
5. that we couldn't hear the TV
6. that we talked for hours
7. that all the hotels were full
8. that we cried

C
1. The Smiths are such nice people.
2. correct
3. Thanks for the party. We had such a good time.
4. correct
5. correct
6. Bob's an expert. He knows so much about computers.

Review: Cycle 3 – Units 50-65

A
1. must
2. should
3. can't
4. must
5. ought to
6. can't
7. can't
8. must
9. can't
10. should
11. must

B
1. May/Could I have another drink, please?
2. Could you give me directions to the nearest bank, please?
3. Could you tell me when I can see Mr Smart?
4. May/Could I have some more chocolate cake?
5. Could you tell him what time the film starts?
6. Could/May we leave now?
7. Could Janet have a quick talk with the manager, please?
8. It's very hot. Could they take their jackets and ties off?

Answer Key

C
1 can't
2 are not allowed to
3 don't need to/needn't
4 needn't
5 don't need to/needn't
6 can't

D
1 My father dislikes doing the washing-up.
2 How about going to the beach this weekend?
3 Young children normally enjoy watching adventure films.
4 Nature lovers often enjoy going camping.
5 You must tell us about your holiday.
6 How about letting me do the cooking this evening?
7 I don't mind listening to classical music.
8 I hated sleeping in the dark when I was a child.
9 Do you fancy coming with us to the disco?

E
1 promised to buy his wife
2 agreed not to smoke
3 hope to get there
4 asked her husband to give her a hand
5 decided not to
6 ordered the soldiers not to leave
7 advised the students to use a dictionary to check
8 told the artist not to show anyone
9 asked me whether you know how to ski

F
1 help   5 let
2 let   6 made
3 let   7 make
4 help   8 made

G
1 singing   4 swimming
2 play   5 come
3 get   6 acting

H
1 take   6 had
2 give   7 go
3 take   8 Take
4 gave   9 having
5 have   10 taking

I
1 Hurry up   5 looked up
2 stay up   6 go on
3 look after   7 kept on
4 found out   8 take up

J
1 about   5 about
2 to   6 for
3 into   7 for
4 on   8 to

K
1 Actually I made it myself.
2 Enjoy yourselves.
3 No, I think you should change.
4 . . . he cut himself while he was shaving.
5 . . . people who talk to themselves are a little strange.
6 The washing machine will turn itself off . . .
7 Mrs Banks got up, washed and went to work as normal.
8 I have two uncles who live by themselves.

L
1 fascinating   5 interested
2 interesting   6 relaxing
3 impressed   7 amusing
4 bored   8 disappointed

M
1 anybody   5 They
2 anybody   6 nobody
3 something   7 nothing
4 anything   8 anywhere

N
1 The video we watched last night was easily the funniest I have seen for a long time.
2 It's far hotter today than it was yesterday.
3 I feel a good deal more relaxed now.
4 This is by far the best book she's written.
5 This exercise is rather more difficult than I thought.
6 A lot more people went to the exhibition than expected.
7 The things they sell in the shops nowadays are much more expensive than last year.
8 I think it would be a much better idea to go on holiday in the spring when there aren't so many tourists.

O
1 more exciting
2 more competitive
3 most expensive
4 expensive
5 long
6 biggest
7 best/most famous/most expensive
8 luckiest
9 lucky
10 better
11 longer
12 better/more famous

P
1 so 2 such 3 such 4 so 5 such
6 so 7 so 8 such 9 such 10 such

General review B: Cycle 1

A
1 moved   7 was
2 came   8 is
3 had gone/went 9 has found
4 had finished   10 is
5 wanted   11 has made
6 was worried   12 is going

B
1 isn't going
2 didn't hear
3 isn't
4 hasn't felt/ hasn't been feeling
5 isn't
6 hasn't finished
7 isn't working
8 hasn't arrived
9 isn't raining
10 wasn't

C
1 the   21 the
2 you   22 a
3 me   23 a
4 the   24 no article
5 we   25 it
6 no article   26 the
7 me   27 the
8 a   28 it
9 no article   29 a
10 a   30 the
11 the   31 a
12 you   32 a
13 some   33 the
14 some   34 a
15 it   35 no article
16 some   36 the
17 some   37 the
18 some   38 it
19 you/I   39 the
20 the   40 a

D
1 that   5 that/she
2 These, those   6 that, it
3 those   7 her
4 one   8 This

E
1 want to come   6 it
2 are you going to 7 does it cost/
3 of film is that   will it cost
4 does it start 8 is it
5 does it last

F
1 recently   10 since
2 ago   11 ago
3 in   12 in
4 probably   13 since
5 very much   14 hardly ever
6 until, in   15 very much
7 since   16 until
8 from, until   17 probably
9 hardly ever   18 often

General review C: Cycle 2

A
1 must, can't   7 may/might/
2 couldn't, had to   could
3 could   8 must/have to
4 may/might   9 mustn't
5 will be able   10 mustn't/shouldn't
6 Would

B
1 I like it here.
2 What time is it?
3 It will be stormy tomorrow.
4 It is almost a year since we had a holiday.
5 It was very kind of your sister to lend me some money.
6 Who is it?
7 It is a pity they weren't here with us.
8 It can be frightening to drive in a city.

C
1 post you your exam results
2 buy something for me
3 bring that dictionary to me
4 to read them a story
5 to find a present for my mother
6 postcards to their friends
7 their version of what happened to the policeman
8 you another piece of cake
9 what to get my father for his birthday
10 cups of tea for everyone

Answer Key

D 1 make   4 made
   2 do   5 doing
   3 making 6 did

E 1 There was so much traffic on the
     road that we arrived late.
   2 Both Bournemouth and Brighton are
     on the coast.
   3 None of my friends can speak
     Japanese.
   4 Most of the luggage was already on
     the plane.
   5 We bought a few souvenirs for
     family and friends.
   6 You can buy stamps in any post
     office.
   7 I've listened to most of the records
     in the school library.
   8 All the students in our class have
     travelled abroad.
   9 Most of the information you gave me
     was wrong!
  10 He wrote me a one hundred pound
     cheque.

F 1 real   6 opposite
   2 on   7 on
   3 at   8 at
   4 hard   9 next to
   5 in   10 in a lonely
             manner

General review D: Cycle 3

A 1 The   6 to
   2 his   7 are going to meet
   3 arrived 8 the
   4 at   9 dinner
   5 their   10 in

B 1 The   10 a
   2 who   11 exploded
   3 in   12 over
   4 when   13 in
   5 didn't   14 of
   6 the other 15 is
   7 luckier 16 longest
   8 a   17 a
   9 came

C 1 On   11 out of
   2 had   12 it up
   3 taken   13 all
   4 was waiting 14 was
   5 felt   15 had taken
   6 drove   16 nothing
   7 had   17 looked
   8 dropped 18 saw
   9 in   19 into
  10 got   20 were

D 1 must   6 Do
   2 will   7 seeing/watching
   3 can't   8 to take, to go
   4 Can/May 9 Let, help
   5 going

E 1 talking 6 for
   2 at   7 his
   3 told   8 take
   4 funny   9 out
   5 who   10 looked at

Unit 66 Practice

B 1 looks   3 smells
   2 sounded 4 smell/taste

C 1 A: Hello what are you doing?
     B: Hi! I'm reading this book.
     A: That looks interesting.
     B: Yes it is very good.
     A: Do you like reading?
     B: Yes I love it.

   2 A: Can I borrow your pen?
     B: I'm sorry. I am using it.
     A: What about this one? Who does
       this belong to?
     B: I think it's Carol's. I know she has
       one like that. You can ask her. She
       works/is working in the next room.

   3 A: Do you remember Fred Johnson?
     B: Yes I know him well. Why?
     A: I am writing him a letter.
     B: Great! Say 'Hello' to him from me.

   4 A: That coffee smells great!
     B: Would you like some or do you
       prefer tea?
     A: Are you making tea as well?
     B: I can make some tea if you like.
     A: Thank you. I think a cup of tea
       would be very nice.

Unit 67 Practice

A 1 were   5 is
   2 is   6 are
   3 was   7 are
   4 were   8 were

B 1 been   4 being
   2 being   5 been
   3 be   6 been

C 1 have been reduced
   2 were killed
   3 was brought up
   4 are not allowed
   5 was directed
   6 are sold
   7 has been cancelled
   8 be bought

D Picture 1
   1 The washing-up hasn't been done.
   2 The radio hasn't been turned off.
   3 The dustbin hasn't been emptied.
   4 The windows haven't been cleaned.
   5 The pots and pans have not been
     washed.
   6 The floor has not been cleaned.
   7 The clock has not been changed.
   8 The table has not been cleaned.

   Picture 2
   1 The washing-up has been done.
   2 The radio has been turned off.
   3 The dustbin hasn't been emptied.
   4 The windows haven't been cleaned.
   5 The pots and pans have been put
     away.
   6 The floor has been cleaned.
   7 The clock hasn't been changed.
   8 The table has been cleaned.

Unit 68 Practice

A 1a, 2a, 3b, 4b, 5a, 6b, 7b

B 1 she was meeting a client
   2 she had to visit her mother in
     hospital
   3 he would be in Glasgow
   4 she had already arranged something
     important
   5 he had stayed late the last time
   6 he didn't think he would be

C 1 asked, told, thought
   2 asked, told, asked
   3 told
   4 said, told

Unit 69 Practice

A 1 Yes, I do./No, I don't
   2 No, I'm not.
   3 Yes, I have.
   4 Yes, it is.
   5 No, they aren't.
   6 No, I don't./Yes, I do.
   7 Yes, you can.
   8 No, there isn't.

B 1 No, they can't.
   2 No, it isn't.
   3 Yes, they do.
   4 No, it doesn't.
   5 Yes, it has./No, it hasn't.
   6 Yes, she was.
   7 No, they didn't.
   8 No, it wasn't.
   9 No, I wasn't./Yes, I was.
  10 No, they aren't.

C 1 Where? When?
   2 Which one? Where?
   3 Which one? Why?
   4 Why? Where?
   5 Which one? Where?
   6 Why? Which one?

D 1 I expect so. I don't expect so.
   2 I think so. I don't think so.
   3 I hope so. I hope not.
   4 I'm afraid so. I'm afraid not.

Unit 70 Practice

A 1 wasn't it   4 can they
   2 have you 5 is there
   3 did they

B a 1 're   6 used to be
     2 're   7 should
     3 was   8 shouldn't be
     4 was, were 9 shouldn't
     5 _____ 10 didn't

   b 1 are you?   6
     2 aren't we? 7 shouldn't they?
     3 wasn't it? 8 should you?
     4 wasn't he? 9 should you?
     5 _____ 10 _____

Answer Key

c 5 didn't it
6 didn't it
10 did they

C 1 I think it is less than a million, isn't it?
2 I think they were held in Montreal, weren't they?
3 I think he died in 1947, didn't he?
4 I think they started playing in the 1960s, didn't they?
5 I think there are 11 players on a cricket team, aren't there?
6 I think Istanbul is bigger, isn't it?
7 I think it means a fear of light, doesn't it?

Unit 71 Practice

A 1 So have I. 5 So was I.
2 So will we. 6 So do you.
3 So are mine 7 So did we.
4 So does mine. 8 So can I.

B 1 Neither do I. 5 Neither was I.
2 Neither could we. 6 Neither can I.
3 Neither have I. 7 Neither did we.
4 Neither can mine. 8 Neither will I.

C 1 Greenland is an island. So is Australia.
2 The whale is an endangered species. So is the rhino.
3 My mother can't ski. Neither can my brother.
4 Smoking isn't good for you. Neither is eating a lot of chocolate.
5 The Beatles became famous in the 60's. So did the Rolling Stones.
6 Paul didn't write to me. Neither did Mandy.
7 Mozart was a composer. So was Beethoven.
8 Dictionaries aren't allowed in the exam. Neither are computers.

Unit 72 Practice

A 1 who/that 5 who
2 which/that 6 which/that
3 that 7 who/that
4 which/that

* Sentences 1, 2, 3, and 4 do not need a relative pronoun.

B 1 who cuts hair.
2 who cuts hair
3 who sells fruit and vegetables
4 who writes newspaper articles
5 which/that opens tins
6 who sells meat
7 which/that protects you from the sun.

D 1 Mr Davies is the dentist my family goes to.
2 Euro-net is the marketing company my sister works for.
3 Wine and cheese are the local products this region is famous for.
4 Simon is the friend of mine who has just gone to New Zealand.

Unit 73 Practice

A 1 It's unlikely to rain in August.
2 The football match is due to start at 3 p.m.
3 Will your brother be able to lend us some money?
4 There's so much traffic we're bound to be late.
5 The price of petrol is likely to go up next year.
6 When will you be ready to go out tonight?
7 Some people are prepared to do anything to get rich.
8 The doctors were unable to save the patient's life.

B 1 It's easy to criticize young people.
2 It isn't easy to learn how to use a computer.
3 It's essential to have a clean driving licence.
4 It's important to be polite to customers.
5 It's very rude to arrive late.
6 It's stupid and dangerous to drive long distances when you're tired.
7 It's difficult to make everyone happy at the same time.

C 1 I was frightened to watch the film on my own.
2 My cousin was afraid to go home on foot.
3 I was sad to hear the bad news.
4 We were surprised to meet an old friend in Japan.
5 The boys were glad to go home early.
6 Eric was disappointed to do badly in the test.

D 1 I was pleased that everyone was on time.
2 My parents were happy that we got home before dark.
3 The restaurant manager is worried that the price of food is going up.
4 We were surprised that Henry couldn't find the right address.
5 The tourists were disappointed that the weather wasn't very good.

Unit 74 Practice

A 1 too many 5 enough
2 well enough 6 too many
3 too much 7 clearly enough
4 not enough 8 too little

B 1 My brother's too young to drive a car.
2 You look too tired to go out tonight.
3 That dress looks too expensive to buy.
4 The book is too long to finish now.
5 It's too cold outside to play football.
6 This question is too difficult to do.

C 1 too busy
2 old enough
3 enough sugar
4 too long
5 big enough
6 too old
7 too much
8 too many, enough drink
9 enough chairs
10 too soon

Unit 75 Practice

A 1 if it rains.
2 if we can get tickets.
3 before you go to bed?
4 if you take a taxi.
5 as soon as your father gets home.
6 if anyone comes to the door.

B 1 When you go to town tomorrow I will look after the children.
2 If Mary is late I will meet her at the station.
3 I will tell you all Bill's news when he writes to me.
4 If you go to the supermarket you can buy some bread.
5 I won't go to bed until Peter gets home at midnight.
6 She can't go out until after she finishes her homework.
7 The weather will probably be very bad next week while we are on our holidays.
8 When you get your exam results next week you can write to Mary.
9 If you don't get home till after midnight your mother will be very worried.
10 I will pay you the money as soon as I get a job.

Unit 76 Practice

A 1 I wish it wasn't raining.
2 I wish I knew the answer.
3 I wish Jack would help us.
4 I wish I had seen Angela this morning.
5 I wish we didn't live here.
6 I wish Mary would telephone.
7 I wish Paul would write.
8 I wish I had enough time.

B 1e, 2h, 3f, 4a, 5d, 6g, 7b, 8c

C 1 If I wasn't ill I could play basketball.
2 If I had enough money I could buy it.
3 If she was tired she would go to bed.
4 If we had more time we could wait for him.
5 If he was smaller it would fit him.
6 If it was warmer we could go out today.
7 If they had a map they would be able to find the way.
8 If they knew the way they wouldn't need a map.
9 If I hadn't got them all wrong I wouldn't do the exercise again.

Answer Key

Unit 77 Practice

A *Gaps in the song*
She swallowed the bird to catch the spider

In order to
She swallowed the cow in order to catch the goat.
She swallowed the goat in order to catch the dog etc.

Questions and answers
Why did she swallow the dog?
She swallowed the dog to catch the cat.
Why did she swallow the cat?
She swallowed the cat to catch the bird.
Why did she swallow the cow?
She swallowed the cow to catch the goat.

Unit 78 Practice

A 1 He was so pleased that he wrote a letter to thank me for my help.
2 They worked so hard that they finished everything in one afternoon.
3 She is so kind that she will help anyone who asks her.
4 It's so nice that we should go out for a walk in the fresh air.
5 She had such a bad cold that she could not possibly go to work.
6 He had such a big car that there was plenty of room for everybody.
7 The flat was so small that three of us had to share a room.
8 They have such a lot of friends that they go out almost every evening.

B 1 too busy/I'm afraid I'll be too busy to come tomorrow.
2 old enough/She's certainly old enough to go to school by herself.
3 too cold/It's much too cold to go out without an overcoat.
4 too late/It will be too late to telephone you when we get back.
5 close enough/It's close enough to walk there in about ten minutes.
6 too far/It's too far to drive there in a day.
7 fit enough/She's still fit enough to cycle to the shops every day.
8 too expensive/It's too expensive to stay in a hotel.

Unit 79 Practice

A 1 we were really hungry
2 We are very good friends
3 he still didn't earn very much
4 We don't see her very often
5 we drove very fast
6 He was looking very well
7 I was very angry
8 it's much more expensive
9 the sun was shining
10 he looked very fierce
11 I haven't finished it yet
12 They didn't hear us

B 1 in spite of getting lost on the way.
2 in spite of being over seventy.
3 In spite of being injured
4 in spite of being much younger.
5 in spite of having three children to look after.

Unit 80 Practice

A
1 where	5 who
2 when	6 when
3 which	7 which
4 where	8 who

B 1e, 2h, 3j, 4l, 5i, 6g, 7k, 8m, 9a, 10c, 11b, 12f, 13n, 14d

C 1 when the First World War started.
2 where he was born.
3 who was studying mathematics.
4 when they left university.
5 which is in the south of England.

Review: Cycle 4 – Units 66-80

A
1 are you cooking		7	Is
2 smells		8	think
3 am making		9	belongs
4 Do you like		10	know
5 love		11	has
6 tastes			

B 1 (a) is having
2 (b) think
  (c) can hear
3 (d) were seeing
4 (e) doesn't like
  (f) doesn't understand
5 (g) owned
6 (h) am trying
  (I) am thinking
7 (j) looks
  (k) belonged
8 (l) is learning
  (m) sounds

C 1 are kept in this cupboard.
2 was found lying in the street.
3 can be obtained at your local library.
4 was told to park my car outside in the street.
5 was sold for over £200,000.
6 has not been heard of since he went to live in America.
7 are sold at most corner shops.
8 are not allowed to borrow more than three books.
9 was given a computer for her birthday.
10 must be worn in the factory.

D
1 was attacked		9	won
2 had just left		10	beat
3 was stopped		11	were beaten
4 tried		12	was won
5 fought back		13	was born
6 took		14	was elected
7 was badly cut		15	was shot
8 was taken		16	was shot

E
1 was getting		8	could
2 shouted		9	was
3 asked		10	was
4 was going		11	had broken down
5 told		12	would not start
6 was going		13	was not going
7 asked		14	could

F
1 wanted		5	didn't have
2 had		6	had been studying
3 had used		7	had
4 had been		8	was going

G 1 was looking
2 saw
3 were carrying
4 called out
5 asked
6 were doing
7 explained
8 were being taken
9 thought
10 would like
11 could
12 would return
13 had been stolen
14 had given

H 1 Yes she did.
2 Yes, they were.
3 Yes, they were.
4 No, she didn't.
5 Yes, she did.
6 Yes, they could.
7 No, they wouldn't.
8 Yes, she was.

I
1 don't you		10	can you
2 am I		11	doesn't he
3 didn't he		12	is it
4 are you		13	did you
5 won't you		14	aren't I
6 have we		15	shouldn't you
7 isn't there		16	don't we
8 haven't you		17	will you
9 didn't you		18	won't we

J
1 too		5	too
2 neither		6	either
3 so		7	so
4 either			

K 1 he was carrying looked really heavy.
2 who/that drive too fast are really dangerous.
3 we went to in London wasn't very good.
4 I saw in your shop yesterday.
5 that/who live very near you.

L
1 enough		5	enough
2 too much		6	too much
3 too many		7	too many, enough
4 enough		8	too much

M
1 too late		6	do you
2 are we		7	too expensive
3 haven't we		8	warm enough
4 went		9	Is it
5 you haven't visited		10	Haven't you

Answer Key

N
1. is
2. can have
3. rains
4. will eat
5. will get
6. catch
7. want to
8. can stay
9. come
10. will look after
11. go
12. will come round
13. has
14. will fall
15. get home

O
1. would you do, were
2. knew, would go
3. can, haven't
4. were, I'd
5. are, will
6. had telephoned
7. was, was, would know
8. see, will you give

P
1. She used a corkscrew to open the bottle.
2. I used the dictionary to find what the word meant.
3. He used a piece of string to mend the chair.
4. She used a wet cloth to polish her shoes.
5. I used a trap and a big piece of cheese to catch the mouse.
6. Our teacher always used a red pen to mark our books.
7. She used a microscope to look at the leaf.
8. He used a bucket to bathe the baby.

Q
1. I was so tired that I couldn't work any more.
2. It was such a wet day that we couldn't go out.
3. My bicycle was so old that it was always breaking down.
4. Don is such a good friend that he will always help me if I ask him.
5. My father lives such a long way from his office that he has to drive to work every day.
6. The journey took so long that it was dark when we arrived.
7. He was so angry that he wouldn't speak to me.
8. I was so frightened that I didn't know what to do.

R
1. even though
2. because
3. even though
4. because
5. even though
6. even though
7. because

S
1. We are going on holiday to Brighton, where my mother was born.
2. I'll telephone you at six o'clock, when I get home.
3. She comes from Sofia, which is the capital of Bulgaria.
4. This is my old friend Tom, who is staying with us this week.
5. I'm reading a book about Ronald Reagan, who used to be President of the USA.
6. This is the garage, where we keep all the garden furniture.
7. Pele is a famous footballer, who played for Brazil at the age of seventeen.
8. We visited Buckingham Palace, where the royal family lives.

T
1. who
2. because
3. enough
4. If
5. so / and
6. because
7. because
8. Although
9. to
10. if
11. so / and
12. to
13. because
14. so
15. enough
16. If
17. if/when

General review E

A
1. have lived, was
2. am trying
3. has just gone, went
4. got, had been travelling
5. had not finished
6. is
7. don't hurry
8. was waiting
9. was, could drive
10. could
11. went
12. have not played, broke
13. learnt, was working
14. will telephone, get
15. had just gone, rang
16. don't like
17. saw, don't remember
18. lived

B
1. What time is it?
2. How old will you be next birthday? or How old are you?
3. Is there any milk in the fridge?
4. Have you ever met Marie?
5. Who does Jack look like?
6. What are you doing tomorrow?
7. What kind of car have you got?
8. Where do you live? or What is your address?
9. Where to?
10. When?

C
1. on, on
2. at, on
3. at
4. in, in
5. by, in
6. off
7. at
8. no preposition required.
9. on
10. no preposition required.

D
1. We often go to the cinema at the weekend.
2. George can certainly tell you what you want to know.
3. I don't play football very much now, but I play tennis a lot.
4. I saw Fred a while ago but he isn't here now.
5. It rained quite a lot last night.
6. The door was definitely locked when I went out.
7. We hardly ever watch television at the weekend.
8. It is one of the best films I have ever seen.
9. I didn't enjoy the film very much, but I enjoyed the play a lot.
10. I met Helen a week ago, but I haven't seen her since then.
11. I read the instructions on the medicine bottle carefully/ I carefully read the instructions on the medicine bottle.
12. We always see Richard when we are in Oxford.

E
1. take/have
2. do
3. make
4. take
5. have
6. do
7. make
8. have
9. Give
10. do

F
1c, 2c, 3c, 4a, 5c, 6b, 7a, 8c, 9a, 10a, 11a, 12c, 13a, 14b, 15b 16b, 17b, 18c, 19b, 20b, 21a, 22a 23a, 24b, 25b, 26b

Pronunciation

A
1. have
2. far
3. learn
4. fool
5. eat
6. lost
7. forget
8. but
9. saw
10. sit
11. get
12. good
13. blood
14. do
15. word
16. about
17. give
18. piece
19. start
20. agreed

B
1. weather
2. young
3. lovely
4. hat
5. judge
6. pleasure
7. dog
8. money
9. winter
10. kicking
11. thick
12. watch
13. leg
14. hurry
15. brother
16. summer
17. running
18. runs
19. singer
20. see
21. coffee
22. happy
23. reaching
24. woman

C 1 seven 2 one 3 six 4 ten 5 four 6 two 7 three
The right order is:
one, two, three, four, six, seven, ten
The three missing are:
five, eight and nine

D
1. there
2. paint
3. alive
4. nearly
5. flower
6. going
7. sound
8. coin
9. higher
10. sure
11. again

E London – England;
Paris – France;
Madrid – Spain;
Lisbon – Portugal;
Tokyo – Japan;
Moscow – Russia;
Washington – The United States;
Athens – Greece;
Rome – Italy;
Amman – Jordan;
Damascus – Syria;
Canberra – Australia;
Cairo – Egypt;
Jakarta – Indonesia.

red – tomato;
green – grass;
brown – coffee;
white – milk;
blue – the sky;
black – ink;
yellow – the sun.

Answer Key

bread – butter;
salt – pepper;
shoes – socks;
pen – ink;
fish — chips.

F
1 banana
2 sister
3 lessons
4 elephant
5 London
6 pleasure
7 apple
8 father
9 tiger
10 Australia
11 summer
12 measure
13 brother
14 mother
15 Lisbon
16 Japan
17 weather
18 mister

G
1 I'm a teacher.
2 I'm a boy.
3 I am married.
4 I have a sister.
5 I live in a house.
6 I'm a student.
7 I'm a girl.
8 I am not married.
9 I have a brother and sister.
10 I like English lessons.
11 I live in London.
12 My name is Peter.
13 I have a brother.
14 I live in a flat.
15 I don't like English lessons.

H
cow   desk   train
horse chair   bus
sheep table   car

shirt   apple   tiger
jacket banana   elephant
blouse orange   lion

I
/ðə/ name coin man day car
/ði/ orange address eye ink elephant

J
/ə/ bike boy glass house
/ən/ apple office actor engine egg

K
1 enough
2 explanation
3 general
4 everything
5 enjoyment
6 university
7 intention
8 children
9 careful
10 December
11 Wednesday
12 government

L
1 borrow
2 importance
3 magazine
4 position
5 everybody
6 necessary
7 forgotten
8 accent
9 American
10 probably
11 September
12 syllable

N 1-h; 2-f; 3-e; 4-b; 5-g; 6-a; 7-c; 8-d.

O
1 Where do you live?
2 What are you going to do tomorrow?
3 Tell them to come at four o'clock.
4 I want to go home.
5 I didn't know what to do.
6 What do you want to do?
7 I don't know what you mean.
8 Who's that over there?
9 I have to go home now.
10 You can do what you want.
11 I've got a lot of money.
12 I'm going to get a cup of tea.
13 Who do you want to see?
14 I'll tell you what I want.
15 How do you know? c

Numbers Practice

A
1 second
2 fourth
3 sixth
4 first
5 fifth
6 third

B
1 oh
2 nil
3 oh
4 love
5 nil
6 nought
7 nought nought nought
8 zero

C
1 three-day
2 eighty-mile-per-hour
3 five-pound
4 three-hour
5 twenty-two-pound
6 three-course

D
1 four times
2 twice
3 five times
4 once

Letters

A
1A	8H	15O	22V
2B	9I	16P	23W
3C	10J	17Q	24X
4D	11K	18R	25Y
5E	12L	19S	26Z
6F	13M	20T	
7G	14N	21U	

C
1Z	14S
2H	15F
3G	16M
4E	17U
5W	18C
6Y	19T
7B	20J
8A	21N
9K	22D
10X	23P
11L	24R
12Q	25V
13I	26O

D
1 /ju: keɪ/
2 /dʒɪ: bɪ:/
3 /eɪ em/
4 /pi: em/
5 /pi: ti: oʊ/
6 /si: di:/
7 /di: dʒeɪ/
8 /bi: bi: si:/
9 /ti: vi:/
10 /neɪtoʊ/
11 /i: si:/
12 /ju: es eɪ/
13 /vi: aɪ pi:/
14 /ju: ef oʊ (ju:fəʊ)/
15 /dʌbəlju: dʌbəlju: ef/

Appendices

Appendices

Contents

Regular Verb Tenses

tense name	active	passive	use
present continuous (Unit 2)	he/she/it **is helping** her I **am helping** her you/we/they **are helping** her	he/she/it **is being helped** I **am being helped** you/we/they **are being helped**	● to talk about something happening now ● to talk about a future plan
present simple (Unit 3)	he/she/it **helps** her I/you/we/they **help** her	he/she/it **is helped** I/you/we/they **are helped**	● to talk about things that are always true ● to talk about regular actions
present perfect (Unit 5, 6)	he/she/it **has helped** her I/you/we/they **have helped** her	he/she/it **has been helped** I/you/we/they **have been helped**	● to talk about something which happened in the past with an effect in the present
present perfect continuous (Unit 6)	he/she/it **has been helping** her I/you/we/they **have been helping** her	he/she/it **has been being helped*** I/you/we/they **have been being helped***	● to talk about something which started in the past and is still happening now or has recently finished
past simple (Unit 8)	I/you/he/she/it/we/they **helped** her	he/she/it **was helped** I/you/we/they **were helped**	● to talk about things that happened in the past ● to talk about regular actions in the past

*not often used

242

Regular Verb Tenses

tense name	active	passive	use
past continuous (Unit 9)	*I/he/she/it* **was helping** *her* *you/we/they* **were helping** *her*	*I/he/she/it* **was being helped** *you/we/they* **were being helped**	• to talk about an action in the past which was not finished or was interrupted
past perfect (Unit 10)	*I/you/he/she/it/we/they* **had helped** *her*	*I/you/he/she/it/we/they* **had been helped**	• to talk about something that happened before a particular time in the past
past perfect continuous (Unit 10)	*I/you/he/she/it/we/they* **had been helping** *her*	*I/you/he/she/it/we/they* **had been being helped***	• to talk about something that happened over a period of time before a particular time in the past
future (Unit 12)	*I/you/he/she/it/we/they* **will help** *her*	*I/you/he/she/it/we/they* **will be helped**	• to talk about an action in the future

*not often used

Nouns and Countability

type of noun	examples	determiners	singular or plural verb?	some uses
singular count noun	holiday, tooth, bus, potato, baby, child	• always used with a determiner such as a/an, the, this, every, another, possessives such as my, his etc. or one	• only used with a singular verb: A bus is coming.	
plural count noun	holidays, teeth, buses, potatoes, babies, children	• never used with a/an • sometimes used with the, these, possessives such as my, his etc. or numbers • can be used without a determiner	• only used with a plural verb: The babies were crying.	• used without a determiner to talk about people or things in general: I don't like spiders.
singular noun	air, future, sun, chance, rest	• always used with a determiner such as a/an, the or possessives such as my, his etc.	• only used with a singular verb: The sun was shining.	• often used with the to refer to unique things: the air, the future • singular nouns formed from verbs are often used with a to talk about common activities: a snooze, a rest
plural noun	clothes, feelings, police, scissors	• usually used with the or possessives such as my, his etc.	• only used with a plural verb: The police are coming.	• often used to talk about tools and clothes with two similar parts: trousers, glasses, scales

Nouns and Countability

type of noun	examples	determiners	singular or plural verb?	some uses
collective noun	*team, audience, staff*	• usually used with *the* or possessives such as *my, his* etc.	• used with a singular or a plural verb: *Which team is winning?* *Our team are wearing red.*	• used to talk about a group as one unit: *My family **is** in Brazil.* • or as many individuals: *His family **are** all strange.*
uncount noun	*food, electricity, music*	• never used with *a/an*, *these/those* or numbers • often used without a determiner • can be used with *the, this/that* or possessives such as *my, his* etc	• only used with a singular verb: *Electricity is dangerous.*	• used with *some, much* and *any* to talk about quantities: *There's not much food in the house.* *I need to buy some bread.* • often used to talk about abstract ideas such as feelings: *It was a year of sadness and happiness.*

Position and Order of Adjectives

Position of Adjectives

A Most adjectives can be used before a noun as part of a noun group. They come after determiners and numbers if there are any, and immediately before the noun.

*He had a **beautiful** smile.*
*She bought a loaf of **white** bread.*
*In the corner of the room there were two **wooden** chairs.*

B Most adjectives can also be used after a link verb such as 'be', 'become', or 'feel'.

*I'm **cold**.*
*She felt **angry**.*
*Nobody seemed **happy**.*

C Some adjectives are only used after the verb 'be' or other link verbs such as 'become', 'seem' or 'feel'.

For example, you can say 'She was glad', but you do not talk about 'a glad woman'.

Some examples of adjectives like this are:

| afraid | alive | alone | asleep | glad | ill |
| ready | sorry | sure | unable | well | |

*I wanted to be **alone**.*
*We were getting **ready** for bed.*
*I'm not quite **sure**.*
*He didn't know whether to feel **glad** or **sorry**.*

D Some adjectives are normally only used before a noun.

For example, you talk about 'the main problem', but you do not say 'The problem was main'.

Some examples of adjectives like this are:

| absolute | atomic | indoor | main |
| other | total | utter | |

*Some of it was **absolute** rubbish.*
*The hotel has an **indoor** swimming pool.*

E Some adjectives that describe size or age can come after a noun that indicates a unit of measurement.

Some examples of adjectives like this are:

| deep | high | long | old |
| tall | thick | wide | |

*He was about six feet **tall**.*
*The water was several metres **deep**.*
*The baby is nine months **old**.*

F A few adjectives with a special meaning are used immediately after a noun.

Some examples of adjectives like this are:

| designate | elect | galore | incarnate |

*She was now the president **elect**.*
*There are empty houses **galore**.*

G A few adjectives have a different meaning depending on whether they come before or after a noun.

For example, 'the concerned mother' means a mother who is worried, but 'the mother concerned' means the mother who has been mentioned.

Some examples of adjectives like this are:

| concerned | involved | present | proper |
| responsible | | | |

*I'm worried about the **present** situation.* (= the situation that exists now)
*Of the 18 people **present** (= the 18 people who were there), I knew only one.*

Position and Order of Adjectives

Order of Adjectives

A You can use adjectives to describe various qualities of people or things. For example, you might want to talk about their size, their shape, or the country they come from.

Descriptive adjectives belong to seven main types, and two or three different types are often used together. If you use more than one type, you would normally put them in the following order:

1st	2nd	3rd	4th	5th	6th	7th
opinion	size	age	shape	colour	nationality	material
beautiful	large	old	round	black	Chinese	wooden

This means that if you want to use an 'age' adjective and a 'nationality' adjective, you put the 'age' adjective first.

*We met some **young Chinese** girls.*

Similarly, a 'shape' adjective normally comes before a 'colour' adjective.

*He had **round black** eyes.*

You would put a 'size' adjective before a 'shape' or 'colour' adjective, and a 'shape' or 'colour' adjective before a 'material' adjective.

*There was a **large round wooden** table in the room.*
*The man was carrying a **small black plastic** bag*

But if you want to use two 'colour' adjectives, you put *and* between them.

*He was wearing a **long red** and **blue** t-shirt.*

With three 'colour' adjectives, you link the last two with *and* and put a comma after the first.

*France has a **red**, **white** and **blue** flag.*

B You can use more than one adjective to describe a noun. When you use two or more adjectives before a noun, you usually put an adjective that gives your opinion before an adjective that just describes something.

*You live in a **nice big** house.*
*He is a **naughty little** boy.*
*She was wearing a **beautiful pink** suit.*

C When you use more than one adjective to give your opinion, an adjective with a more general meaning such as 'good', 'bad', 'nice', or 'lovely' usually comes before an adjective with a more specific meaning such as 'comfortable', 'clean', or 'dirty'.

*I sat in a **lovely comfortable** armchair.*
*He put on a **nice clean** shirt.*
*It was a **horrible dirty** room.*

D You usually put comparative adjectives such as 'cheaper', 'better' or superlative adjectives such as 'hardest', 'best' before other adjectives.

*That plant has **larger** purple flowers.*
*Some of the **best** English actors have gone to live in Hollywood.*

E When you use two adjectives after a link verb such as 'be', 'seem', or 'feel', you use a conjunction like *and* to link them. With three or more adjectives, you link the last two with a conjunction, and put commas after the others.

*The day was **hot** and **dusty**.*
*The room was **large** but **square**.*
*We felt **hot**, **tired** and **thirsty**.*

Prepositions: *in*, *on*, *at*

The prepositions *in*, *on* and *at* are used very frequently in English to talk about times and places. Sometimes it can be difficult to know which one you should choose in a particular phrase or sentence. The table below shows some of the very common uses of these prepositions that have been talked about in this book. It gives examples to help you learn them.

	in	*on*	*at*
TIME	months/years: *in February* *in 1996* *in the last century* parts of the day: *in the morning* seasons: *in winter* *in (the) summer* to say when something will happen in the future: *I'll talk to you in ten minutes.*	days: *on Monday* parts of days: *on Tuesday evening* dates: *on the ninth of May* *on Friday 29th* special days: *on my birthday* *on Christmas Eve*	clock times: *at 10 o'clock* *at midnight* meals: *at breakfast* festivals: *at Christmas* *at Easter*
PLACE	geographical regions: *in Spain* *in the mountains* cities/large areas: *in York* *in the park* roads/streets: *There are lots of shoe shops in that street.* rooms/buildings: *I heard a noise in the kitchen.* *There's a wedding in the church.* containers: *in a box* *in the fridge* liquids: *I'd like sugar in my coffee.*	surfaces: *on the wall/roof* *on the table/shelf* *on the first floor* *on a piece of paper* roads/streets: *The bank is on Kings Road.*	specific places: *at the bus stop* *at home/work* *at Amy's house* *at the back of the book* addresses: *She lives at 5, Regent Street.* public places: *at the station/theatre* *at the doctor's* shops: *at the supermarket* events: *at Steve's party* *at last year's conference*

British and American English

There are very few differences in the grammar of British and American English. Below are the main ones.

A Using the present perfect tense

The present perfect tense (*have/has* + past participle, Units 5 and 6)) is used less in American English than in British English. American speakers often use the past simple (Unit 8) instead.

This is especially true:

(a) In sentences with *yet*, *just* and *already* (Unit 5):

British English/ American English	American English
A: Is your mother here? B: No, she **has** just **left**.	A: Is your mother here? B: No, she just **left**.
A: Is he going to the show tonight? B: No. He**'s** already **seen** it.	A: Is he going to the show tonight? B: No. He already **saw** it.
A: Can I borrow your book? B: No, I **haven't finished** it yet.	A: Can I borrow your book? B: No, I **didn't finish** it yet.

(b) In sentences which talk about an action in the past that has an effect in the present (Unit 5):

British English/ American English	American English
Arthur doesn't feel well. He's **eaten** too much.	Arthur doesn't feel well. He **ate** too much.
I can't find my glasses. **Have** you **seen** them?	I can't find my glasses. **Did** you **see** them?

B Using collective nouns

In British English, nouns for special groups of people or things, called collective nouns, can have a singular or plural verb because you can think of the group as one idea, or as many individuals (Unit 17):

My team **is** losing.
His team **are** all wearing red.

In American English, these nouns normally take a singular verb:

Which team **is** winning?

C Use of *needn't*

In British English, you can use *needn't* in the same way as *don't need to* to say that something is not necessary (Unit 51):

You **don't need to** come to work today.
You **needn't** come to work today.

In American English, *needn't* is very unusual. The usual form is *don't need to*:

You **don't need to** come to work today.

D Use of *have* and *take*

In British English, *have* is used with some nouns to talk about common activities (Unit 56).

eating and drinking:
Let's have a drink.

relaxation:
I think we all need to have a rest.

washing:
She wants to have a shower first.

In American English, *have* is not used when talking about washing. Americans use *take* instead.

She wants to take a shower first.
Do you mind if I take a bath?

Americans also usually use *take* when talking about relaxation:

Let's take a vacation.
I think we all need to take a rest.

E Use of *do* as an auxiliary verb

British people sometimes use *do* as an auxiliary verb as a substitute for a verb in response to a question:

'Do you think you will vote in the future?' 'I might **do**.'

Americans do not use *do* in this way.

'Do you think you might vote for Judith Ryan?' 'I might.'

British and American English

F Use of *at*, *on*, and *in*

In British English, *at* is used with many time expressions (Unit 30):

at *ten o'clock* **at** *Easter*
at *the weekend*

In American English, you cannot use *at* when talking about the weekend. Americans always use *on*.

*Will he still be there **on** the weekend?*
*He'll be coming home **on** weekends.*

Americans, when talking about universities and institutions, use *in*:

*We both took calculus **in** university.*

In British English, *at* is used:

*Thomas Dane studied history of art **at** university.*

G Use of articles

Americans always use the definite article *the* when referring to a hospital:

*I'm going to **the** hospital.*

British people do not use *the* in this way:

I'm going to hospital.

H Use of the pronoun *one*

British people sometimes use the pronoun *one* to refer to a particular person or to anyone in general.

*'What can **one** say?' she whispered.*

*How can **one** know about things like that in advance?*

Americans use *a person*, *I*, or *we* instead.

*What can **I** say?*

*How can **a person** ask about a problem they don't know anything about?*

I Past simple and past participle forms

Some verbs have different past simple and past participle forms in British and American English:

infinitive	past simple *(Br)*	past simple *(Am)*	past participle *(Br)*	past participle *(Am)*
burn[1]	burned/burnt	burned/burnt	burned/burnt	burned/burnt
bust	bust	busted	bust	busted
dive	dived	dove/dived	dived	dived
dream[1]	dreamed/dreamt	dreamed/dreamt	dreamed/dreamt	dreamed/dreamt
get	got	got	got	got/gotten
lean	leaned/leant	leaned	leaned/leant	leaned
learn	learned/learnt	learned	learned/learnt	learned
plead	pleaded	pleaded/pled	pleaded	pleaded/pled
prove	proved	proved	proved	proved/proven
saw	sawed	sawed	sawn	sawn/sawed
smell	smelled/smelt	smelled	smelled/smelt	smelled
spell	spelled/spelt	spelled	spelled/spelt	spelled
spill	spilled/spilt	spilled	spilled/spilt	spilled
spit	spat	spat/spit	spat	spat/spit
spoil[1]	spoiled/spoilt	spoiled/spoilt	spoiled/spoilt	spoiled/spoilt
stink	stank	stank/stunk	stunk	stunk
wake	woke	waked/woke	woken	woken

[1]For the verbs *burn*, *dream* and *spoil* the irregular past forms (*burnt*, *dreamt*, *spoilt*) are possible in American English, but less common than the forms ending in *-ed*.

Prefixes and Suffixes

Prefixes are beginnings of words, which have a regular and predictable meaning.

Suffixes are word endings which can be added to words, usually to make a new word with a similar meaning but different part of speech.

Prefixes

a- forms adjectives which have 'not', 'without', or 'opposite' in their meaning. For example, *atypical* behaviour is not typical of someone.

aero- forms words, especially nouns, that refer to things or activities connected with air or movement through the air. For example, an *aeroplane* is a vehicle which flies through the air.

astro- is used to form words which refer to things relating to the stars or to outer space. For example, an *astronaut* is a person who travels in space.

anti- forms nouns and adjectives which refer to some sort of opposition. For example, an *anti-government* demonstration is a demonstration against the government.

auto- forms words which refer to someone doing something to, for, or about themselves. For example, your *autobiography* is an account of your life, which you write yourself.

be- can be added to a noun followed by an '-ed' suffix to form an adjective that indicates that a person is covered with or wearing the thing named. For example, a person who is *bespectacled* is wearing spectacles.

bi- forms nouns and adjectives which have 'two' as part of their meaning. For example, if someone is *bilingual*, they speak two languages.

bi- also forms adjectives and adverbs which refer to something happening twice in a period of time, or once in two consecutive periods of time. A *bimonthly* event happens twice a month, or once every two months.

bio- is used at the beginning of nouns and adjectives that refer to life or to the study of living things. For example, a *biography* is a book about someone's life.

co- forms verbs and nouns which refer to people sharing things or doing things together. For example, if two people *co-write* a book, they write it together. The *co-author* of a book is one of the people who has written it.

counter- forms words which refer to actions or activities that oppose another action or activity. For example, a *counter-measure* is an action you take to weaken the effect of another action or situation.

de- is added to some verbs to make verbs which mean the opposite. For example, to *deactivate* a mechanism means to switch it off so that it cannot work.

demi- is used at the beginning of some words to refer to something equivalent to half of the object or amount indicated by the rest of the word. For example, a *demigod* is a god which is half god and half human.

dis- can be added to some words to form words which have the opposite meaning. For example, if someone is *dishonest*, they are not honest.

e- is used to form words that indicate that something happens on or uses the Internet. 'e-' is an abbreviation for 'electronic'. For example, *e-business* is the buying, selling, and ordering of goods and services using the Internet.

eco- forms nouns and adjectives which refer to something related to the environment. For example, *eco-friendly* products do not harm the environment.

em- is a form of 'en-' that is used before 'b-', 'm-' and 'p-'. SEE **en-**.

en- is added to words to form verbs that describe the process of putting someone into a particular state, condition or place, or to form adjectives and nouns that describe that process or those states and conditions. For example, if you *endanger* someone or something, you put them in a situation where they might be harmed or destroyed.

euro- is used to form words that describe or refer to something which is connected with Europe or with the European Union. For example, If you describe something as *Eurocentric*, you disapprove of it because it focuses on Europe

Prefixes and Suffixes

and the needs of European people, often with the result that people in other parts of the world suffer in some way.

ex- forms words which refer to people who are no longer a particular thing. For example, an *ex-policeman* is someone who is no longer a policeman.

extra- forms adjectives which refer to something being outside or beyond something else. For example, Britain's *extra-European* commitments are its commitments outside of Europe.

extra- also forms adjectives which refer to something having a large amount of a particular quality. For example, if something is *extra-strong*, it is very strong.

geo- is used at the beginning of words that refer to the whole of the world or to the Earth's surface. For example, *geology* is the study of the Earth's structure, surface, and origins.

great- is used before some nouns that refer to relatives. Nouns formed in this way refer to a relative who is a further generation away from you. For example, your *great-aunt* is the aunt of one of your parents.

hyper- forms adjectives which refer to people or things which have a large amount of, or too much of a particular quality. For example, *hyperinflation* is very extreme inflation.

il-, im-, in-, and **ir-** can be added to some words to form words which have the opposite meaning. For example, if an activity is *illegal*, it is not legal. If someone is *impatient*, they are not patient.

inter- forms adjectives which refer to things that move, exist, or happen between two or more people or things. For example, *inter-city* trains travel between cities.

ir-. SEE **il-**.

kilo- forms words which refer to things which have a thousand parts. For example, a *kilometre* is a thousand metres.

macro- is added to words in order to form new words that are technical and that refer to things which are large or involve the whole of something. For example *macroeconomic* means relating to the major, general features of a country's economy, such as the level of inflation or unemployment.

mal- forms words which refer to things that are bad or unpleasant, or that are unsuccessful or imperfect. For example, if a machine *malfunctions*, it does not work properly.

mega- forms words which refer to units which are a million times bigger. For example, a *megawatt* is a million watts.

micro- forms nouns which have 'small' as part of their meaning. For example, a *micro-organism* is a very small living thing that you cannot see with the naked eye.

mid- forms nouns and adjectives which refer to the middle part of a particular period of time, or the middle part of a particular place. For example, *mid-June* is the middle of June.

milli- forms nouns which refer to units which are a thousand times smaller. For example, a *millimetre* is a thousandth of a metre.

mini- forms nouns which refer to things which are a smaller version of something else. For example, a *minibus* is a small bus.

mis- forms verbs and nouns which refer to something being done badly or wrongly. For example, if you *miscalculate* a figure, you wrongly calculate it.

mono- forms nouns and adjectives which have 'one' or 'single' as part of their meaning. For example, *monogamy* is the custom of being married to only one person.

multi- forms adjectives which refer to something that consists of many things of a particular kind. For example, a *multi-coloured* object has many different colours.

narco- is added to words to form new words that relate to illegal narcotics. For example, a *narco-trafficker* is a person who illegally buys or sells narcotics.

neo- forms nouns and adjectives which refer to modern versions or styles and particular groups of the past. For example, *neo-classical* architecture is based on ancient Greek or Roman architecture.

neuro- is used to form words that refer to or

Prefixes and Suffixes

relate to a nerve or the nervous system. For example, *neurology* is the study of the structure, function, and diseases of the nervous system.

non- forms nouns and adjectives which refer to people or things that do not have a particular quality or characteristic. For example, a *non-smoker* does not smoke. A *non-fatal* accident is not fatal.

non- also forms nouns which refer to situations where a particular action has not taken place. For example, someone's *non-attendance* at a meeting is the fact of their not having attended the meeting.

out- forms verbs which refer to an action as being done better by one person than by another. For example, if you can *outswim* someone, you can swim further or faster than they can.

over- forms words which refer to a quality of action that exists or is done to too great an extent. For example, if someone is being *over-cautious*, they are being too cautious.

pan- is added to the beginning of adjectives and nouns to form other adjectives and nouns that describe something as being connected with all places or people of a particular kind. For example, a *pandemic* is an occurrence of a disease that affects many people over a very wide area.

para- forms nouns and adjectives which refer to people or things which are similar to other things. For example, a *paramilitary* organisation is organized like an army, and a *paramedic* is a person whose training is similar to that of a nurse and who helps to do medical work.

para- also forms nouns and adjectives which refer to situations which are beyond or more important than normal. For example, a *paranormal* event cannot be explained by scientific laws and is thought to involve strange, unknown forces.

part- forms words which refer to something that is partly but not completely a particular thing. For example, *part-baked* bread is only partly baked.

poly- forms nouns and adjectives which have 'many' as part of their meaning. For example, a *polysyllabic* word contains many syllables.

post- forms words that refer to something that takes place after a particular date, period, or event. For example, a *post-Christmas* sale takes place just after Christmas.

pre- forms words that refer to something that takes place before a particular date, period, or event. For example, a *pre-election* rally takes place just before an election.

pro- forms adjectives which refer to people who strongly support a particular person or thing. For example, if you are *pro-democracy*, you support democracy.

proto- is used to form adjectives and nouns which indicate that something is in the early stages of its development. For example, a *prototype* is a new type of machine or device which is not yet ready to be made in large numbers and sold.

pseudo- forms nouns and adjectives which refer to something which is not really what is seems or claims to be. For example, a *pseudo-science* is something that claims to be a science, but is not.

psycho- is added to words in order to form other words which describe or refer to things connected with the mind or with mental processes. For example, a *psychoanalyst* is someone who treats people who have mental problems.

re- forms verbs and nouns which refer to an action or process being repeated. For example, if you *re-read* something, you read it again.

semi- forms nouns and adjectives which refer to people and things that are partly, but not completely, in a particular state. For example, if you are *semi-conscious*, you are partly, but not wholly, conscious.

sub- forms nouns which refer to things that are part of a larger thing. For example, a *subcommittee* is a small committee made up of members of a larger committee.

sub- also forms adjectives which refer to people or things that are inferior. For example, *substandard* living conditions are inferior to normal living conditions.

super- forms nouns and adjectives which refer to people and things that are larger, better, or more advanced than others. For example, a *super-fit* athlete is extremely fit, and a *supertanker* is a very large tanker.

techno- is used at the beginning of words that refer to technology. For example, if you refer to someone as a *technophobe*, you mean that they do not like new technology, such as computers or mobile telephones, and are afraid to use it.

trans- is used to form adjectives which indicate that something moves or enables travel from one side of an area to another. For example, *transatlantic* flights go across the Atlantic.

trans- is also used to form words which indicate that someone or something moves from one group, thing, state or place to another. For example, a blood *transfusion* is a process in which blood is injected into the body of a person who is badly injured or ill.

tri- forms nouns and adjectives which have 'three' as part of their meaning. For example, a *tricycle* is a cycle with three wheels.

ultra- forms adjectives which refer to people and things that possess a quality to a very large degree. For example, an *ultra-light* fabric is extremely light.

un- can be added to some words to form words which have the opposite meaning. For example, if something is *unacceptable*, it is not acceptable.

under- forms words which refer to an amount or value being too low or not enough. For example, if someone is *underweight*, their weight is lower than it should be.

vice- is used before a rank or title to indicate that someone is next in importance to the person who holds the rank or title mentioned. For example, a *vice-president* is next in importance to the president.

Suffixes

-ability and **-ibility** replace '-able' and '-ible' at the end of adjectives to form nouns which refer to a particular state or quality. For example, *reliability* is the state or quality of being reliable.

-able forms adjectives which indicate what someone or something can have done to them. For example, if something is *readable*, it can be read.

-al forms adjectives which indicate what something is connected with. For example, *environmental* problems are problems connected with the environment.

-ally is added to adjectives ending in '-ic' to form adverbs which indicate how something is done or what something relates to. For example, if something is done *enthusiastically*, it is done in an enthusiastic way.

-ance, **-ence**, **-ancy** and **-ency** form nouns which refer to a particular action, state, or quality. For example, *brilliance* is the state or quality of being brilliant, and *reappearance* is the action of reappearing.

-ancy. SEE **-ance**.

-ation, **-ication**, **-sion** and **-tion** form nouns which refer to a state or process, or to an instance of that process. For example, the *protection* of the environment is the process of protecting it.

-cy forms nouns which refer to a particular state or quality. For example, *accuracy* is the state or quality of being accurate.

-ed is added to verbs to make the past tense and past participle. Past participles formed are often used as adjectives which indicate that something has been affected in some way. For example, *cooked* food is food that has been cooked.

-ence. SEE **-ance**.

-ency. SEE **-ance**.

-er and **-or** form nouns which refer to a person who performs a particular action, often because it is their job. For example, a *teacher* is someone who teaches. *-er* and *-or* also form nouns which refer to tools and machines that perform a

Prefixes and Suffixes

particular action. For example, a *mixer* is a machine that mixes things.

-er is also added to many short adjectives to form comparatives. For example, the comparative of 'nice' is *nicer* and the comparative of 'happy' is *happier*. You also add it to some adverbs that do not end in '-ly'. For example, the comparative of 'soon' is *sooner*.

-est is added to many short adjectives to form superlatives. For example, the superlative of 'nice' is *nicest*, and the superlative of 'happy' is *happiest*. You also add it to some adverbs that do not end in '-ly'. For example, the superlative of 'soon' is *soonest*.

-fold combines with numbers to form adverbs which say how much an amount has increased by. For example, if an amount increases *fourfold*, it is four times greater than it was originally.

-ful forms nouns which refer to the amount of a substance that something contains or can contain. For example, a *handful* of sand is the amount of sand that you can hold in your hand.

-ibility. SEE **-ability**.

-ic forms adjectives which indicate that something or someone is connected with a particular thing. For example, *photographic* equipment is equipment connected with photography.

-ication. SEE **-ation**.

-icity replaces '-ic' at the end of adjectives to form nouns referring to the state, quality, or behaviour described by the adjective. For example, *authenticity* refers to the quality of being authentic.

-ify is used at the end of verbs that refer to making something or someone different in some way. For example, if you *simplify* something, you make it easier to understand or you remove the things which make it complex.

-ing is added to verbs to make the -ing form, or present participle. Present participle forms are often used as adjectives describing a person or thing who is doing something. For example, a *sleeping* baby is a baby that is sleeping and an *amusing* joke is a joke that amuses people. Present participle forms are also used as nouns

which refer to activities. For example, if you say you like *dancing*, you mean that you like to dance.

-ise. SEE **-ize**.

-ish forms adjectives which indicate that someone or something has a quality to a small extent. For example, if you say that something is *largish*, you mean it is fairly large, and something that is *yellowish* is slightly yellow in colour.

-ish also forms words that indicate that a particular time or age mentioned is approximate. For example, if someone is *fortyish*, they are about forty years old.

-ism forms nouns which refer to particular beliefs, or to behaviour based on these beliefs. For example, *professionalism* is behaviour that is professional and *racism* is the beliefs and behaviour of a racist.

-ist replaces '-ism' at the end of nouns to form nouns and adjectives. The nouns refer to the people who have particular beliefs. For example, a *fascist* is someone who supports fascism. The adjectives indicate that something is related to or is based on particular beliefs.

-ist also forms nouns which refer to people who do a particular kind of work. For example, a *geologist* is someone who works in the field of geology.

-ist also forms nouns which refer to people who play a particular musical instrument, often as their job. For example, a *violinist* is someone who plays the violin.

-ity forms nouns which refer to a particular state or quality. For example, *solidity* is the state or quality of being solid.

-ize is used at the end of many verbs to describe processes by which things or people are brought into a new state. For example, to *standardize* things means to change them so that they all have the same features. The spelling *-ise* is also used, especially in British English.

-less forms adjectives which indicate that someone or something does not have a particular thing. For example, someone who is *childless* does not have any children.

Prefixes and Suffixes

-logical. SEE **-ological**.

-logist. SEE **-ologist**.

-logy. SEE **-ology**.

-ly forms adverbs which indicate how something is done. For example, if someone whistles *cheerfully*, they whistle in a cheerful way.

-ment forms nouns which refer to the process of making or doing something, or to the result of this process. For example, *assessment* is the process of assessing something or the judgment made as a result of assessing it.

-nd is added to written numbers ending in 2, except for numbers ending in 12, in order to form ordinal numbers, for example *22nd February...2nd edition*.

-ness forms nouns which refer to a particular state or quality. For example, *gentleness* is the state or quality of being gentle.

-ological or **-logical** is used to replace *-ology* or *-logy* at the end of nouns in order to form adjectives that describe something as relating to a particular science or subject. For example, *biological* means relating to biology.

-ologist or **-logist** is used to replace *-ology* or *-logy* at the end of nouns in order to form other nouns that refer to people who are concerned with a particular science or subject. For example, a *biologist* is concerned with biology.

-ology or **-logy** is used at the end of some nouns that refer to a particular science or subject, for example *biology* or *sociology*.

-or. SEE **-er**.

-ous forms adjectives which indicate that someone or something has a particular quality. For example, someone who is *courageous* shows courage.

-phile occurs at the end of words which refer to someone who has a very strong liking for people or things of a particular kind. For example, if you describe a non-British person as *Anglophile*, you mean that they admire Britain and British culture.

-phobe occurs at the end of words which refer to someone who has a very strong irrational fear or hatred of people or things of a particular kind. For example, if you refer to someone as a *technophobe*, you mean that they do not like new technology, such as computers or mobile telephones, and are afraid to use it.

-phobia occurs at the end of words which refer to a very strong irrational fear or hatred of something. For example, someone who suffers from *claustrophobia* feels very uncomfortable or anxious when they are in small or enclosed places.

-phobic occurs at the end of words which describe something relating to a strong, irrational fear or hatred of people or things of a particular kind. For example, you describe a place or situation as *claustrophobic* when it makes you feel uncomfortable and unhappy because you are enclosed or restricted.

-rd is added to written numbers ending in 3, except for numbers ending in 13, in order to form ordinal numbers, for example, *September 3rd...the 33rd Boston Marathon*.

-sion, -tion. SEE **-ation**.

-st is added to written numbers ending in 1 except for numbers ending in 11, in order to form ordinal numbers, for example, *1st August 1993...the 101st Airborne Division*.

-th is added to written numbers ending in 4, 5, 6, 7, 8, 9, 10, 11, 12 or 13 in order to form ordinal numbers, for example, *6th Avenue...the 25th amendment to the American Constitution*.

-y forms adjectives which indicate that something is full of something else or covered in it. For example, if something is *dirty*, it is covered with dirt.

-y also forms adjectives which mean that something is like something else. For example, if something tastes *chocolatey*, it tastes like chocolate, although it is not actually chocolate.

Glossary of Grammar Terms

abstract noun

An abstract noun is a noun used to refer to a quality, idea, feeling, or experience, rather than a physical object, for example, *size, reason, joy.*

active voice

The active voice refers to verb groups such as 'gives', 'took', 'has made', which are used when the subject of the verb is the person or thing doing the action or responsible for it. Compare with **passive voice**.

adjunct

An adjunct is another name for **adverbial**.

adjective

An adjective is a word used to tell you more about a person or thing, such as their appearance, colour, size, or other qualities.

EG   *She was wearing a pretty blue dress.*

adverb

An adverb is a word that gives more information about when, how, where, or in what circumstances something happens, for example, *quickly, now.*

adverbial

An adverbial is an adverb, or an adverb phrase, prepositional phrase, or noun group which does the same job as an adverb, giving more information about when, how, where, or in what circumstances something happens, for example, *then, very quickly, in the street, the next day.*

adverbial of degree

An adverbial of degree is an adverbial which indicates the amount or extent of a feeling or quality.

EG   *She felt extremely tired.*

adverbial of duration

An adverbial of duration is an adverbial which indicates how long something continues or lasts.

EG   *He lived in London for six years.*

adverbial of frequency

An adverbial of frequency is an adverbial which indicates how often something happens.

EG   *She sometimes goes to the cinema.*

adverbial of place

An adverbial of place is an adverbial which gives more information about position or direction.

EG   *They are upstairs.*
       Move closer.

adverbial of probability

An adverbial of probability is an adverbial which gives more information about how sure you are about something.

EG   *I've probably lost it.*

adverbial of time

An adverbial of time is an adverbial which gives more information about when something happens.

EG   *I saw her yesterday.*

adverb of manner

An adverbial of manner is an adverbial which indicates the way in which something happens or is done.

EG   *She watched carefully.*

adverb phrase

An adverb phrase is two adverbs used together.

EG   *She spoke very quietly.*
       He did not play well enough to win.

Glossary of Grammar Terms

affirmative

An affirmative is a clause or sentence which does not contain a negative word such as 'not' and which is not a question.

apostrophe s

An apostrophe s is an ending ('s) added to a noun to indicate possession.

EG *She is Harriet's daughter.*
    He married the Managing Director's secretary.

article

SEE **definite article, indefinite article**

auxiliary

An auxiliary is another name for **auxiliary verb**.

auxiliary verb

An auxiliary verb is one of the verbs 'be', 'have', and 'do' when they are used with a main verb to form tenses, negatives, and questions. Some grammars include modals in the group of auxiliary verbs.

bare infinitive

A bare infinitive is the form of the infinitive without 'to'.
SEE ALSO **'to'-infinitive**

base form

A base form is the form of a verb without any endings added to it, which is used in the 'to'-infinitive and for the imperative, for example, *walk, go, have, be.* The base form is the form you look up in a dictionary.

cardinal number

A cardinal number is a number used in counting, for example, *one, seven, nineteen.* Compare with **ordinal number**.

clause

A clause is a group of words containing a verb.
SEE ALSO **main clause** and **subordinate clause**

collective noun

A collective noun is a noun that refers to a group of people or things, and which can be used with a singular or plural verb, for example, *committee, team, family.*

comparative

A comparative is an adjective or adverb with '-er' on the end or 'more' in front of it, for example, *slower, more important, more carefully.*

complement

A complement is a noun group or adjective, which comes after a link verb such as 'be', and gives more information about the subject of the clause.

EG *She is a teacher.*
    She is tired.

complex sentence

A complex sentence is a sentence consisting of a main clause and a subordinate clause.

EG *She wasn't thinking very quickly because she was tired.*

compound

A compound is a compound noun, adjective or verb made up of two or more words, for example, *fat-cat corporate types, a stick of chewing gum.*

compound sentence

A compound sentence is a sentence consisting of two or more main clauses linked by 'and', 'or' or 'but'.

EG *They picked her up and took her into the house.*

Glossary of Grammar Terms

conditional clause

A conditional clause is a subordinate clause, usually starting with 'if' or 'unless', which is used to talk about possible situations and their results.

EG   *They would be rich if they had taken my advice.*
We'll go to the park, unless it rains.

conjunction

A conjunction is a word such as 'and', 'because', or 'nor', that links two clauses, groups, or words.

consonant

A consonant is a sound such as 'p', 'f', 'n' or 't'. Compare with **vowel**.

continuous tense

A continuous tense is a tense which contains a form of the verb 'be' and a present participle.

EG   *She was laughing.*
They had been playing badminton.

SEE **tense**.

contrast clause

A contrast clause is a subordinate clause, usually introduced by 'although' or 'in spite of the fact that', which contrasts with a main clause.

EG   *Although I like her, I find her hard to talk to.*

coordinating conjunction

A coordinating conjunction is a conjunction such as 'and', 'but', or 'or', which links two main clauses.

countable noun

A countable noun is another name for **count noun**.

count noun

A count noun is a noun which has both singular and plural forms, for example, *dog/dogs*, *foot/feet*, *lemon/lemons*. Compare with **uncount noun**.

declarative

A declarative is another name for **affirmative**.

defining relative clause

A defining relative clause is a relative clause which identifies the person or thing that is being talked about

EG   *I like the lady who lives next door.*
I wrote down everything that she said.

definite article

The definite article is the determiner 'the'. Compare with **indefinite article**.

delexical verb

A delexical verb is a common verb such as 'give', 'have', 'make', or 'take', which has very little meaning in itself and is used with a noun as object that describes the action.

EG   *She gave a small cry.*
I've just had a bath.

demonstrative

A demonstrative is one of the words 'this', 'that', these', and 'those'.

EG   *This woman is my mother.*
That tree is dead.
That looks interesting.
This is fun!

demonstrative adjective

A demonstrative adjective is another name for **demonstrative**.

descriptive adjective

A descriptive adjective is an adjective which

Glossary of Grammar Terms

describes a person or thing, for example indicating their size, age, shape, or colour, rather than expressing your opinion of that person or thing. Compare with **opinion adjective**.

determiner

A determiner is one of a group of words including 'the', 'a', 'some', and 'my', which are used at the beginning of a noun group.

direct object

A direct object is a noun group referring to the person or thing affected by an action, in a clause with a verb in the active voice. Compare with **indirect object**.

EG   *She wrote her name.*
      I shut the windows.

direct speech

Direct speech is the actual words spoken by someone. Compare with **indirect speech**.

ditransitive verb

A ditransitive verb is another name for a verb with two objects, such as 'give', 'take', or 'sell'.

EG   *She gave me a kiss.*

double-transitive verb

A double-transitive verb is another name for **ditransitive verb**.

'-ed' adjective

An '-ed' adjective is an adjective which has the same form as the '-ed' form of a regular verb, or the past participle of an irregular verb, for example, *boiled potatoes, a broken wing.*

'-ed' form

The '-ed' form is the form of a regular verb used for the past simple and for the past participle.

ellipsis

An ellipsis is the leaving out of words when they are obvious from the context.

emphasizing adverb

An emphasizing adverb is an adverb such as 'absolutely' or 'utterly', which modifies adjectives that express extreme qualities, such as 'astonishing' and 'wonderful'.

EG   *You were absolutely wonderful.*

ergative verb

An ergative verb is a verb which is both transitive and intransitive in the same meaning. The object of the transitive use is the subject of the intransitive use.

EG   *He boiled a kettle.*
      The kettle boiled.

first person

SEE **person**

future tense

SEE **tense**

gerund

The gerund is another name for the '-ing' form when it is used as a noun.

'if'-clause

SEE **conditional clause**

imperative

The imperative is the form of a verb used when giving orders and commands, and is the same as its base form.

EG   *Come here.*
      Take two tablets every four hours.
      Enjoy yourself.

Glossary of Grammar Terms

impersonal 'it'

The impersonal 'it' is used as an impersonal subject to introduce new information.

EG   *It's raining.*
      It's ten o'clock.

indefinite adverb

Indefinite adverbs are a small group of adverbs including 'anywhere' and 'somewhere' which are used to indicate place in a general way.

indefinite article

The indefinite articles are the determiners 'a' and 'an'. Compare with **definite article**.

indefinite pronoun

Indefinite pronouns are a small group of pronouns including 'someone' and 'anything' which are used to refer to people or things without saying exactly who or what they are.

indirect object

An indirect object is an object used with verbs that take two objects. For example, in 'I gave him the pen' and 'I gave the pen to him', 'him' is the indirect object and 'pen' is the direct object. Compare with **direct object**.

indirect question

An indirect question is a question used to ask for information or help.

EG   *Do you know where Jane is?*
      I wonder which hotel it was.

indirect speech

Indirect speech is the words you use to report what someone has said, rather than using their actual words. Compare with **direct speech**.

infinitive

The infinitive is the base form of a verb.

EG   *I wanted to go.*
      She helped me dig the garden.

'-ing' adjective

An '-ing' adjective is an adjective which has the same form as the present participle of a verb, for example, *a smiling face, a winning streak.*

'-ing' form

The '-ing' form is a verb form ending in '-ing' which is used to form verb tenses, and as an adjective or a noun. Also called the **present participle**.

interrogative pronoun

An interrogative pronoun is one of the pronouns 'who', 'whose', 'whom', 'what', and 'which', when they are used to ask questions.

interrogative sentence

An interrogative sentence is a sentence in the form of a question.

intransitive verb

An intransitive verb is a verb which does not take an object. Compare with **transitive verb**.

EG   *She arrived.*
      I was yawning.

irregular verb

An irregular verb is a verb that has three forms or five forms, or whose forms do not follow the normal rules. Compare with **regular verb**.

link verb

A link verb is a verb which takes a complement rather than an object, for example, *be, become, seem, appear.*

main clause

A main clause is a clause which does not

Glossary of Grammar Terms

depend on another clause, and is not part of another clause.

main verb

Main verbs are all verbs which are not auxiliaries or modals.

manner clause

A manner clause is a subordinate clause which describes the way in which something is done, usually introduced with 'as' or 'like'.

EG   *She talks like her mother used to.*

modal

A modal is a verb such as 'can', 'might', or 'will', which is always the first word in a verb group and is followed by the base form of a verb. Modals are used to express requests, offers, suggestions, wishes, intentions, politeness, possibility, probability, certainty, obligation, and so on.

EG   *I might go after all.*

mood

The mood of a clause is the way in which the verb forms are used to show whether the clause is a statement, command, or question.

negative

A negative clause, question, sentence, or statement is one which has a negative word such as 'not', and indicates the absence or opposite of something, or is used to say that something is not the case. Compare with **positive**.

EG   *I don't know you.*
      I'll never forget.

negative word

A negative word is a word such as 'never', 'no', 'not', 'nothing', or 'nowhere', which makes a clause, question, sentence, or statement negative.

non-defining relative clause

A non-defining relative clause is a relative clause which gives more information about someone or something, but which is not needed to identify them because we already know who or what they are. Compare with **defining relative clause**.

EG   *That's Mary, who was at university with me.*

non-finite clause

A non-finite clause is a 'to'-infinitive clause, '-ed' clause, or '-ing' clause.

noun

A noun is a word which refers to people, things, ideas, feelings, or qualities, for example, *woman, Harry, guilt.*

noun group

A noun group is a group of words which acts as the subject, complement, or object of a verb, or as the object of a preposition.

object

An object is a noun group which refers to a person or thing that is affected by the action described by a verb. Prepositions also have noun groups as objects. Compare with **subject**.

object pronoun

An object pronoun is one of a set of pronouns including 'me', 'him', and 'them', which are used as the object of a verb or preposition. Object pronouns are also used as complements after 'be'. Compare with **subject pronoun**.

EG   *I hit him.*
      It's me.

Glossary of Grammar Terms

opinion adjective

An opinion adjective is an adjective which you use to express your opinion of a person or thing, rather than just describing them. Compare with **descriptive adjective**.

ordinal number

An ordinal number is a number used to indicate where something comes in an order or sequence, for example, *first, fifth, tenth, hundredth*. Compare with **cardinal number**.

participle

A participle is a verb form used for making different tenses. Verbs have two participles, a present participle and a past participle.

particle

A particle is an adverb or preposition which combines with verbs to form phrasal verbs.

passive voice

The passive voice is verb groups such as 'was given', 'were taken', 'had been made', which are used when the subject of the verb is the person or thing that is affected by the action. Compare with **active voice**.

past form

The past form is the form of a verb, often ending in '-ed', which is used for the past simple tense.

past participle

A past participle is a verb form which is used to form perfect tenses and passives. Some past participles are also used as adjectives, for example, *watched, broken, swum*.

past tense

SEE **tense**

perfect tense

SEE **tense**

person

A person is one of the three classes of people who can be involved in something that is said. The person or people who are speaking or writing are called the first person ('I', 'we'). The person or people who are listening or reading are called the second person ('you'). The person, people or things that are being talked about are called the third person ('he', 'she', 'it', 'they').

personal pronoun

A personal pronoun is one of the group of words including 'I', 'you', and 'me', which are used to refer back to yourself, the people you are talking to, or the people or things you are talking about.

SEE ALSO **object pronoun** and **subject pronoun**

phrasal verb

A phrasal verb is a combination of a verb and a particle, which together have a different meaning to the verb on its own, for example, *back down, hand over, look forward to*.

plural

A plural is the form of a count noun or verb, which is used to refer to or talk about more than one person or thing.

EG   *Dogs have ears.*
     The women were outside.

plural noun

A plural noun is a noun which is normally used only in the plural form, for example, *trousers, scissors*.

positive

A positive clause, question, sentence, or

Glossary of Grammar Terms

statement is one which does not contain a
negative word such as 'not'. Compare with
negative.

possessive

A possessive is one of the determiners 'my',
'your', 'his', 'her', 'its', 'our', or 'their', which is
used to show that one person or thing belongs
to another.

EG   *I like your car.*

possessive adjective

A possessive adjective is another name for
possessive.

possessive pronoun

A possessive pronoun is one of the pronouns
'mine', 'yours', 'hers', 'his', 'ours', or 'theirs'.

preposition

A preposition is a word such as 'by', 'with' or
'from', which is always followed by a noun
group.

prepositional phrase

A prepositional phrase is a structure consisting
of a preposition followed by a noun group as
its object.

EG   *I put it on the table.*
        They live by the sea.

present participle

SEE **'-ing' form**

present tense

SEE **tense**

progressive tense

The progressive tense is another name for
continuous tense.

pronoun

A pronoun is a word which you use instead of a
noun, when you do not need or want to name
someone or something directly, for example, *it,
you, none.*

proper noun

A proper noun is a noun which is the name of a
particular person, place, organization, or
building. Proper nouns are always written with
a capital letter, for example, *Nigel, Edinburgh,
the United Nations, Christmas.*

purpose clause

A purpose clause is a subordinate clause which
is used to talk about the intention that
someone has when they do something.

EG   *I came here in order to ask you out to
      dinner.*

qualifier

A qualifier is a word or group of words, such as
an adjective, prepositional phrase, or relative
clause, which comes after a noun and gives
more information about it, for example, *the
person involved, a book with a blue cover, the
shop that I went into.*

quantifier

A quantifier is a word or phrase such as 'plenty'
or 'a lot' which you use to refer to a quantity of
something without being precise. It is often
followed by 'of'.

EG   *There was still plenty of time.*
      He drank lots of milk.

question

A question is a sentence which normally has an
auxiliary verb in front of the subject, and which
is used to ask someone about something.

EG   *Do you have any money?*

Glossary of Grammar Terms

question tag

A question tag is an auxiliary or modal with a pronoun, which is used to turn a statement into a question.

EG *He's very friendly, isn't he?*
    I can come, can't I?

reason clause

A reason clause is a subordinate clause, usually introduced by 'because', 'since', or 'as', which is used to explain why something happens or is done.

EG *Since you're here, we'll start.*

reciprocal verb

A reciprocal verb is a verb which describes an action that involves two people doing the same thing to each other.

EG *I met you at the dance.*
    We've met one another before.
    They met in the street.

reflexive pronoun

A reflexive pronoun is a pronoun ending in '-self' or '-selves', such as 'myself' or 'themselves', which you use as the object of a verb when you want to say that the object is the same person or thing as the subject of the verb in the same clause.

EG *He hurt himself.*

reflexive verb

A reflexive verb is a verb which is normally used with a reflexive pronoun as object.

EG *He contented himself with the thought that he had the only set of keys.*

regular verb

A regular verb is a verb that has four forms, and follows the normal rules. Compare with **irregular verb**.

relative clause

A relative clause is a subordinate clause which gives more information about someone or something mentioned in the main clause.
SEE ALSO **defining relative clause** and **non-defining relative clause**

relative pronoun

A relative pronoun is 'that' or a 'wh'-word such as 'who' or 'which', when it is used to introduce a relative clause.

EG *I watched the girl who was carrying the bag.*

reported clause

A reported clause is the clause in a report structure which indicates what someone has said.

EG *She said that I couldn't see her.*

reported question

A reported question is a question which is reported using a report structure rather than the exact words used by the speaker.
SEE ALSO **indirect question**

reported speech

Reported speech is the words you use to report what someone has said, rather than using their actual words. Also called **indirect speech**.

reporting clause

A reporting clause is the clause in a report structure which contains the reporting verb.

reporting verb

A reporting verb is a verb which describes what people say or think, for example, *suggest, say, wonder.*

Glossary of Grammar Terms

report structure

A report structure is a structure which is used to report what someone says or thinks, rather than repeating their exact words.

EG   *She told me she'd be late.*

result clause

A result clause is a subordinate clause introduced by 'so', 'so...that', or 'such...(that)', which indicates the result of an action or situation.

EG   *I don't think there's any more news, so I'll finish.*

second person

SEE **person**

semi-modal

A semi-modal is a term used by some grammars to refer to the verbs 'dare', 'need', and 'used to', which behave like modals in some structures.

sentence

A sentence is a group of words which express a statement, question, or command. A sentence usually has a verb and a subject, and may be a simple sentence with one clause, or a compound or complex sentence with two or more clauses. In writing, a sentence has a capital letter at the beginning and a full-stop, question mark, or exclamation mark at the end.

short form

A short form is a form in which one or more letters are omitted and two words are joined together, for example an auxiliary or modal and 'not', or a subject pronoun and an auxiliary or modal, for example, *aren't, couldn't, he'd, I'm, it's, she's.*

simple tense

A simple tense is a present or past tense formed without using an auxiliary verb.

EG   *I wait.*
       She sang.

SEE **tense**

singular

A singular is the form of a count noun or verb which is used to refer to or talk about one person or thing.

EG   *A dog was in the back of the car.*
       That woman is my mother.

singular noun

A singular noun is a noun which is normally used only in the singular form, for example, *the sun, a bath.*

strong verb

A strong verb is another name for **irregular verb**.

subject

The subject is the noun group in a clause that refers to the person or thing who does the action expressed by the verb.

EG   *We were going shopping.*

subject pronoun

A subject pronoun is one of the set of pronouns including 'I', 'she', and 'they', which are used as the subject of a verb.

subordinate clause

A subordinate clause is a clause which must be used with a main clause and is not usually used alone, for example a time clause, conditional clause, relative clause, or result clause, and which begins with a subordinating conjunction such as 'because' or 'while'.

Glossary of Grammar Terms

subordinating conjunction

A subordinating conjunction is a conjunction such as 'although', 'as if', 'because' or 'while', which you use to begin a subordinate clause.

superlative

A superlative is an adjective or adverb with

t,

)f

ɔe'

ɪre

'

ɪuture periect cuntmuous: ᴡɪɪ ᴏɪ shall' with 'have been' and a present participle, used to refer to future events.

EG   *I will have been walking for three hours by then.*

past simple: the past form of a verb, used to refer to past events.

EG   *They waited.*

past continuous: 'was' or 'were' with a present participle, usually used to refer to past events.

EG   *They were worrying about it yesterday.*

past perfect: 'had' with a past participle, used to refer to past events.

EG   *She had finished.*

past perfect continuous: 'had been' with a present participle, used to refer to past events.

EG   *He had been waiting for hours.*

present simple: the base form and the third person singular form of a verb, usually used to refer to present events.

EG   *I like bananas.*
     My sister hates them.

present continuous: the present simple of 'be' with a present participle, usually used to refer to present events.

EG   *Things are improving.*

present perfect: 'have' or 'has' with a past participle, used to refer to past events which exist in the present.

EG   *She has loved him for ten years.*

present perfect continuous: 'have been' or 'has been' with a present participle, used to refer to past events which continue in the present.

EG   *We have been sitting here for hours.*

Glossary of Grammar Terms

'that'-clause

A 'that'-clause is a clause starting with 'that', used mainly when reporting what someone has said.

EG   *She said that she'd wash up for me.*

third person

SEE **person**

time clause

A time clause is a subordinate clause which indicates the time of an event.

EG   *I'll phone you when I get back.*

time expression

A time expression is a noun group used as an adverbial of time, for example, *last night, the day after tomorrow, the next time.*

'to'-infinitive

A 'to'-infinitive is the base form of a verb preceded by 'to', for example, *to go, to have, to jump.*

transitive verb

A transitive verb is a verb which takes an object. Compare with **intransitive verb**.

EG   *She's wasting her money.*

uncountable noun

An uncountable noun is another name for **uncount noun**.

uncount noun

An uncount noun is a noun which has only one form, takes a singular verb, and is not used with 'a' or numbers. Uncount nouns often refer to substances, qualities, feelings, activities, and abstract ideas, for example, *coal, courage, anger, help, fun.* Compare with **count noun**.

verb

A verb is a word which is used with a subject to say what someone or something does, or what happens to them, for example, *sing, spill, die.*

verb group

A verb group is a main verb, or a main verb with one or more auxiliaries, a modal, or a modal and an auxiliary, which is used with a subject to say what someone does, or what happens to them.

EG   *I'll show them.*
     She's been sick.

vowel

A vowel is a sound such as the ones represented in writing by the letters 'a', 'e', 'i', 'o' and 'u'. Compare with **consonant**.

'wh'-question

A 'wh'-question is a question which expects the answer to give more information than just 'yes' or 'no'. Compare with **'yes/no'-question**.

EG   *What happened next?*
     Where did he go?

'wh'-word

A 'wh'-word is one of a group of words starting with 'wh-', such as 'what', 'when' or 'who', which are used in 'wh'-questions. 'How' is also called a 'wh'-word because it behaves like the other 'wh'-words.

'yes/no'-question

A 'yes/no'-question is a question which can be answered by just 'yes' or 'no', without giving any more information. Compare with **'wh'-question**.

EG   *Would you like some more tea?*

Index